Dogs: A Historical Journey

Dogs

A HISTORICAL JOURNEY

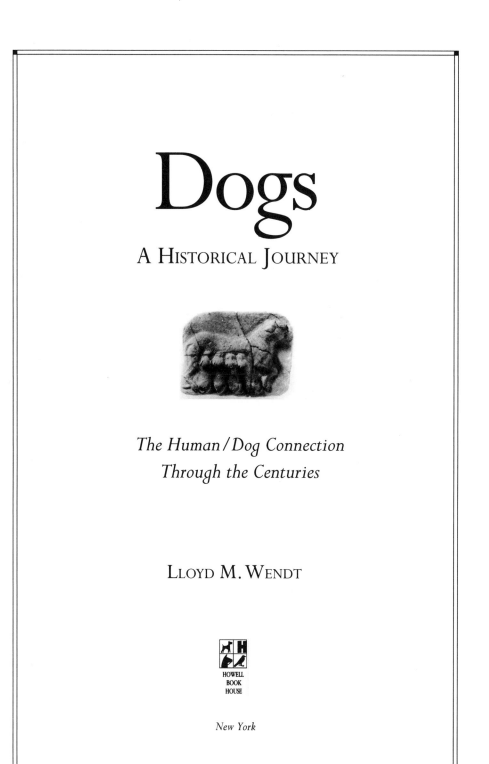

*The Human/Dog Connection
Through the Centuries*

LLOYD M. WENDT

HOWELL
BOOK
HOUSE

New York

Howell Book House
MACMILLAN
A Simon & Schuster Macmillan Company
1633 Broadway
New York, NY 10019

MACMILLAN is a registered trademark of Macmillan, Inc.
Library of Congress Cataloging-in-Publication Data
Wendt, Lloyd M.
     Dogs : a historical journey : the human/dog connection through the centuries / Lloyd M. Wendt.
       p. cm.
     ISBN 0-87605-533-1
     1. Dogs—History.   2. Human-animal relationships.   I. Title.
    SF422.5.W46   1996
    636.7'009—dc20   96-35960
                                              CIP

Manufactured in the United States of America
10 9 8 7 6 5 4 3 2 1

Book Design by George Mckeon

CONTENTS

Acknowledgments

∾ʘʍʍʘ∾

In 1953 Herman Kogan, my friend and co-author of five books, introduced me to a stunning literary event, *Great Books of the Western World,* published by Encyclopaedia Brittanica, Inc. (Chicago, Illinois), while in the same year Walter P. Paepcke, chairman of the board, Container Corporation of America, presented me with a compendium of environmental knowledge, *World Geographic Atlas*, edited by Herbert Boyer (privately published). Later I had accumulated all fifty-four *Great Books* and added the American edition of *The Evolution of Man and Society*, written by Oxford professor C. D. Darlington, FRS (Simon & Schuster, New York). This, with the edition of the books from Bennett Cerf's Modern Library (Random House, New York) that he recommended to us when Herman Kogan and I became book reviewers for rival Chicago newspapers, provided the seed that would initially lie dormant but ultimately result in the creation of this book.

Both Herman and I had pets for a long time. Herman's dog Charlie and his cats clearly merited print, and my beloved Boxers were always close behind, but we never really considered doing books about cats and dogs though the resources were there. Herman would write seventeen books and I ten, all of sterner stuff than tales of dogs and cats. Herman Kogan was walking with his cat, Missy, during the last hour of his life, his wife, Marilew, recalls. Shortly after that time Kiwi, a Border Collie, entered my life, thanks to my wife, Martha. The seminal book gifts of 1953 finally flowered for me after forty years. I had discussed genetics, chromosomes, and DNA with mutual friend Ruth Moore in early years, and I brought out her book *Evolution* (Time-Life Books, New York), recalling her explanation of those subjects, especially genetics. Meanwhile, our new pup was herding ducks, cows, and horses with no training. What might such a phenomenon have meant? It meant that I should go back to the literary acquisitions of 1953 and give them closer attention. Our modest library, taken to our mountain cottage at Sassafras Gap in the Smoky Mountains of North Carolina, was teeming with data on the role of canines in human history. All this was saying I should go back to work. Martha agreed, as wives of newly retired husbands nearly always do.

So the book manuscript slowly began to take shape. Martha suggested quite correctly that early history of dogs would be preserved graphically in ceramic pottery to be found in caves and tombs and sunken ships. A former teacher of arts and crafts, she became art director of our project. Dr. George DeVore, former chairman of geology at Florida State University, came into our neighborhood around Sassafras Gap from a mission in the mountains of Asia and tolerantly listened to my writing problems after becoming a close friend of our dog Kiwi and us. "An idea," he said, in the beginning, "Kiwi deserves." A few friends passing through had called this book idea bizarre. Dr. DeVore acquainted me with science disciplines sufficient for my purpose—geology, paleontology, archaeology—guiding me into proper restraints. He also responded to my request for a quartenary chart of the Pleistocene based on his synthesis, establishing the glacial events for this book. Thus the work eventually came to the veteran editor Seymour Weiss at Howell Book House in New York, who was able to shape the manuscript to publication standards.

I am deeply grateful for those who have helped me in a fascinating but difficult undertaking and who have graciously provided permissions to use quotations and graphics relating to the story of canines in the rise of civilization. Kind staffs at libraries and museums from National Musée du Bardo in Algiers to the National Museum of New Zealand have encouraged me to proceed, as did James B. Malloy, president of Container Corporation of America, by granting permission to cull the *World Geographic Atlas* for data and maps. I am indebted to Dr. Donald Patterson from the University of Pennsylvania, who guided me to treasures from the ancient Middle East in the University Museum's collection in Philadelphia, and De Hamchi Hafio Bardo, of the Museum of Bardo, who provided access to the rich lore of cave art and artifacts of northern Africa, who most kindly advised: "As for permission there is no problem, just underwrite 'National Museum of Bardo, Algiers.'" This has been done reverently. Michael

Walters reviewed the publications of the American Veterinary Medical Association, Chicago, according me permissions to quote, and Dr. Kevin O'Neil guided me to useful lanes into genetics, chromosomes, and DNA via the Memorial Hospital Library, Sarasota, Florida.

I am indebted also to writers and publishers of other vital sources consulted for this book that seeks to follow the injunction Samuel Eliot Morison, the American historian, gave himself for his excellent *Oxford History of the American People* (Oxford University Press, New York): "Since this is not primarily a textbook but a history to read and enjoy, footnote references, bibliographies, and other 'scholarly apparatus' have been suppressed." I gladly follow his example; my notes are intended to identify and thank sources that have made this book possible. Nothing more.

Historian Morison's books, read many times over, crowd the shelves of our mountain cottage library. Many books specifically on canine natural history include Dr. Fernand Mery's *Le Chien* (Cassell); Gino Pugnetti's *Cani* (Simon & Schuster) and Austrian biologist and zoologist Konrad Lorenz's classic "Covenant," which appears in *King Solomon's Ring* (HarperCollins, New York), have provided basic research for this book. I have relied heavily on the work of Miriam Magregor Redwood of New Zealand, who has written a most complete account of New Zealand shepherds' dogs, *A Dog's Life, Working Dogs in New Zealand* (A.H. & A.W. Reed, Wellington), and American naturalist Peter Matthiessen, who has allowed generous quotation from his book *The Tree Where Man Was Born* (E.P. Dutton, New York).

Our research team has been mostly family—Martha directing graphic research, assisted by Jeannie Skinner, library adviser of the New Zealand National Library in Auckland; Sabine Callaris, of Paris and Athens, provided many photographs and also Greek and French translations. Mark Sandlin, teacher of art and president of Direct Drive Design in Atlanta, has sketched and computer-enhanced faded and damaged cave-wall and tomb art and has created the maps based on those in the previously acknowledged *World Geographic Atlas*. Daughter Bette Jore brought in early Egyptian finds, including Adolf Erman's classic *Life in Ancient Egypt* (Dover Publications, New York). Lloyd W. King and Brooks King covered the Pacific rim areas; Julia King, partner of Sandlin, handled maps and graphics. Also, thanks go to Mrs. Jay Biel, for American dog genome data; Cyndi Toale, for the veterinary profession; Peter Guldager and Brooks King, for Internet research; and Ann Jenkins and Allen Ramey, for manuscript preparation.

Throughout the history of man, relics have been discovered in many cultures that point to the valuable place dogs have had in life and developing society of mankind. This neo-Hittite relief depicts a lion hunt with charioteers and dogs. (Courtesy Museums of Anatolian Civilizations, Ankara)

Thanks also to the Crown Publishing Group, New York, for rock art showing hunters with dogs in prehistoric Spain, and to *The Westerners* (Chicago Corral), for dog lore and sketches in *This Is the West*, edited by Robert West Howard (Rand McNally & Company, Chicago).

I am deeply grateful to Encyclopaedia Britannica, Inc. (Chicago), for permission to reprint from *Great Books of the Western World* extracts from Charles Darwin's *The Origin of Species* and *The Descent of Man* and briefer references from Aristotle to Zoroaster; and to Oxford University Press (London and New York), for permission to quote from *The Dialogues of Plato*, and from Homer and Aristotle in the *Great Books* series, and from Morison's *Oxford History of the American People*. I conducted interviews in various parts of the world, the results of which appear in this book, and I wish to thank all those responding, providing words and pictures. I am grateful also to good friends Hal and Polly Cooke for their continuing assistance to me in the field of local history in the Carolinas, Georgia, and Tennessee where their ancestors settled in the late eighteenth century; and to Gert McIntosh for her fine local history *Highlands, North Carolina, a Walk into the Past*; and to the always helpful librarians of Hudson Library, Highlands, and Macon County Library, Franklin, North Carolina; Clemson University Library, South Carolina; and Manatee County Library, Bradenton, and Selby Library, Sarasota, Florida. Their generous assistance over the years is appreciated.

Dogs: A Historical Journey

1

CONTEMPLATING THE JOURNEY

Ͼᴛᴍᴍᴐ

Her name is Kiwi. We were told that she is descended from Australian stock dogs, locally called Heelers, but my wife Martha's intuition prevailed. So, she is called Kiwi, unquestionably a fine New Zealand name. She has the look of those canines that can manage a mob of sheep with minimum human direction, quelling the most stubborn ewe or ram with her steady "strong eye." Kiwi's shaggy marl coat, round eyes, and drop ears can be identified in the portrait designated as a "typical New Zealand sheepdog" in that country's famed Alexander Turnbull Library. Why is such ancestry of consequence? It marks the end of a global trek that began when Kiwi first fixed her strong eye on us. That small, taffy-colored bundle of fur and toothy yearning squirmed and struggled for our attention. Her underbite, the breeder conceded, would bar her from any show ring. She was the runt of her litter, Martha agreed, but then, so were we. I was fascinated by Kiwi's coy smile, which concealed a secret she would soon reveal. While Martha settled the business of price and papers, the pup leveled her amber eyes on me— I was hypnotized like a Merino lamb.

Three days later, when our new pup with a New Zealand name established herself by herding mallard ducklings along the pond near our Florida home, I recalled similar scenes on South Island sheep stations. The Kiwi shepherd dogs instinctively herd ducks even before they learn to bark. They grow up able to hypnotize and control the world's most stubborn domestic animal, the Merino ram. I prowled through my books and learned that the "strong-eye" dog actually originated in the highlands of Scotland where in the late eighteenth century Lord Gordon crossed a Border Collie with his black-and-tan strong-eye Setter. The

Collie was probably descended from dogs brought into Europe by ancestors of the Basques, who were kin of the Celts and Berbers, whose speech was that of a shepherd people, as noted by the English botanist and historian C. D. Darlington. Shepherds from the British Isles later took the strong eye and Gordon Setter black-and-tan of the "typical sheepdog" to New Zealand in the mid nineteenth century. Thus dogs and shepherds at last had circled the globe together. Many had walked out of Africa and across Asia all the way to Australia via "island stepping stones."

Kiwi had other secrets besides her New Zealand past. She loved to hunt, and her behavior while chasing swamp rabbits in the marshes of Florida and raccoons and deer in North Carolina reminded me of the scenario provided by Dr. Konrad Lorenz, the famed Austrian biologist and animal behavior specialist, explaining the characteristic behavior pattern of a Lupus dog, one having a bit of wolf blood. "When you walk with him in the woods you can never have him stay near you," Lorenz wrote. "The Lupus dog will give his life for you but not obey you." Kiwi exhibited both signs of a Lupus past that probably came with the ancestry of a Basque dog since she would also, when called, zig-zag wolflike after sitting and staring at me from any distance—the pattern of the wolf itself.

Martha readily explained why Kiwi came straight on to her. "She comes to me because she thinks I'm her mother," Martha said. "She thinks you are her sibling."

"Yeah, an older brother," I admitted. "But she may have Dingo blood, not wolf. She's got Dingo qualities—tough, a strong jaw and bite like a Heeler." So I had read in the work of Dr. D. J. Mulvaney, the Australian prehistorian, no special friend of the wild dog. "Man has had the privilege of living with dogs for three hundred generations, but the Dingo at times will go his own way," Mulvaney writes. Yet the wild dog still hunts with the Bindibu aboriginal in north Australia precisely as other feral canids do with traditional hunters in modern Africa. Many wild dogs stay faithful.

So, our small, eager Kiwi, avid hunter but also a herder, has, by her behavior, revealed her secret, shared with many if not most working and hunting dogs. The genes and DNA of the working canine also guide the instincts of wild dogs and may have brought them into companionship and partnership with humans during prehistoric times. They were then directed by breeding and training into becoming faithful, dependable friends and partners of humans.

When and where might such a relationship have begun? It may have been born where the fossil bones of earliest humankind, succeeding the prehuman hominids, have been found, in Tanzania, Kenya, and Ethiopia. Here Louis and Mary Leakey and other paleontologists dug up crude tool kits as well as fossil bones of *Australopithecus afarensis* and *Homo erectus*, who, after ages of collecting and scavenging for food, learned to hunt big game because they had the help of wild dogs.

Kiwi's personality of hunter and herder, surely conflicting instincts, sent me into a search for the reasons why, a retracing of steps back into global experiences and into new vistas unveiled by modern research. This mystical walk with Kiwi, seeking the reason and pattern for the global marches of primitive man with his wives, children, and canines, has taken us from east-central Africa when dogs first hunted with the aborigines, into Berber country of North Africa, where canines and human hunters are shown working together in ancient cave and rock shelter paintings, on to Egypt, where humankind worshiped the dog god Anubis, into Greece, home of the philosophers in Plato's dialogues who advised humans to try to behave like well-bred dogs in their efforts to create an ideal state, and on into the Basque country of Spain and into and across Asia. The final steps came into the Americas by way of the Bering Strait land bridge and, via Malaysia and South Pacific stepping stone islands, to Australia and New Zealand by Maori canoe.

Throughout history our dogs have assisted in the rise of civilization as attested on the record by fossil discoveries and the testimony of many world leaders and scholars. So Kiwi leads us into stories of remarkable canine feats in ancient and modern times when dogs and humans did and continue to hunt and work together in war and peace and on a global odyssey enduring more than 80,000 years.

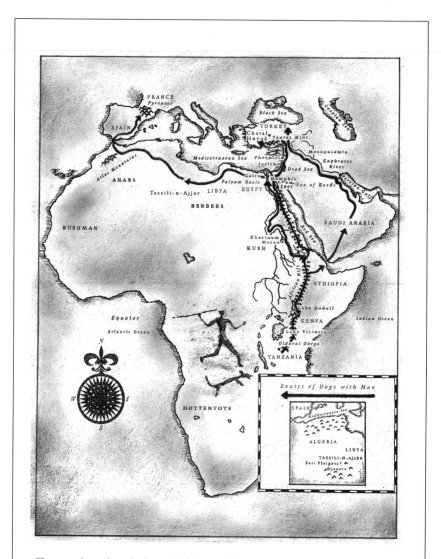

This map shows the wide dispersal of dogs and humans in Africa 80,000 years ago but provides only the mass-migration routes begun in the past 15,000 years when glaciers peaked, locking up great bodies of water and exposing the land bridges that made global migrations possible.

2

Out of Africa

〇IIII〇

An unexpected telephone call from a special friend reminded me that on several occasions I had visited territories where dogs and mankind may have developed the world's oldest business partnership, that of hunting, termed euphemistically by Dr. Konrad Lorenz as "the Covenant." A renewal of my old acquaintance with my friend Seymour seemed indicated. Seymour, arriving in Atlanta from Israel, wished to come by to chat. He was welcomed. I remembered my awe at his journalistic feats in the Yom Kippur War of 1973 and the days following. He covered it well on the Egyptian front in the morning and on the Golan Heights that same afternoon, for example, making all our *Chicago Today* editions. I was freelancing now. Martha was away. I offered him potluck with Kiwi and me, and he arrived over ice-covered mountain roads that reminded us of the time we ditched our vehicle in a Golan Heights snowstorm during the war. That night we reviewed some experiences by a good log fire.

Our old Seymour yielded little about his new job with a South African publication for which he'd become a special correspondent, and he probed my activities as usual. I asked questions about South African wild dogs and got a short answer. "They're a scruffy lot," he said. I had forgotten he was allergic to dogs. Kiwi seemed to sense this and kept her distance. I did learn he was still based in Israel and his daughters were both in the Israeli army. They planned to create a vacation resort on the Red Sea when their military service ended. I had seen the site, a delightful beachfront area, and was sure they would do well there.

"I need information about the Red Sea," I said, and told him about my writing project on the covenant of man and dogs and their part in human migrations beginning in Africa about 80,000 years ago. Since I had forgotten about his antipathy toward canines, I expected his cooperation. His response quickly reminded me of his feelings.

"I can tell you about Abraham and God," he offered. "After several centuries in Egypt, the Children of Israel wanted no relationship with dogs. Dogs were worshiped in Egypt, and for the Jews that was too much. Abraham had a covenant with God. His people were in; dogs were out."

"You are right, and I've got the Talmud, so I'll work it out," I said. "What I need to know is about the crossing of the Red Sea. Could it have been done without the direct intervention of God? Dogs would have been inconvenient there, I'll admit."

"When the wind was right it could have been done," Seymour said. "I doubt that it was a common occurrence. But it was done, along the Gulf of Suez. What's more amazing was the silence of those Egyptian dogs. They didn't betray the Exodus. I don't think Moses was properly grateful for that. Crossing the Gulf of Suez may have been relatively easy, if the moon was right and the prevailing winds held back the waters. And not a single Egyptian guard dog sounded the alarm! The people slipped away, fled the towns, awaited the high winds, and crossed into the Wilderness of Etham. Perhaps Moses had a covenant, too."

We discussed the recent archaeological finds at Faiyum Oasis in Egypt and in Qafzeh, Israel, each estimated by modern dating methods to be nearly 100,000 years old. Then Seymour mentioned what he'd really come about. He had been a student in my writing class at Northwestern University in Chicago. He was thinking of history of the Yom Kippur War. "Do you still hold to those quaint views you discussed with the Prime Minister back in 1974?" he asked.

I did. Menachem Begin was head of the Likud party at that time. Our formal interview had ended, and I was invited to stay behind. My view continued to be that the United States would strongly support Israeli policy because of our debt to Judaic religious, cultural, and ethical concepts, not because Israel represented the military power of a strong ally. I believed most midwestern Americans, if not most Americans, felt that way. That idea had not gone down well with the Likud leader, who was not yet the new prime minister. "You are right for all the wrong reasons," Seymour said.

"I remember that the prime minister did not in 1974 think that the cease-fire signed with Egypt would endure," I reminded him. "He publicly said so the day of the signing."

"And Israel has proved a powerful ally to America ever since," Seymour replied, rather sharply.

At this point, I turned our discussion back to my developing research project.

"I don't think I've ever seen a dog in Israel," I said. "They were at the peace signing with Egypt at Kilometer 101 in the desert, but they were United Nations animals. I was so impressed seeing dogs there that I mentioned their presence in my dispatch."

"Read Job," Seymour suggested. "He had thousands of sheep and hundreds of dogs. The people of Egypt worshiped dogs. Abraham's people believed in one God, Yahveh, and Abraham made his Compact with Him. As for dogs in Israel, in the newspaper business we generally see what we're looking for."

"I remember now, I did see a dog in Israel," I recalled. "It was a Saluki . . . in an Arab tent somewhere near Beersheba."

Seymour departed in the morning. "When you come, bring Kiwi," he called. "We'll introduce her to our military dogs . . . the world's best."

I now began studying the maps of Kenya and northern Africa and the territory along the Great African Rift reaching into Asia to the Dead Sea. I had to conclude that early humans with their domestic dogs had crossed the upper area above the Red Sea and perhaps the lower, into Palestine just above the Gulf of Suez, or into Arabia and Yemen from the tip of Abyssinia about 100,000 years ago. I would learn that fossils and artifacts fixed at about 92,000 years by uranium thorium dating methods have been discovered in recent digs in those areas.

Back to the books. It was in 1924 that a certain skull was found by anatomist Raymond Dart, of Witterand University, in a South African quarry. He called it *Australopithecus*, *austral* meaning southern and *pithecus* meaning ape in Greek. Dart somewhat shyly suggested that the fossil might represent the "missing link" in the theory of the evolution of man, postulated seventy-five years earlier by Charles Darwin and Arthur Russel Wallace and hotly contested since. Wallace had described beginning man as a frail, helpless, and hairless creature who had abandoned an arboreal existence for a somewhat incredible life on the ground. *Australopithecus* proved him right.

Further fossils found in southern Africa and north into Kenya by Louis S. B. Leakey and his wife, Mary, provided a changing portrait of *Australopithecus*. This controversial early hominid appeared to have wandered about, mostly in the northern part of the area. Complete skeletons were discovered in Kenya, indicating that early man indeed originally fitted the Wallace description but also that he was growing a bit taller, from about four to five feet. He had found a way to improve his diet of fruit, nuts, insects, and berries by adding plants and roots, and he began to leave occasional evidence that he feasted on the flesh of game animals, perhaps acquired by scavenging or a lucky kill of an ill or aging beast.

These bones and petrified evidence of a collector's diet were accompanied by crude artifacts, tools and weapons created from stones, sticks, and flints that primitive man had found on his travels. He had become *Homo habilis,* the tool maker. He would become *Homo sapiens* (wise man); the skulls found in Kenya indicated that early man had also evolved a larger brain. Surrounding the Kenya fossils and tools were evidences of an improved diet—rats, lizards, frogs, birds, shellfish, and some young pigs—but there was little evidence of large game in the diet of early man to this point. The tool maker did not yet possess the equipment for bringing down the bison or gazelle. By the use of potassium argon dating methods, the fossils and artifacts found by the Leakeys were later fixed at 1.75 million years old.

Man was advancing as a collector of plants, roots, and nuts but generally was unacquainted with the taste and various benefits of large game. There were no bones or teeth of big game among the initial fossil finds in camps, rock shelters, and caves where primitive humans dwelled in Kenya or Abyssinia (Ethiopia). Man's tools continued to show improvement, until they reached a level of Stone Age quality called Acheulean by scientists. These contrivances, fashioned of bone, wood, and stone, endured with little change for a million years.

The early fossil discoveries tell a of story of the wanderings of a once-arboreal creature who found a sparse existence on the ground. Yet he persisted. In time he added the flesh of large game to his diet, but only occasionally. He evoved into *Homo erectus,* able to walk and run, use his hands to catch and throttle small game, and carry his surplus plants and animal flesh to his camp or cave. At times his improved food supply gave him the time and energy to play, to create rudimentary tools, and to explore. He found pebbles, rocks, and splinters of stone that amused him and also aided in cracking and softening nuts, roots, and the bones of small prey. He was the Leakey find called "*Homo habilis* the tool maker," who left traces along the seashore and the lakes, where he consumed shellfish, and on a trail north to what is now Tanzania, Kenya, and Ethiopia. Some of the skulls found had teeth well worn by the chewing of grains, indicating that man had discovered nutrition in a weed he would plant and domesticate, a kind of barley.

Early man etched this vivid portrait of a leashed hunting dog on a cave wall in Algeria about 10,000 years ago above the then-green Sahara. Henri Dhote, the French ethologist, discovered this petroglyph at Tassili-n-Ajer. It may be the earliest clear picture of the prototype sight hounds that illustrates how early man hunted them. (Courtesy Musée du Bardo, Algiers)

The scene on a cave wall in Tassili-n-Ajer shows a group of dogs surrounding a wild sheep, possibly closing in for the kill. It may also depict the capture of live sheep, for early man to tame and begin the development of domestic livestock.

10

The Meeting of Man and Dog

Man became a scavenger, following predators that killed big game. He killed some himself—beasts wounded by stronger predators, dying of old age, or trapped in bogs and marshes. But bones of large animals were rarely found in his campsites, shelters, and caves. Man continued to move about, seeking food while avoiding animals that might attack him. At times he appears to have joined forces with a creature that neither feared nor attacked him, perhaps the African wild dog, universally known today as the Cape Hunting Dog. At other times and in other places during man's evolution, his wild ally may have been the Dhole or Pariah dog of India or the Dingo of Australia, the latter name now in general use in designating many types of wild dogs.

Until man had grown into the rugged, tall, athletic species called Neanderthal, or *Homo sapiens* or, later, Cro-Magnon, he did not extend his habitat beyond the savannahs, deserts, and foothills of Africa. C. D. Darlington, the British botanist and the author of *The Evolution of Man and Society* (New York: Simon & Schuster, 1969), a most dependable book on the rise of man, has likened *Homo habilis* to the African Capoid, or Bushman, a name given to the African primitives by early European settlers. Unquestionably at some time *Homo habilis* learned to hunt big game, a feat requiring extreme strength, dexterity, and weaponry beyond the crude implements he had produced up to this point. Hunting also directly exposed him to the danger from a host of predators stronger than himself.

Earliest fossil finds suggest that humankind originated and developed in Africa, and skeletons indicate both larger cranial capacity and increased height from four to five and a half feet from *Australopithecus* to *Homo erectus*. It therefore seems probable that early man, the scavenger, could keep up with predators such as the wild dog and could share the dog's kills, eventually becoming his partner in the hunt. The elapsed time would span thousands of years. Whether dogs became the first hunting partners of man or the jackal began to follow man the hunter, as suggested by Lorenz, the bonding probably became effective in the area of East Kenya about 80,000 years ago. In providing evidence of such a development, we must concede that some prehistorians insist that the canine/human relationship did not begin with the hunter dog but rather with man as the hunter and dog his prey.

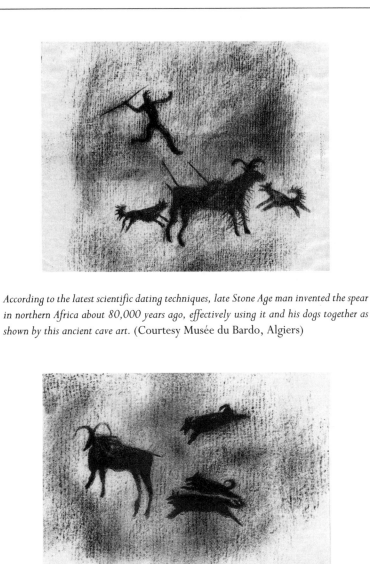

According to the latest scientific dating techniques, late Stone Age man invented the spear in northern Africa about 80,000 years ago, effectively using it and his dogs together as shown by this ancient cave art. (Courtesy Musée du Bardo, Algiers)

Ancient hunting dogs worked wild game just as modern dogs do, selecting and separating one animal from the herd. These early dogs worked cooperatively in packs, using movements seen in many of today's most competent working stock dogs. (Courtesy Musée du Bardo, Algiers)

Exactly how may it have happened? We can examine the evidence in the light of recent fossil finds. Did man engage in scavenging and thus achieve friendship with the wild dog or encourage the relationship as a friendly hunter? Let's turn back to the essay by Lorenz, "The Covenant."

"How did the Stone Age man come by his dog?" Lorenz asks. "Very probably without intending it," he answers, and offers a scenario. Packs of jackals must have accompanied the hominid migrants from the south who were following herds of bison, mammoth, and auroch moving north as the glacial ice slowly retreated in Asia and Europe. The jackals were scavenging for their food, keeping up with the human hunters and surrounding the camps and settlements by night as they continue to do today in Africa and the Middle East. The jackals were probably welcomed by the hunters, often scavengers themselves.

So Lorenz conjectures. "The Stone Age hunters," he writes, "for whom the large beasts of prey were still a serious menace, must have found it quite agreeable to know that their camp was being watched by a broad circle of jackals which, at the approach of the saber-toothed tiger or the marauding cave-bear, gave tongue in the wildest tones.

"It is very easy to imagine how this prehistoric dog would develop an interest in larger game animals (once he had a taste by scavenging) that he could not bring down," Lorenz continues. "He might even by a stroke of canine genius have called the hunters' attention to the track." (A tracking dog could discover game by its sense of smell, which is thousands of times superior to that of humankind.) "It is a strongly appealing and elevating thought that the age-old covenant between man and dog was signed voluntarily and without obligation by each of the contracting parties."

Others, following Lorenz, have projected the rest of the scenario. Dogs could find game by their superior sense of smell and capture it by their superior speed; man had superior eyesight and the ability to climb trees. Their natural talents complemented each other and made the hunt more successful for both. Early humans, aware of the value of their canine helpers, lured them to their caves and camps, where they could share the warmth of shelter and fire as the migrations continued north and also share the food man learned to preserve with salt or fire.

Lorenz is internationally recognized as one of the most devoted and wise scientists of his time, with pragmatic knowledge of the behavior patterns of mammals and birds. Yet not everyone agrees with his premise that descendants

This cave painting shows a dog holding a wild sheep and, evidently, a boar at bay. Swine are believed to be the first animals to have become domesticated. (Courtesy Musée du Bardo, Algiers)

Another example of cave painting that shows hunting dogs surrounding and capturing wild sheep. The original rendition may have been drawn from actual events or from a recollection in the mind of the primeval artist. Henri Dhote himself helped copy this example of cave art. (Mark Sandlin, after Dhote; courtesy Musée du Bardo, Algiers)

of the golden jackal *(Canis aureus)* learned to hunt while traveling with man, and thus became domesticated dogs. Man himself began as a collector of food, subsisting on fruit, nuts, berries, plants, roots, and small animals he could capture with his hands or knock out with a stone or club. In time, as *Homo habilis* in Africa, he created crude tools, such as flint points for his spear, and in Africa and Central Asia he invented the bow and arrow. Early on, as *Australopithecus*, "the missing link," man was frail and short; as Neanderthal and Cro-Magnon, he achieved the proportions of modern man. He was then hunting big game, probably with the help of dogs descended from the golden jackal and the African wild dog. He would become the adventurer who would lead the way into Asia and Europe as a Neanderthal. "The legbones of Neanderthal were heavily built," says Erick Trinkhaus, anthropologist at the University of New Mexico. "They're strongly built in an inside-outside direction that implies to us that the Neanderthal had a side-to-side movement, the kind implying you were running over a very irregular terrain, or if you were chasing something that was moving. . . . "

Those Neanderthals were chasing big game and had grown tall and strong on a diet of the flesh of their prey as well as plants they found. It is doubtful they could supply themselves regularly as only scavengers. Some, at least, were working with dogs. Their tree-dwelling relatives also thrived from a vegetarian diet, but did so by spending most of their time collecting food. The hominids following the predators, whether as scavengers or helpers in the hunt, found added energy from the flesh of large game, and thus had time to experiment with stones and pebbles they used in play, in time creating tools. They could employ their hands to carry extra food, when the hunting was good, to a cave or cache for future need. They discovered fire, started by lightning, and carried it to their camps and rock shelters. Fossil remains in such caves suggest dogs living with the *Homo habilis* 100,000 years ago, small canines perhaps acquired for food but others whole and unharmed, pups taken in and cared for as companions and pets.

Contrary to the contention that asserts that the wolf is the sole progenitor of the dog and that early man alone destroyed the woolly mammoth, auroch, and bison without help, there is evidence of an early canine presence 100,000 years ago that included large dogs. These are assumed previously to have appeared only in the North, where they descended from the wolf. "Contrary to the wide-spread opinion that the wolf plays an essential role in the ancestry of the larger dog breeds," Lorenz writes, "comparative research in behavior has revealed the fact

This rendering of the bowman and his dog was found in the cave art of Tassili-n-Ajer. Archers such as this may have ventured north from what is present-day Zaire, where migrant craftsmen were well advanced in creating weapons. The bow and arrow, said to have originated in central Asia, may have actually come from central Africa instead. (Mark Sandlin, after Dhote; courtesy Musée du Bardo, Algiers)

that European dogs, including the largest ones such as Great Danes and wolf-hounds, are pure descendants of *Canis aureus* and contain, at the most, a minute amount of wolf blood." Even the first dogs in Lapland are basically *C. aureus*, Lorenz finds, since the Lapps followed the reindeer north, taking dogs with them—these the dogs that subsequently hybridized with wolves. Lorenz found the pure *C. aureus* dog as far north as the Baltic Sea. Later in Luristan (now a province of Iran), Afghanistan, and other northern areas, a large Mastiff with wolf ancestry would be developed to herd large flocks of sheep and oxen and to protect them from wolves and bears.

When the Neanderthal peoples began departing northern Africa for Asia and Europe, not all may have taken dogs. Cave paintings in southern Africa show some small, indistinct creatures that may have been canines aiding in the hunt. However, the famous pictures of the hunt found in the caves of France and Spain, the art of the Neanderthal and Cro-Magnons, depict no dogs. Thus some say that late Stone Age man hunted alone with his flint-stone spears and arrows. Biologist J. Bronowski, however, takes a different view.

"For us, the cave paintings re-created the hunter's way of life as a glimpse of history," Bronowski writes. "We look through them into the past. But for the hunter, I suggest, they were a peep-hole into the future . . . the men who made the weapons and the men who made the paintings . . . anticipating the future as only man can do." The hunter, Bronowski says, "was a puny, slow, awkward, unarmed animal . . . he had to invent . . . a flint, knife and spear . . . in his pictures. He saw the bison as he would have to face him, he saw the running deer, the turning boar."[1]

An ancient rock artist working on a cave wall in Tassili-n-Ajer left this record of a ring-tailed canine. In spite of its obvious exaggeration, this rendering could have been an attempt to portray an ancestor of the family of Northern breeds that gave rise to Samoyeds, Akitas, and Siberian Huskies.

Historian Philip Van Doren Stern's careful explanation of prehistoric rock art found hidden in caves in France and Spain provides another answer to the seemingly strange absence of dogs, an answer going beyond Bronowski's explanation and helping to clarify the assertion by Stern himself and others that Paleolithic hunters had no dogs.[2] Probably some of the first people to enter Europe in an early stage of the ice age warming period crossed some water barriers in small leather boats. Thus they didn't bring dogs or sheep, nor did they try to domesticate the fierce northern wolves. More likely, Stern suggests, the Neanderthals did not enter Eurasia—especially the cold, damp European areas—until improved weapons enabled them to bring down large game on their own.

In recent years, some fossil sites in Europe have yielded canine bones dating back 17,000 years. For years the excavations at Starr Carr, south of Scarborough in England, were believed to have provided fossils of the first known domesticated dog, dated at 7,500 B.C. Starr Carr was probably a winter camp, Stern suggests. The Mesolithic people (middle Stone Age) had reached Denmark when the ice retreated. They were dependent on the sea for food but also hunted with half-wild dogs similar to Huskies. Stern concludes, "They did domesticate the dog." But other early peoples, in Africa and other places, had also domesticated the dog.

When and where did the domestic dog become man's partner as a hunter and warrior? As primitive man was a scavenger and collector, he followed the African wild dog and the scavenging jackal northward after the vast game herds toward what are now Kenya and Ethiopia, about 80,000 years ago. They reached northern Africa hunting together, as shown by cave art discovered in Algeria depicting dog and man with spears pursuing wild oxen. Such canines appear to have originated among Capoid migrants and later Berber nomads moving north along the African rift. Those Berber nomads at a later time, perhaps 10,000 years ago, began supplying tribes along the Nile, in Cush (Sudan) and Egypt, with the hunting Greyhound, the Basenji, and the small red wolf-dog that would guard goats and sheep. Several early breeds are still found in Africa and around the world: the Greyhound, the Basenji, and the Rhodesian Ridgeback.

Such canines evidently associated voluntarily with humankind and became changed by hybridization, mutations, and selective breeding directed by humans according to their needs. The planned breeding of dogs sometimes resulted in extremes—from enormous Mastiffs used as "guard dogs" and later as war dogs to tiny Toy breeds used by the Chinese and Mediterranean peoples as "sleeve dogs" and by Paleo-Indians in Mexico both as pets and for food. The canines that remained the least changed were the Dingos and similar types, those that stayed close to their primitive hunting companion, Stone Age man—unchanged in Africa, the Canary Islands, Australia, and Patagonia.

The story has been made quite clear. Together the hunters, man and dog, could find, run down, and bring down more game than they could devour and, in the case of wild dogs, regurgitate to their young. Man, walking and running erect, used his hands to carry the surplus to camp or shelter and ultimately to

The ancient Portuguese Peat Dog was a prototype of the Northern breeds family.

Jackals are believed by some authorities to be in the bloodline of modern dogs. The world-renowned scholar Konrad Lorenz believes that the Aureus dog derives from a member of this branch of the canid family. (Courtesy Union of South Africa Parks)

According to Fernand Mery, the well-known African wild dog was the ancestor of the Cape Hound, a popular South African hunting dog. (Courtesy Union of South Africa Parks)

make and use weapons such as the stone ax and the spear. The dog, its powers of scent thousands of times keener than that of humans, could locate herds of game at a distance and wear down the animals, slowing them to a pace at which man could use his ax or spear, or, later, his bow and arrow.

Was early man—"frail, hairless and helpless . . . puny and awkward," about four and a half feet tall—teaching the jackals how to hunt, as Lorenz has suggested, or was man being led in the hunt by the African wild dog and the Dingo found later in Egypt, India, Malaysia, and Australia? The Algerian cave art indicates that man may have domesticated the dog and the jackal at about the same time, acquiring their services as guardians of the camp and the rock shelter as well as helpers in the hunt. The Aureus dog by definition is descended from the jackal. In the north, the migrating domesticated dog evidently met the wolf. In far off Luristan, now a province of Iran in the foothills of the Zagros Mountains, the canines pictured on the cave walls of shepherd kings are either wolves, dogs, or hybrids—no one can be sure. Those shown at the Archaeological Museum in Teheran and on the painted pottery of Suza, the ancient capital of Persia, are definitely the kind of fighting dogs shown escorting war chariots of Nineveh. The southern dog had met the northern wolf. The Assyrian Mastiff and the great Molossian Dog appear to be the fruit of that union.

How did the partnership begin in the Lorenz scenario? He tells us that the earliest dogs to be domesticated descended from the golden jackal (*Canis aureus*) and suggests that they became acquainted with humans by following them in the hunt. By night the jackals surrounded the hunters' encampment, hoping for entrails and other scraps of food. When large predators appeared, the jackals sounded an alarm, a service welcomed by the humans. In time the jackals became responsible sentinels, guarding the camp. They also helped in the hunt, using their superior sense of smell to discover the prey, though no jackal attacked large game on its own. Eventually the semi-domesticated animals took to running ahead of the human hunters to wear down and help contain the prey. But we must ask, how could humans successfully pursue large game with their puny weapons? Bows and arrows had not yet been created, and these hunters were generally under surveillance and attack by lions, tigers, and other large predators. How could they bring down the running bison, the woolly mammoth, the powerful auroch, or even the swift gazelle with rocks, clubs, and crude knives and spears? Early fossil finds indicate that some humans used a flintstone hand ax to kill obviously injured, aged, or trapped large beasts, or they made an occasional kill by surrounding large animals with fire or by driving them into a bog or over a cliff. Eventually learning to follow the herds in order to share the kill, they sometimes made a kill on their own with the hand ax. As scavengers, the humans probably followed the wild dog, a predator that allowed hyenas and his relatives the jackals to share his kills, as they continue to do today.

The deduction that dogs and these first hominids, whose descendants are today known as the Bushmen of the African deserts, may have formed an early partnership can be made from the fact that such dogs still work with man today. They can be found not only in Africa but in other distant parts of the world, among primitive people similar in size and appearance to the Bushmen, in Australia and at the southern tip of South America. Naturalists Stern and Carl C. Saur scoff at such deduction, Saur asserting flatly that "the great hunters of the Upper Paleolithic had no dogs."[3]

They do not agree on the origin of the domestic dogs, however. "It is generally agreed that the ancestor of the European dog was the wolf with some possible inbreeding of the jackal," Stern writes. Sauer, on the other hand, writes, "The dog is considered as originating from a wild dog, native to Southeastern Asia, living in a forested monsoon land, perhaps resembling the fox in food and social habits," thus disagreeing also with Lorenz.

This superb example of Tassilli cave art depicts Neolithic migrant herdsmen together with their sheep and oxen and their herd dogs (faintly visible in the top row and at the fringes of the herd). They were among the many races that came to North Africa some eight to ten thousand years ago and whose activity marked the beginning of the Neolithic period.

Frederick Zeuner, the British prehistorian, suggests that early hunters tossed morsels of food to wild dogs that invaded the camps of Neolithic man (late Stone Age) or lurked about them before the domestication of dogs, and adds, "It must be noted, however, that the animals in their wild state do not become friendly with other species. Much work must be done."

Zeuner then concludes that the dog was not really domesticated until relatively modern times, fixing the date at about 10,000 years ago.[4] Francois Bourliere of the University of Paris states, "The earliest certain domestic dog thus far discovered is one with wolflike teeth dating to 7,500 B.C.," evidently referring to the dogs found at Starr Carr. His caveat "thus far discovered" is well taken. The intact skeletons of dogs buried intentionally with human families, dating back 30,000 years, have been found in China and North America. Bourliere makes a useful contribution to the dissonant discussions by adding, "Transitional stages between true wolf and true dog unfortunately do not exist as fossils—or if they do, they have not been discovered. But dogs themselves go back a long way."[5] Stern adds: "The dog, the hearth, fire, meat, fruit, berries, and edible roots are about all we have left of far-off days when man was a professional hunter and the whole world was his domain."

The earliest evident pattern of human and dog migrations and partnership activity began in southeastern Africa, extending to Lakes Turkana and Omo in Ethiopia and the Nile tributaries, the Nile itself, and may have reached past the deserts of Sudan and on to Faiyum Oasis, not far from where Memphis would become a great Egyptian port city. The impenetrable Nile Delta marshes turned some of the southern migrants west to Arabia, toward the Mediterranean shores, and on to Mesopotamia (now Iraq and Iran) where the Tigris and Euphrates would provide fertile if flood-prone lands for herdsmen and farmers as well as game for hunters. Other migrants and dogs reached Arabia by routes above the Red Sea and went on to Palestine, Syria, Anatolia (Turkey), and the Caspian Sea. In addition to their dogs and growing flocks and herds, some migrants carried seeds, plants, and roots, collecting additional specimens washed down from the mountains and plateaus en route. Along the foothills of the Zagros Mountains and the rivers flowing into the Persian Gulf, they would begin the first modern civilization at Zawi Chemi Shanidar, where archaeologists have found the bones of sheep 9,000 years old at Mureybit on the Euphrates. At Jericho, in the desert near the Dead Sea, people hunting with their dogs halted to begin farms watered by the uncertain Jordan River. Jericho would become a wealthy town on a camel route when trade began, using its dogs against the robbers who attacked the oncoming caravans and the approaching shepherds seeking water.

The age of war dogs was near. At Byblos, a Mediterranean population center (known today as Jubayl, Lebanon) that claims to be the world's oldest inhabited place, dogs defended that port town, where the farmers and the herdsmen also engaged in trade. Eventually they built a navy that would carry grains, tools, lumber, and dogs to the entire Middle East. The first domesticated canines appear to have originated in central and north Africa among the Nomadic Berber tribes and the Capoid hunters-turned-herdsmen in Kenya and the foothills of Abyssinia. Many of the migrants from southern Africa made their way along the African rift and the Nile to settle at Meroe and in the lands of Cush and Egypt. They also took their cattle and dogs into the highlands of Ethiopia. Some found precious ores, iron for tools and armor, and gold. Women were the cultivators; Darlington credits them with creating edible grains such as millet and barley from wild weeds. Dogs helped to capture the wild progenitors of livestock and later herd domesticated pigs, sheep, and goats, guard the working women and their children, and hunt with the men. They would help to guard the caravans as trade developed. Meroe became a vital trading center, in time attracting some migrants who had proceeded on to Egypt, Mesopotamia, Anatolia, and even India. The Bushmen hunters, on the other hand, tended to retreat south and west, taking their semi-domesticated dogs with them.

During the thousands of years of migration, humans as well as dogs changed. Humans developed a capacity for speech and the ability to create tools. And, as Darlington points out, humankind evolved differing genetic patterns and blood types. The genetic differences changed the larynx, palate, and teeth in a way that enabled humans to utter complex sound signals called speech. Genetics also altered patterns of behavior and appearance. The migrants in Africa manifested varied colors, differences in size, and other adaptations to the environment. Thus Bushmen remaining in the African deserts remained smaller than those who migrated north, and they ranged from brown and yellow-brown to black and white in color. The white descendants were to be found among the hill and mountain people. Some bronze- and yellow-tinted tribes developed the eye pattern of people now inhabiting much of Asia. Some primitives developed the dark characteristics of tribes designated as Negroid, dark-pigmented people; others remained pygmy in size, while the Watusis became warriors six feet and more in height. Genetics, DNA patterns, environmental differences, and hybridization governed the development of African tribes moving about and beyond the continent of origin.

The dogs controlled by genetics, DNA, and blood types in time were altered by the control of their breeding by humans. In the desert, the Berbers developed large, strong "gazehounds" that could see game at a distance, since there was little verdure to catch and hold the spoor of game. In the north, Hittites developed large hunting dogs to pursue big game and to guard livestock. The herds continued to move north, finding the grazing better, until they approached the areas of perpetual ice. The early hominids followed. Many Capoids remained in Africa, some turning back south to live in the deserts as they continue to do today, as expert hunters, using spears and stone axes and working with their dogs, content with hunting as a way of life.

They also learned the uses of plants and herbs. Botanist Darlington tells us that fifty such species are known to the Bushmen of the Kalahari. Some migrants continued to collect plants and roots that they planted in the Nile Valley. They developed settlements and found caves for refuge. As they wandered they encountered obstacles, rivers and lakes, marshes and deserts. They learned to make rafts, canoes of animal skins, bark, and logs dug out by use of fire and flintstone axes. Some discovered that salt would preserve animal flesh, and they came to employ it in trade with those who learned to collect fish and shellfish.

The more aggressive hunters pushing north entered Asia and Europe and were "much more robustly built than modern humans," according to anthropologist Erik Trinkus. They became Neanderthals, named so for their fossils found in the Neander Valley of Germany, and Cro-Magnons, named for a village in France where their fossils were first discovered. They were followed in time by "a more lightly built Mediterranean type," according to archaeologist Jaquetta Hawkes, reporting on the discovery of this hominid in Northern Africa, "possibly the ancestor of the Berber tribes."[6] The Berbers wandered about northern Africa, becoming famous for the hunting, shepherd, and guard dogs that they bred and in time would supply to the Egyptians, Minoans, and Phoenicians, the latter two carrying them in their ships to the nations of the known world to help build their civilizations.

Few can doubt that modern civilization began in southwest Asia when *Homo sapiens*, a food gatherer and hunter, arrived in the last stages of the ice retreat. He was a Paleolithic tool maker who followed Neanderthal man into Europe, bringing his dogs with him. These dogs have been found buried in family plots in Chatal Hüyük, Eridu, Babylon, Nineveh, Ur, Byblos, and in the Danube Valley in Europe. "The appearance of the domesticated dog made hunting more effective," *The Cambridge Ancient History* tells us. Men with spears and bows and arrows took up the hunting of auroch and bison and smaller game such as gazelle, deer, and squirrel. They began smelting ores and creating pottery, and they also had learned to create fire by striking flint against iron pyrites, producing sparks. The country in which he would hunt was cold, but big game was plentiful when the ice retreated. Man had now improved his weapons, enabling him to bring down the formidable woolly mammoth, reindeer, rhinoceros, and bison that favored regions of Asia, southwest France, and northern Spain, according to Jacquetta Hawkes and Christopher Hawkes. He was mostly Cro-Magnon, described by the Hawkeses as "tall robust men with round but strongly-boned faces" whose fossil bones were found among those of extinct animals. They conclude, "Those arriving late brought their dogs along with their pygmy flints."[7]

Humans also had changed in appearance and cranial capacity. The early Bushmen of Africa, as we have noted, had varied considerably during the course of their long migrations. Originally yellow-brown according to biologists, some— as among the Berbers and Tauregs in the northern deserts—ranged in color from

Clay dogs such as these were found in the ruins of Sumeria (now southern Iraq). Amulets of this kind were often used as talismans to protect the homes of farmers and townspeople who lived along the Euphrates River. (Sketch by Mark Sandlin from *Man and Animals;* courtesy University of Pennsylvania Museum Press)

yellow-brown to black, yellow, brown, and white, and those tribes electing to live in eastern mountains were and continue to be blue-eyed blonds.

Man and dogs began to develop larger brains than did other creatures, as did the horse in a lesser degree after it was captured and trained by man 6,000 years ago. William T. Keaton of Cornell University states that "horses and dogs have large, well-developed brains with the same parts as a human brain."[8] The dog, however, a social animal and intelligent organizer of his family and the hunt, evidently joined humankind voluntarily and showed a capacity to lead.

The civilizations of "anatomically modern humans" that began in Mesopotamia, Anatolia, and Palestine about 100,000 years ago were initially tribal and nomadic. Some hunters, however, paused to capture and domesticate goats and sheep or to plant grains. Yet they also continued to seek new lands when they overhunted and overgrazed. The invention of the bow and arrow, the use of big dogs to protect the flocks from large predators, including human thieves, and the taming of the horse gave some nomadic marauders great power over peoples inclined to farming and trade. Strife arose between migrants and settlers, usually involving the townsmen against the warlike shepherds in the mountains.

The Paleolithic migrants had also carried mankind and dogs to the Nile Delta, where marshes and thick vegetation turned them aside. Many marched east into the deserts, some pausing at Faiyum Oasis in what is now Egypt, which they saved for a time from the encroaching desert by creating a system of canals. Others became bedouins, hunters who also created flocks and herds and bred domestic dogs in the desert. Many crossed a narrow strip of marsh and desert above the Gulf of Suez on the Red Sea into the vast Eurasian continent, moving along the Mediterranean into Palestine and Anatolia to the north, or across the Arabian desert to find fertile lands and favorable climate in Mesopotamia, between the Tigris and Euphrates Rivers, and on to prairie steppes and forest lands bordering the Arabian Sea and the Indian Ocean.

The farmers and herdsmen reaching Palestine and areas of the Fertile Crescent, past the Zagros Mountains of Iran, and those remaining along the Nile River discovered highly favorable conditions for crops and herds. Those Neolithic migrants became farmers and builders of towns and cities. They discovered ores, improved their Stone Age tools, and prospered with their canine helpers. Their dogs continued to assist hunters and herdsmen, and now turned to additional duties such as protecting homes and property and safeguarding and herding livestock, especially in areas where large wolves, bears, lions, and human predators threatened. The shepherds breeding bigger dogs found a ready market for them and sold some to wealthy merchants and land owners who used them as guard dogs. Shepherd kings in the deserts and mountains in time outmatched hunting, farming, and pastoral peoples and became wealthy landed gentry. In Palestine on the Dead Sea, a sheepherder who acquired a flock of 100,000 became a king—Mesha of Moab, scourge of the Israeli people. In Meroe and Cush and in the mountains of Anatolia, shepherds who knew the uses of fire also discovered ores they could smelt, and thus began a trade in iron and bronze tools and weapons.

By 8,000 B.C.E. hundreds of villages and many cities lined the banks of the Tigris and Euphrates Rivers, where the earliest known civilizations—Sumer, Akkad, Babylonia, Elam, and Assyria—flourished. In Anatolia (modern Turkey) hardy shepherds generated vast flocks and created shepherd kingdoms, began the craft of weaving, smelted ores, and engaged in trade with settlements in Egypt, supplying bronze and iron tools, pottery, and textiles. In return, the Anatolians received Egyptian grain and dogs. Anatolia, according to Darlington, also supplied Egypt with cave artists from Chatal Hüyük who would become the creators of the rock art of Egypt.

This clay relief pressed from a mold was discovered in Sumeria and shows a Molossian bitch suckling a litter of puppies. The relic is reliably dated circa 2025–1763 B.C. (Courtesy Oriental Institute, University of Chicago)

The rock artists of Africa were evidently among the earliest migrants into Europe accompanied by dogs. This is believed to have occurred about 10,000 years ago when these wanderers reached Scandinavia, Spain, and Britain. The deer hunt scene reproduced here, though from Spain, is highly reminiscent of the cave paintings of Tassili-n-Ajer. Note that the dog in this hunt bears strong similarities to the hunting dogs in African cave paintings.

The Role of the Waterways

Early in the African migrations the nomads used log rafts and dugout canoes to move along the Nile and Niger Rivers and to cross streams not fordable. Later Nile boats were fashioned of wood and papyrus, seventy feet long and some fitted with sails, though Egypt had few trees suitable for masts. Their dhows, however, made their way from the Gulf of Suez into the Red Sea, reaching Arabia Felix (Yemen) when winds were favorable, where their grain and dogs were traded for spices, gems, and gold.

The earliest ships into the Mediterranean, however, were probably those from Anatolia, where Minoans set out to trade, founded a base, and created the legendary civilization of Crete. The arts show a close association with Anatolia and Egypt, including fine glazed pottery showing sketches of graceful Egyptian Greyhounds hunting, as well as statuettes of a variety of canines. The Phoenician navy, based at Byblos and Ugarit, brought the world's first alphabet to Egypt, along with pottery, glass, and lumber. Both Crete and Phoenicia penetrated the Nile marshes after the Egyptians created canal systems, later reaching the wharves at Memphis. In addition to handling Egypt's export of grain, artifacts, spices, myrrh, gold, and gems from Arabia Felix, the Phoenicians endlessly carried cargoes of dogs.

All were eager to exchange their produce for Egyptian grains, the working dogs bred or obtained from the Berber tribes and in Cush, and iron tools produced at Meroe to the south. As a small agricultural and merchant land, Egypt would for many generations remain free from the growing strife and warfare in the outside world.

A Growing Commerce in Dogs

In time the warlike kings of towns and cities of the Middle East imported huge dogs from Aryan tribes in the north, said to have originated in India. These tribes may have obtained some of their canines in trade with shepherd tribes in Afghanistan and Tibet. They fought one another as Medes and Persians and ultimately united to form a power that would conquer much of the known world. The large and fierce dogs from the Persians were in great demand among their warrior neighbors, the Assyrians, Hittites, Sumerians, and Babylonians.

The Assyrians and later the Hittites of Anatolia largely provided the machinery of war—armored men, chariots, iron and bronze, war dogs, the uses of fire in combat—which they would employ against one another and in the conquest of Egypt. In Anatolia, Persia, and Afghanistan, breeders of the big hybrid wolf dogs that could battle fierce wolves, bears, and even lions had a ready market for their canines. Some were even imported from Tibet, where the dogs herded the huge mountain sheep. Soon Mesopotamia would acquire large Egyptian Greyhounds, Persian Mastiffs, and later Greek Molossians, needed to keep down the Arab bedouins who sought to drive their flocks from coastal areas into the highlands through towns and farms and the limited pastures near urban areas. As pottery arts improved, their decorative images depicted the gods and the life scenes of townspeople, especially dogs; Greyhounds, Mastiffs, and "lion dogs" were shown mostly in scenes of hunt and war. As civilization spread, the work and responsibilities of the dogs increased.

THE RISE OF THE PERSIAN EMPIRE

Meantime, migrants from the Mesopotamian lowlands moved higher and farther north with their dogs and herds to establish a hunting-pastoral society chiefly devoted to growing bread grains of superior quality. Hittites invaded Anatolia using their battle axes and war dogs to conquer earlier migrants in lands from Luristan to the Caspian Sea; their rule would endure nearly 1,000 years. The Achaemenes family arose among them, Cyrus the Great creating his dynasty by uniting two of the remaining powerful tribes in the declining Hittite empire, the Medes and Persians. Cyrus, the Persian Empire's first king, proved wise in diplomacy and skillful in using his troops, camel corps, and war dogs to create the first of world empires.

Herodotus, the Greek historian, in writing of the Persian might, accused Cyrus of continuing the Hittite practice of using war dogs to dispose of the bodies of their male dead. "It is said that the body of a male Persian is never buried," Herodotus charges in his *Persian Wars: Book II,* "until it is torn either by a big dog or birds of prey. That the Magi [the priests of Persia] has this custom is beyond doubt." Herotodus further asserted that the fierce Persians themselves "killed animals of all kinds with their own hands, excepting dogs."

Thus, in the course of creating a vast empire, the Persians spread wide their vicious practice of desecrating the dead. Later Zoroaster, a religious leader reared among the Medes, preached the brotherhood of man and had good words to say about dogs. This founder of Zoroastrianism deplored the Magi blood sacrifices and worship of idols. Even in view of this controversy, the canines that tore up human bodies also served as war dogs throughout the Persian Empire. The repulsive reputation of those Persian dogs, and of jackals that resembled early dog breeds and actually devoured human carrion, spread throughout the nations of the earth. A revulsion against some dogs spread wide and has been preserved, especially in the sacred Hebrew, Christian, and Islamic literature emerging near that time.

THE DOG'S PLACE IN THE HOLY BIBLE

We must choose our time carefully if we are to walk with Kiwi along the partnership path of man and dog from a significant beginning. The New Testament tells us that a day is as a thousand years in the mind of God (2 St. Peter 3:8), so the date of the creation of Earth may not have been precisely 4004 B.C. as fixed by Archbishop James Ussher of Armagh in 1654. Not long after the creation, God directed Noah to build an ark and then sent the flood. According to ancient legend, the dog got his cold nose by faithfully using it to plug a leak in Noah's ark. Thus Kiwi would be at home with her kind of antediluvian days. But we must also consider astronomical discoveries suggesting that the creation of the universe, including the Earth, was in the mind of God in a time when a day or night might span a million years. We must choose our own time as we understand it.

The invention of new methods of dating the geological and biological past, the discovery of many new fossil and artifacts sites in various parts of the world, and new data generally from astronomy to zoology are drastically changing our concept of prehistoric times. Was the Pleistocene age of advancing and retreating ice caps two million, one million, or merely 600,000 years ago? Were there four or ten melting periods? The answers so far have changed our perception of human development in relatively modern times by some 50,000 years or more. *Homo erectus* probably emerged 300,000 years ago"; "anatomically modern man," once estimated at 40,000 years, has been pushed back by recent finds in Israel to 92,000 years.

CARBON DATING—A VITAL DIAGNOSTIC

It began when Willard Libby of the University of Chicago, who had worked on the atom bomb development in World War II, created a method of carbon isotope dating of the world's past, based on the rate of disintegration of radioactive carbon-14. Photosynthesis in growing plants consumed by animals and humans creates the carbon from the atmosphere. When death occurs, the process ceases, and carbon disintegration begins at a constant measurable rate, precisely one half in 20,000 years. Thus in 40,000 years the process has ended. Science now has an accurate clock for that span of time. Other improvements in measurement have vastly expanded the time span. Potassium argon dating is good for 50,000 or more years; uranium thorium dating is preferred for ages between 50,000 and 500,000 years; and oxygen-18 covers millions of years. So our story of dogs traveling with man changes. The crossing of the Bering Strait may not have occurred 15,000 years ago, as Darlington suggested in 1968, but perhaps 50,000 years or longer into the past. By new dating methods, archaeological finds on Santa Rosa Island off the California coast, near Calico Hills in California, and at sites near Folsom and Clovis in southwestern parts of the United States generally show that human-kind left artifacts some 70,000 years ago.

Yet we can only deduce, as many have done. Botanist and naturalist Darlington early on relied on carbon-14, the somewhat limited measuring method developed shortly after World War II, to fix the time of the "first domesticated dog" included in discoveries of fossils in the caves of Choukoutien in China, where humans were buried with their dogs. Carbon-14 dating fixed the age of the skeletons at 15,000 years. Since the skeletons of the dogs buried with humans had not been harmed, we infer that those dogs were friends of the humans with whom they were buried, possibly guardians for those within the "cave." Darlington also suggests that Australoids departed Asia for New Guinea "whence, taking with them their domesticated dog, the Dingo, they passed over into Australia. . . . Similarly the Capoid or Bushmen-like people from North Africa expanded into South Africa. . . . Other early peoples with their dogs crossed the Bering Straits and spread during a period of about 80,000 years all over America." When did this happen relative to other events? It happened during the most recent glacial warming periods. "Of these," Darlington writes, "the most recent three occurred 115,000, 72,000, and 24,000 years ago. . . . The last glaciation locked up so much water in great ice caps . . . that the level of the sea fell about 200 meters [650 feet]." The Bering Strait crossings of animals and humans thus occurred from about 100,000 to 8,000 years ago, over a dry-land area about 300 miles wide by 600 miles in length.

Recent dating of fossils and artifacts from finds made at sites as far from Africa as Lake Baikal in Siberia and Old Crow in the Yukon Territory of Canada now fixes the Bering Strait passages of humans with domesticated dogs at 30,000 years ago. The domestic dog fossils found in England date from 7,000 to 17,000 years ago. "They were brought in by the Tardenosians," the Hawkeses report, without, however, fixing the precise date. They add wryly, "The Tardenosians, therefore, can claim to have originated the institution of canine friendship that has survived as one of the most cherished and most hated of our national foibles."[9]

3

EGYPT: THE ANCIENT LAND OF DOG LOVERS

⟨ơᵐᵘ⟩

Nothing in travel is more warming and thrilling to me than a visit to Egypt, that land of magnificent architecture, awesome mysteries of an ancient past, and the charm of the green countryside along the Nile. The Greek Herodotus, "Father of History," said it to his people long ago: "No country possesses so many wonders . . . not only the climate is different from that of the rest of the world . . . but the people also, in the most of their manners and their customs, they exactly reverse the common practices of mankind." Women went to the marketplace while men sat at home at the loom, Herodotus marveled. "All other men pass their lives separate from animals, but the Egyptians have animals living with them. Dough for bread they mix with their feet, mud they mix with their hands."

Our visit was in the course of tracing the rise of the canines amid civilization, and it had become obvious that nowhere else on earth but in Egypt had dogs risen so quickly and completely to their high position among humankind. We had come again to the Gulf of Suez along the line of migration of primitive peoples with their dogs, to visit the descendants of those who remained to create one of earth's most admirable civilizations and a close, even religious, relationship with their canines. Domesticated trained dogs not only lived with the ancient Egyptian, they guarded the children, carried burdens for the family, pulled carts, led the way in the hunt, herded and guarded domestic stock, and attended royalty and nobility as they were carried about on their palanquins. Dogs sat at the feet of the Pharaoh on his throne as his officials, priests, and scribes attended him. Dogs guarded

him in his bed chamber and, in death, joined him in his tomb, either personally
or in a sculptured likeness.

DEJA VU

We had come again to the pyramids, tombs, and museums, but also to seek out,
in the desert beyond Port Said, the probable routes of prehistoric peoples who
passed from Africa to Asia with their canine helpers at a time when the marshes
of the Nile Delta were too lush and thick to penetrate for the purposes of ordinary travel. En route I began to recall the remarkable difference between my
present quest and a previous trip into the Gulf of Suez less than a decade earlier.
It was the time of the Yom Kippur War, shortly after the Egyptians had launched
a surprise attack on Israeli forces in the Sinai and the Syrians simultaneously invaded from the Golan Heights on the north. My friend Seymour had been covering the war alone for our paper: the Egyptian front in the morning and Syrian
front in the afternoon. The fronts were quiet now in mid-January 1974. The time
for truce had come, as Israel's General Yariv had arrived at Kilometer 101 on the
Suez road to discuss the terms with Egypt's Abdul Gamazi. We correspondents
arrived later by air: I had time to visit the battlefield where in about six days the
Israeli forces, recovering fast from the Yom Kippur surprise, had taken more territory from Egypt than Neolithic African migrants had covered in some 6,000
years. On the day of our arrival the contending generals and their entourages,
including guard dogs, had assembled under bright yellow tents and pennants and
blue United Nations flags, a scene reminiscent of the days of medieval military
pageantry in the eighth century when Charles Martel and his Franks stopped the
Arab invaders of Europe, in the Battle of Tours.

As I sought the briefing tent, a pair of German Shepherd dogs came out to
inspect me. They halted, stiff-legged, while the United Nations honor guard, re-
splendent in blue helmets and battle dress with bayonets fixed, passed by. The
dogs ignored me. I was free to move on.

That afternoon I heard the terms of the cease-fire that had been signed and
flew back to the airfield nearest Jerusalem to telephone my story in time to make
the final edition of *Chicago Today*. Within two hours from Kilometer 101 we made
the deadline. The banner headlines that same afternoon, January 18, 1974, read:
"Mideast Pact Signed/Syria Talks to Open." I managed to include the war dogs
in my story. They had been serving all sides in hundreds of wars for 8,000 years

and were rarely mentioned in the history books. A simple acknowledgment seemed appropriate.

Now, in October 1984, we were in Egypt again, a land once more at peace. The pleasant people welcomed us to their magnificent museums, ancient tombs, temples, and pyramids.

TRACING THE EGYPTIANS

The origin of the Egyptians is not known with certainty. Botanist and historian C. D. Darlington has the support of others in suggesting that the original settlers along the Nile "came from Palestine along the Mediterranean coastal strip." He also credits the Egyptians or Copts as being ancestors of the Berbers who roamed the adjacent deserts and the mountains beyond. Darlington was writing prior to the 1989 discovery at Faiyum Oasis of fossil and primitive artifacts dating back nearly 100,000 years. At about the same time, other fossils and Stone Age "tool kits" dating back some 92,000 years were discovered in Israel. This suggests that

The ancient Egyptians worshiped dogs very early in the history of their society. This exquisite, gold-plated amulet is said to be a likeness of the god Anubis, also depicted as a man with the head of a jackal. Interestingly, this figure is very similar to the modern Pharaoh Hound which has survived almost unchanged for millennia. (Courtesy the British Museum)

This figure is identified as Oupouaout, the "trail leader," who had many roles in the mythology of Egyptian culture—among them, as a guide for the gods, kings, and the dead. He shares many physical similarities to Anubis but is always depicted standing while Anubis is in repose, a mark of slightly inferior rank. (Courtesy the Louvre, Paris)

This figure of Anubis surmounts a sarcophagus dated at 1,000 B.C. As the cult of Anubis grew older, the figure of the deity appeared more like a dog and less like a jackal. (Courtesy the Louvre, Paris)

some ancient migrants from southern and central Africa halted first in Egypt, while many proceeded into Asia across the sands and marshes above the Gulf of Suez into the Indus Valley of India. Other migrants remaining in northern Africa wandered as bedouins in the deserts or settled in strips about twelve miles wide along five hundred or so miles of the lower Nile. They were stopped by the marshes of the Nile Delta but would build a port city at Memphis, destined to become the capital of Egypt; eventually they would penetrate the delta to the Mediterranean, the Great Sea.

Others turned left to Faiyum Oasis or right toward Palestine, the latter crossing the marshes above the Red Sea, evidently at a place called the Sea of Reeds, as the Red Sea itself was 150 miles wide and a mile and a half deep. The Nile, flooding each September at exact times forecast by the declination of Sothis, the dog star (Sirius to the Greeks), enabled the primitive farmers to regularly harvest indigenous plants, though grains were imported from other places.

Sometime near 5,000 B.C., the people along the Nile were raising bountiful crops for export. They had created governments of Upper and Lower Egypt, established a priesthood, and were engaged in commerce with their neighbors. Their dugout and papyrus canoes plied the Nile between the cataracts, and they created sailing dhows to cross the Red Sea to exchange their exports, including dogs, with Yemen and Arabia. With the help of their domestic dogs brought up from Kenya, Abyssinia, and Meroe, they captured and tamed wild animals, from pigs, oxen, sheep, goats, and wild cats to hippopotami. These traders proudly called themselves "men"—*romet*, according to the German Egyptologist Adolph Erman, writing more than 100 years ago: "Their neighbors they designated as Asiatics, Libyans, and Negroes, but not men."[1] They claimed to be ancestors of the Berber bedouins, who ranged in hues from the dark brown complexion of Egyptian men and the delicate yellow of Egyptian women to the black of Abyssinia, Cush, and Nubis and the white of nomad tribes in the Atlas Mountains.

Early in their history the Egyptians sought to acquire the favorite dog of the Berbers, the Sloughi, a gazehound similar to the Greyhound. The Sloughi is a strong, fleet running hound that finds its prey by sight, since little spoor was left by wild game in the desert. The Greyhound could outrun and take down a lion, according to Erman. The Egyptians themselves bred small red "wolfhounds" that joined the Greyhound in herding sheep and goats, and they bred the Basenji that guarded homes and farms. Eventually, the Egyptians themselves bred Greyhounds since they had discovered a wide market for such dogs, shipping their domesticated cargo abroad by way of the Minoan and Phoenician navies once the Nile Delta had been opened to the Mediterranean.

The Anubis Trinity: three versions of the dog-headed god that attended Egyptian souls to the afterlife. The figure at the right appears to be ocean-oriented and evidently had charge of souls lost at sea. These exquisite depictions appear in the tomb of Horemhab in Biban el-Muluk. (Courtesy the Oriental Institute, University of Chicago)

Anubis, fourth in rank in the Egyptian pantheon of gods, is depicted here tending the mummy of Sen-nedjem I in a painting found on the tomb wall of this ruler in Deir el-Medina. (Courtesy the Oriental Institute, University of Chicago)

Upper and Lower Egypt were divided and relatively remote from the rest of the rising civilizations in Asia and the Mediterranean region until about 3,200 B.C. when King Narmer of Upper Egypt wed Princess Nithotep of Lower Egypt, using his troops and diplomacy to unite the country as well as consolidating the clergy in the worship of the gods Set and Osiris. In the following dynasties the Pharaohs elevated Amon-ra to supremacy and reduced Osiris, god of the Nile and the giver of sustenance via the annual floods, and Isis, his consort and queen of heaven, to lesser ranks. The fourth god, Anubis, the dog, continued as the faithful guide of the souls of the dead to their fate, life with Isis on the dog star Sothis, a return to one's embalmed body on earth for another chance, or condemnation to the realm of Epuat, the wolf god, guardian of the underworld.

EGYPTIAN DOGS IN DAILY LIFE

I was interested in the unusual rise of those canines in ancient Egypt, a status seemingly unique among the early developing civilizations. Ancient Egyptians truly honored their dogs, allowing them to participate in almost every family relationship. Following the invasions of the Hyksos, Hittites, Assyrians, and Persians, the Egyptians became warlike and used war dogs themselves, but they also were the only ancient people who punished a human being for mistreating a dog. And

This painting from the tomb of Ipuy in Deir el-Medina, Egypt, shows a garden scene with a man tending a shaduf (water lifter) and accompanied by a dog. In view of the relative scarcity of water in the region, the dog may have served as a deterrent to thieves. (Courtesy the Oriental Institute, University of Chicago)

according to the writings of Herodotus, when a favorite canine died, the Egyptian owner would shave his own head and body in mourning. However, Egyptians traded in human slaves, forcing their return. The rest of the ancient world for many thousands of years kept their dogs in relative slavery or as ready suppliers of food, in the hunt or as food themselves. In Hittite and Persian civilizations, dogs would become trained killers of human beings and devourers of human carrion.

While high civilizations developed in Mesopotamia and Anatolia, the Egyptians perfected their farming skills and irrigation projects, successfully storing both water and grain. They built their homes of Nile mud and their palaces of brick and stone. They created tools and ornaments from Meroe ores, Nubian gold, Yemeni gems, and glass from Nile sand. The development of glass may have been first accomplished by Phoenicians who arrived to trade for Egyptian grain and dogs and returned with such turbulent cargoes—ancient drawings show ships overloaded with canines—that they also needed to carry bags of Nile sand as ballast in their holds.

Egyptian grain was in heavy demand when the Minoan and Phoenician ships made their way to Memphis on the Nile. So were the dogs. For more than 2,000 years the Egyptians maintained their relative isolation before the invaders came. With the arrival of the merchant ships, Egypt began to open to visitors, the merchants themselves, and refugees from Mesopotamia, Mediterranean coastal towns, and Greek islands. Before he was defeated and dethroned by the Persians, King Amasis, Pharaoh of the Egyptians, welcomed the visitors, especially the Greeks. (The isolation of Egypt may have lasted much longer: The fossil finds of *Aegyptopithecus* may lead to a conclusion that man in Egypt existed as early as the time of *Australopithecus* in South Africa. Also, paleontologists have again found entry into Ethiopia [ancient Abyssinia] where they can once more search for the extensive fossil deposits thought to be there. This and the discovery of what have been described as "anatomically modern humans" at Qafzeh, dated 92,000 B.C., may in time result in further revisions of the time and place where civilization as we know it began. However, for dogs as we know them, it undoubtedly began in ancient Egypt.)

The attachment of dogs and humans was acknowledged by early writers since the time when canines were memorialized in the royal tombs. Why this affinity? The dog is a social animal, but so are many other species. Dogs readily joined early humans in their rock shelters, caves, and at their campfires, as did some wolves, and participated with humans in the hunt, which the wolves did not. In Egypt the working dog, friend and protector of the family, had come into its own.

DOGS IN EGYPTIAN RELIGIOUS LIFE

As noted by Herodotus, the Egyptians loved their animals, especially their canines; they were also devoted to their priesthood. Their religion provided well for the souls of the dead, with the privilege of returning to their earthly bodies if they failed to enter the heavenly world of Osiris and Isis on Sothis, the dog star. The Egyptians consequently became the world's most skilled embalmers and practitioners of the funerary arts, including the construction of massive tombs that survive as modern wonders of the world. They provided in the burial arrangement for the comfort of the individual soul released in death that might, guided by Anubis, return to its human body at any time should it fail to meet the requirements of the heavenly rulers—or escape the bounds of the underworld.

A portion of a scene on walls of the Theban tomb of Nebamun, a scribe and the counter of grain in the granary of divine offerings of Amun. The deceased is shown here with his wife and a small bitch under his wife's chair. (Courtesy the Oriental Institute, University of Chicago)

In the exceptionally dry environment found in the tomb, food would last for some time. This was also true of the fine accouterments and treasures left for nobles, high priests, and members of the wealthy classes. A favorite dog, embalmed or represented by a sculptured likeness, could also be found in the tomb, and it too would remain intact for some time due to the atmosphere.

INSIGHTS INTO ANUBIS

The story of the dog god (to some, the jackal-headed god) Anubis, son of Osiris, god of the Nile and chief of gods after Amon-ra in the ancient Egyptian pantheon, is fascinating as translated from hieroglyphs on the tomb walls of Beni-Hasan by the famed Adolf Erman, director of the Egyptian museum in Berlin, in his book *Life in Ancient Egypt*, and by the French Egyptologist Isha Schwaller de Lubicz, in her book *Her-Bak Egyptian Initiate,* an excellent study of Egyptian religions.[2] The mythological convolutions of ancient Egyptian myths have been a problem for several thousand years, so it is not unusual that two experts disagree from the start on the very name of the dog god Anubis. Among the duties of Anubis was that of directing the wandering soul, *ka*, to one of the thirty-eight assessors, or judges, representing each of the thirty-eight nomes, or provinces, into which Egypt had been districted by the government and priesthood. A judge would make known the individual soul's fate, based on its earthly behavior. Anubis and his assistants then would guide *ka* on its way. Epuat, the wolf god, was assigned to patrol the gates of the underworld, to make sure that an unfortunate spirit condemned to hell would not escape.

There was early controversy about Anubis. He may have been illegitimate. The gods Osiris and Set (first to be portrayed as a dog, with seemingly a jackal head) married sisters—Osiris wedding Nepthys and Set taking Isis. But at some time after the marriages, Osiris took Isis to bed, and she bore him Anubis, shown in ancient Egyptian art as having a dog's head on a human body. In the opinion of Egyptologist Erman, it was a jackal's head; to noted French Egyptologist R. A. Schwaller de Lubicz, the head of Anubis is that of a dog, resembling a montage of all canines within all experiences of the people of that civilization. Madam Schwaller de Lubicz clearly has the best of the argument, when it is considered that the early Egyptian artists, working in stone with their crude chisels, showed the heads of two gods as appearing identical—jackal-like. The best likeness of Anubis is his statue in the Cairo Museum, depicting a beautiful animal whose head has the forward pointing ears of a Basenji (or a jackal), whose body is that of a Greyhound, and whose tail is that of a wolf. Schwaller de Lubicz points out that the mummified skeleton in the base of that statue is that of a dog. "The closest approximation could be the wild dog of Egypt," she concludes.

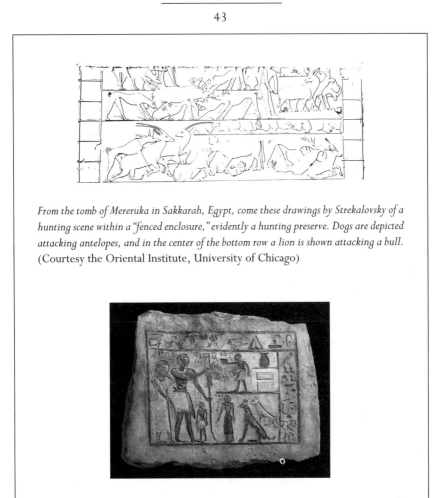

From the tomb of Mereruka in Sakkarah, Egypt, come these drawings by Strekalovsky of a hunting scene within a "fenced enclosure," evidently a hunting preserve. Dogs are depicted attacking antelopes, and in the center of the bottom row a lion is shown attacking a bull. (Courtesy the Oriental Institute, University of Chicago)

Stela of the Nubian mercenary Nenu, 2213–2035 B.C., shows the mercenary, his wife, and son being welcomed to the new Temple of Anubis, built by the conquerors of Nubia. The figure of Anubis himself appears above the head of the cup bearer (top center). (Courtesy Museum of Fine Arts, Boston)

Further answer to the precise nature of the god Anubis can best be provided by considering the relationship of ancient Egyptians to their many gods and to their own way of life. The Egyptians abhorred the habits of jackals that prowled at night and devoured carrion, including the flesh of humans. The tomb of Rameses VI, in the Valley of Kings, contains a mural showing the royal hunting dogs with their trainer. They have Greyhound-like bodies, wolflike tails, and heads precisely like that of the dog god Anubis. The artists may have represented Anubis and Epuat as "jackal-headed" gods, but the models more likely were the Basenji, the small house dog with a rather pointed muzzle and forward-pointing ears, a hybrid of the Dingo or Egyptian wild dogs and jackals.

The history of the dog in Egypt began in the Upper Nile region about 6,000 years ago. Fernand Mery of France, in his excellent book *The Dog*, fixes the time of an official adoption of an Egyptian canine god as "about 4240 B.C. when two deities divided between them the allegiance of all the struggling villages [that] formed Egypt. They were: Set, the Greyhound with the forked tail (in Upper Egypt), and Horus, the hawk (in Lower Egypt and the Delta of the Nile). From the time of the IVth dynasty [3,000 years B.C.] each clan had a sacred animal for its protection, and a canine manufestation appears regularly throughout Egyptian iconography."

When Egypt became a fully united country under Chuen'eten (Amenhotep IV) and his consort, Neferteyte, Egypt was districted into thirty-eight nomes, each having a god of its choosing. The territory of the dog god included the twelfth and thirteenth nomes, and the god Set became known as Anubis.

Anubis would arise to number four in the pantheon of Egypt's national deities. The Amenhoteps and the priests of Thebes, the national capital, were in good part responsible.

From the beginning, when some migrants from southern Africa paused along the Nile north of Meroe to plant their wild grains and create farms, the people showed a special fondness for wild creatures. They used their domesticated dogs to help capture wild animals with nets, traps, and slings that would enable them to capture species they hoped to tame or at least to feed from their wealth of grains, to fatten them for slaughter. The richness of the soil, flooded regularly by the river, enabled those who remained as farmers to feed themselves and their animals and ultimately to sell their produce in a world market. This would attract back the descendants of those migrants who passed on into Asia and even Europe to create their own high civilizations, some exceeding that of Egypt. So, in times of famine and trouble, those Africans who settled between the Tigris and Euphrates Rivers and in India and Asia Minor would return, bringing with them their cultures, their wise men, and their skilled workers, who themselves learned much from Egypt, especially about religion. Most of the Greek gods were conceived and given their names in Egypt, Herodotus tells us. Pythagoras, said to have been the wisest man of his time, traveled from Greece, his homeland, to Egypt, where he developed his theory of transmigration of souls, or metempsychosis. Back in

Greece and in India, he advised the dying to give their final breaths to a dog that could guide their souls to salvation, thus the practice of holding the mouth of a living dog to the mouths of the dying. The canines later began service in hospitals, helping the sick to recover and comforting the dying.

For a time in Egypt, the high position of the canines seemed threatened. After years of wars and struggles, King Narmer by his diplomacy had united the governments of Upper and Lower Egypt and one of his successors, Amenhotep I, drove out invading Hyksos. The Hyksos had brought into Egypt their relatively high culture, as well as their use of war dogs. The Egyptians subsequently began the importation of such dogs, giant Mastiffs from Anatolia and Assyria, to use in battle themselves. Pictographs in the tombs of the period show an Amenhotep (in this instance, Pharaoh Tutankhamen) in his war chariot, drawn by horses and accompanied by his hunting dogs, running down a lion, and again in his chariot, with Mastiffs as guards, shooting his Nubian foes with bow and arrow.

Pharaoh Amenhotep IV veered from Egypt's war policy by turning his attention to alleged interference of the priesthood at Thebes in foreign affairs. He especially held the priests responsible for causing difficulties with gold-rich Nubia. He rejected the idolatry at Thebes and declared his faith in one god—Ra, bringer of light and life. The Pharaoh moved to Heliopolis, city of the sun, with his consort, Neferteyte, and seven daughters, and even changed his name to Chuen'eten, meaning "splendor of the disc."

It appeared that the theocratic might of Thebes and the worship of idols and animals, including the dog gods Set and Anubis, were to end. But the people of Egypt refused to give up their popular deities, and Chuen'eten had to compromise. He accepted Amon, the high god of his ancestors, as well as Ra: Thus Amon-Ra, lord of heavens and earth. Other animal deities, even crocodiles, were worshiped during this period.

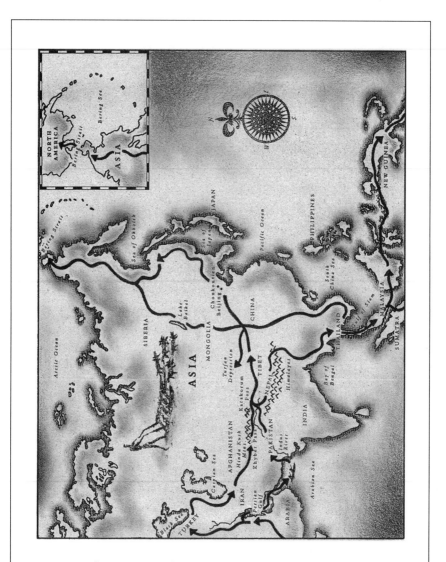

A migration of humans and dogs from Africa into remote areas of Eurasia, across Mongolia and Siberia to the north and China and the Malay Peninsula to the south, occurred between 8,000 and 12,000 years ago. Glaciers held back the great bodies of waters, exposing land bridges. The trails of these ancient migrants have been marked by numerous fossils, artifacts, tool kits, and other records of the development of civilized man.

4

AGE OF THE GIANTS

ᕗᵐᵐᕐ

We were entering Kusudasi, a charmingly beautiful Turkish port town where a summer might be pleasantly spent. At nearby Ephesus we could visit the awesome marble ruins of that ancient Greek capital of religion and learning, first situated on the Turkish coast about 1100 B.C. But our goal was to trace the Neolithic migrants who settled in ancient Anatolia, on the Konya plain beyond the Taurus Mountains about 10,000 years ago. There were wars and rumors of wars to discourage a further trip into the Ararat range beyond Chatal Hüyük, as there have been for several thousand years, so no summer rest stop seemed likely. Chatal Hüyük had been literally unearthed in the 1960s, the mud walls and houses excavated under the direction of James Mellaart of the University of London. It would rival Byblos and Jericho in antiquity. Botanist C. D. Darlington of Oxford would proclaim it the earliest known organized agricultural community. The population of the town, reaching its peak of development about 6500 B.C., has been estimated at 5,000—true Stone Age people who created the world's most advanced Neolithic culture in their time.

The migrants to Chatal Hüyük evidently came around the Mediterranean from the Red Sea nearer Africa as hunters, their women now industrious planters of seeds and roots gathered en route. As they used rafts earlier in their history on the Konya plain to bring down wood and ores from the Arayat and Taurus Mountains, they may have done so to bypass Mediterranean marshes along the way to Anatolia (modern Turkey). That they came from the Gulf of Suez crossing places and along the Mediterranean coast seems indicated by the Red Sea cowrie shells they placed with their dead.

They arrived in Anatolia as Neolithic hunters. Most of their hunting dogs must have been left behind, if the migrants traveled on even quiet coastal waters by raft, but some may have walked along the coast through Palestine and Syria. The men, in any case, continued to hunt at Chatal Hüyük, bringing down big game and predators such as leopards and large northern wolves. In time, dogs were evidently mated with tamed or even wild wolves. In wall paintings, such animals are shown with women as well as men, unlike other primitive art depicting males only at work. Farming, once begun, may have taken 4,000 years to develop fully, Darlington estimates.

Two kinds of people emerged from this 4,000 years of development—the peasant attached to the farm and the grazier or herdsmen, once a hunter and still migratory, who captured wild ruminants with the aid of his dogs. The early herdsmen domesticated and bred his livestock, shifting about as the grazing environment changed. The hunter went on, endlessly seeking better outlook for game, taking his dogs with him. The herdsmen as well continued in a nomadic pattern, but more slowly. Leading their herds and flocks into ever cooler highlands, they developed larger, stronger dogs to contain their stock and to protect against human and animal predators. They discovered copper and iron ore in the highlands and learned the practical art of smelting. In time they created iron tools and weapons and found gemstones they made into beautiful ornaments, later brought downriver to trade with a people who produced grain, milled flour, and baked excellent bread.

In Chatal Hüyük the women continued to plant and tend the hearths in which they baked their bread. They managed the children and domesticated the dogs, including those no longer used for hunting and some that had hybridized with wolves. These imposing dogs, brought down by the herdsmen, proved useful for carrying burdens and guarding people and property. The women became the leaders of their society at Chatal Hüyük, the first organized agricultural town and the world's first matriarchal community. ("The women even had the larger beds," Darlington writes.) But, in four millennia, conditions reversed somewhat. Some-one, man or woman, invented a wooden plow that could be drawn through the tough plateau sod by tame oxen. Only a strong man could have managed such a plow and animals.

Both men and women evidently engaged in creating useful items of stone, bone, wood, and clay. Their tools, weapons, and other artifacts found include copper, bronze, and iron weapons, jewelry with gemstones, and mirrors made of obsidian, a volcanic glass. The mountain craftsmen used their timber rafts to bring their artifacts to trade for ground grain and other products of Chatal Hüyük. Had they used such rafts to reach Anatolia along the coast of the Mediterranean and then crossed over the Taurus Mountains to reach the plateau on which Chatal Hüyük would rise? The skulls of their buried dead usually are found to have had cowrie shells placed in the eye sockets. Such shells, widely scattered in the world, at the least suggest that the Chatal Hüyük migrants had traveled along the Mediterranean coast. How would they reach that coast? From the Red Sea and the Gulf of Suez, near the crossing place of African migrants. Perhaps the first settlers in Anatolia came from Africa, too. Their grisly practice of allowing vultures and possibly dogs to clean the bodies of their dead of all flesh may have been their own invention, as well as the use of the cowrie shells, resembling human eyes.

The shepherds traded in sheep and large herding dogs. They and the herdsmen, alongside the producers of lumber, iron, and copper in the mountains, prospered. Some of the mountain shepherds would eventually become mountain kings, "wild men of the mountains" who worshiped storm gods, men who were enemies of one another until they united to settle trade disputes and land claims of those dwelling in and about Chatal Hüyük and its neighboring towns. The iron mongers made armor and weapons for these men. Eventually they would dominate Anatolia and reach the lowlands of the Middle East and northern Africa from which they came.

Meantime, the migrants reaching the lowlands to the south of the Zagros Mountains, despite their problems with hot dry summers, frequent floods from the rivers flowing down the mountains, and incessant struggle and warfare among the settlements along the rivers, were creating villages, towns, and city-states, among them those destined to become empires—Sumer, Akkad, Elam, Babylonia, and Assyria.

The Sumerians and Akkadians prospered on land that would someday be deeply flooded, according to their legends, but that would also yield productive farms and great city-states near the delta where the Tigris and Euphrates once met; in Assyria along the Tigris to the north; and in Byblos on the Mediterranean.

Was the civilization beginning at Sumer the first of its kind, advanced beyond that of Chatal Hüyük and predating even that of Egypt? Leonard Cottrell, in his authoritative books on both Sumer and Egypt, asks, "Which came first, the civilization of Sumer or that of ancient Egypt? It is difficult to give a positive answer."[1] The civilizations were not the same, though the climate and location, the flowing rivers and the delta marshes, seemed much alike. Both would be within the Fertile Crescent, the area most adaptable to growing crops. Most hunters and herders had gone on to mountains. Only Nimrod, king of Babylon and the possessor of flocks and packs of trained dogs, would be remembered as a great hunter. Sumer and its physical environs lacked the excellent construction rock of Egypt, but it nevertheless built imposing cities and high ziggurats to help them see their gods. They built with baked bricks and stones rolled down from the mountains and dragged to building sites by asses and slaves. Then Sumer invented the wheel, creating heavy work carts pulled by tamed oxen and carts for households and children pulled by dogs.

Sumer would also invent pictogram writing, Akkad created cuneiform signs, and Ugarit would put all this together to create an alphabet. In the writing, on baked clay tables and some chiseled in stone, we can discover a clue to a seeming absence of dogs (many had gone on north to the mountains) and the problems and strife that arose in Sumer's "Garden of the Lord," as they named their flood-prone land. In an epic poem, Sumerians relate the adventures of the mythical hero Gilgamesh, who describes the struggles and ultimately the wars between the shepherds from the deserts and the mountains who descended into the lowlands, following the time of the Great Flood, to raid the cities and ravage the lands. The stories were said to have been written in stone by King Gilgamesh himself. In one of the poems inscribed on clay tablets after the time of Gilgamesh, two short lines suggest that the troubles that arose may have occurred to some degree because most domestic dogs had departed Sumer with the shepherds. The poetry describes the pleasures and delight of Dilmun, the Sumerian heaven, by detailing the absence of certain earthly woes:

> The lion kills not . . . the wolf snatches not the lamb
> Unknown is the kid-devouring wild dog. . . .

Thus is the Gilgamesh story of troubles negatively summarized and confirmed, and a reason provided. The shepherds who attacked and destroyed farms and towns of the lowlands had returned there to repay the villagers for harassment occurring when those same shepherds in earlier days drove their flocks and herds from coastal areas and the valleys toward the highlands. They were not without blame. Their dogs had killed lowland sheep and goats. In the highlands they had found prosperity and power, and they desired more. The shepherds raided one another, and the strongest created tribal relationships and declared themselves kings. In the highlands they bred large Mastiff-type dogs from stocks obtained in the north and created by hybridizing with wolves. They were truly powerful, menacing animals.

Some people in the lowlands no longer had dogs to protect their small herds from wild animals or human predators. Their foes were now skilled in warfare and armed with good weapons made from the ores discovered in the highlands. The time came for them to take vengeance on the villages and to seize or destroy the prospering cities. In 1726 B.C., about the time of the entry of Hebrew shepherd tribes into Egypt following famine in Canaan, the Hyksos in the north descended from the mountains and advanced south into Egypt, bringing in their armored soldiers, war chariots, and large war dogs from Anatolia. They were followed by the Hittites, the Assyrians, and the Persians, all bringing in their cultures, warfare techniques, and war dogs to as far south as Egypt, a land that had been mostly peaceful for 2,000 years.

The Hittites and the Hyksos had been the first to introduce large Mastiffs into Mesopotamia and, perhaps, the first into Anatolia. These tribes initially appeared as a people called Aryans, barbarians in northwest India. Prior to their arrival in India, they may have been on the steppes of Eurasia, according to historian Arnold Toynbee. Possibly, as those who doubt the "Out of Africa" theory suggest, those barbaric tribes may have been the first of primitive humankind and therefore the first to domesticate the wolf.

Asian settlers, especially in times of famine, were eager to exchange their produce for Egyptian grains produced regularly by the flooding of the Nile. This was also true of the working dogs the Egyptians bred or obtained from Berber tribes and in the land of Kush, and iron tools wrought at Meroe to the south. However, as a small agricultural and merchant land protected by the desert and the Red Sea, which few boats could ply, Egypt would for many generations remain free from the growing strife and warfare of the outside world.

In time, the warlike kings of towns and cities of the Middle East imported huge dogs from Aryan tribes in the north. Said to have originated in India, the tribes may have obtained some of their dogs in trade with shepherd tribes in Afghanistan and Tibet. They once fought each other as Medes and Persians, though ultimately uniting to form a power that would conquer much of the known world. The large, fierce dogs of the Persians were in great demand among their warrior neighbors—the Assyrians, Hittites, Sumerians, and Babylonians.

"Choose the Molossian," Aristotle urged in his treatise on animals. This ancient breed probably originated in the mountains of Iran or other northern areas of Mesopotamia when the Kush mountains were still iced over. The great Mastiffs of Greece were named for the Molossian tribe, which settled in Epirus, in northern Greece, about 1000 B.C. (Sketch by Mark Sandlin, from a monument in Keramicus Cemetery, Athens)

The Laconian Hound, another highly regarded breed from Greece, was bred by the Spartans and, like the Molossian, was the subject of praise by Aristotle. The female of the breed, he noted, "was of gentle spirit and more intelligent than the male." While Aristotle did not recommend the female as a war dog, the Laconian remained a fierce, effective factor in battle. (Courtesy, Museum of the Acropolis, Athens; Photographed by Sabine Callaris)

The Assyrians, and later the Hittites of Anatolia, largely provided the machinery of war: flint- and iron-tipped spears and arrows, armored men, chariots protected by iron and bronze, war dogs, and the use of fire in combat, which they would employ in the conquest of Egypt. Anatolian, Persian, and Afghan breeders of mighty hybrid wolf-dogs—able to battle fierce wolves, bears, and even lions—had a ready market for their canines. Some of those fierce dogs came from as far away as Tibet, where they herded huge mountain sheep. Soon Sumer, Akkad, and other warlike city-states of Mesopotamia would acquire large Egyptian Greyhounds and Persian Mastiffs, and later, Greek Molossians, all needed to discourage the bedouins who continued to drive their flocks from coastal areas into the highlands through towns and farms and over the limited pastures near urban areas.

As pottery-making techniques improved, jars, lamps, and other common articles came to be more artistically decorated, now depicting the gods and scenes of everyday life of townspeople. Working dogs, Greyhounds, Mastiffs, and "lion dogs" incorporated into these designs were shown mostly engaged in the hunt and as war dogs. As civilization spread, the work and responsibilities of the dogs also increased.

The Mastiff as he appears today has changed little over the centuries. This basic breed derives from the fearsome war dogs known to Alexander the Great and other commanders from Phoenicia, Rome, and other powerful empires. The Mastiff influence is seen throughout the modern family of Molosser breeds. (Sketch by Mark Sandlin)

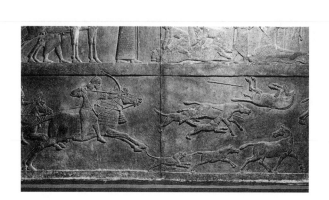

Mastiff-like dogs shown on this bas-relief participate in a wild-horse hunt in the reign of Asshurbanipal II (883–859 B.C.) of Assyria. The style of harnesses and decorations suggests neo-Hittite influences. The hunt itself may have occurred in Hasanlu Tepe in the Solduz Valley of modern Iran, where ancient skeletons of horses and large dogs have been discovered. (Copyright © The British Museum)

From a palace wall in the ancient city of Nineveh came this portion of a bas-relief showing the net bearer and dog handler of an ancient hunting party. (Copyright © The British Museum)

At the same time, migrants from the Mesopotamian lowlands moved higher and farther north with their dogs and herds to establish a hunting-pastoral society chiefly devoted to agriculture, growing bread grains of superior quality. Hittites, Celts, Slavs, and Aryans from Asia invaded Anatolia and Europe using their battle axes and war dogs, conquering earlier migrants in lands from Luristan to the Caspian Sea. The Hittite empire would endure almost one thousand years. As part of their religion, the Hittites worshiped a fertility goddess and were accused of giving over their dead for disposal by wild beasts and their own fierce dogs. The Achaemenes family arose among them, with Cyrus the Great creating his own dynasty by uniting two of the remaining powerful tribes, the Medes and Persians, in the declining Hittite empire. The Persians grew powerful, Cyrus proving wise in diplomacy and skillful in using his troops, camel corps, and war dogs to create the first world empire.

Herodotus, in writing of the Persian might, accused Cyrus of continuing the Hittite practice of using war dogs to dispose of the bodies of their male dead. "It is said that the body of a male Persian is never buried," Herodotus charges in his *Persian Wars: Book II,* "until it is torn either by a big dog or birds of prey. That the Magi has tolerated this evil is well known."

The Hyksos and the Hittites without doubt once invaded Syria and Egypt from the north, bringing in war dogs, after passing through Anatolia and Palestine. The records of those invasions are well dated. The invasion of Anatolia occurred in 1700 B.C. not far from Chatal Hüyük, where dogs and people appear together in stone etchings dating back to 10,000 B.C. Those invaders may have brought with them large Indian dogs, or similar animals from Central Asia descended from wolves. Josephine Z. Rine, in her *World History of Dogs,* reports that large hunting hounds were used to take down big game in India and also in the sport of hunting the indigenous large jackals. Such jackal hunting was a recreation "much in the same fashion as we hunt foxes today," she writes. The pursued jackals didn't behave like African jackals however; they helped one another. "They rushed in to the rescue of the pursued with such fury they routed the huntsmen . . . and inflicted severe injuries upon the dogs," Rine reports. "Thus both wolf and jackal can qualify as ancestors of the dog."[2]

Whether or not the Hyksos and Hittites brought jackals as well as domesticated dogs or wolves into countries later invaded by the Persians, animals Herodotus called "Indian dogs" were used by Cyrus of Persia as he created his empire. In Asia such large dogs, it is said, were accustomed to consuming human flesh. Cyrus is accused by Herodotus and others of forgiving entire cities their war taxes if they agreed to breed and train war canines that would also consume human carrion. The Hittites were additionally credited, or blamed, with introducing the smelting of iron ore and organized military strategies into Mesopotamia, particularly through Assyria.

The German archaeologist Hugo Winckler in 1806 discovered and translated Hittite cuneiform tablets, thereby rescuing the Hittite empire from near oblivion and restoring the Aryan people into civilizations they influenced and dominated for a thousand years. Their contributions to early culture may have outweighed their military record. They were responsible for the checking of Sumerian expansion on the edge of Capadocia in Anatolia. They conquered all of Mesopotamia and drove the Egyptians out of Syria, making effective use of their large war dogs, the same dogs they had previously sold to the Assyrians, Medes, and Persians.

The Hittite empire reached its peak under King Shubbililui (1390–1200 B.C.), who brought some law and order into an otherwise chaotic world. The Hittite war with Egypt, however, exhausted both powers. Hittite use of trained Mastiffs as hunting and war dogs is confirmed by temple and palace bas-relief sketches of their own, as well as Assyrian, kings hunting lions in battle chariots drawn by horses, and by the young King Tutankhamen of Egypt using them in war.

The Assyrians learned from the Hittites and seized the lapse of Hittite power as the opportunity to launch their own aggressions. They too marched down upon the heirs to the Sumerian civilization with soldiers dressed in iron armor, carried by war chariots, and escorted by war dogs. They easily subdued the people of Mesopotamia. Meantime in the north, the Medes and the Persians, freed from Hittite power, were united under Cyrus, who conquered the world from Anatolia to the gateway of Egypt.

Cyrus would become one of the world's great military leaders, but he had lost touch with his priesthood and aroused the opposition of a Mede priest, Zoroaster, who preached the brotherhood of man and deplored blood sacrifice and the worship of idols. Zoroaster praised dogs while the royal family was accused of ordering them into disgraceful practices, including the devouring of human corpses. Herodotus also held the Mazda priests responsible. This seems strange, since the Mazda spoke for the high god Ashuramazda, who was said to have approved the dog as the best of all his creations. "The best of all creatures, self-clothed and self-shod," the priests intoned, "self-clothed, self-shod, and watchful, wakeful and sharp-toothed. Born to watch over man's goods . . . no house could exist on earth but for the shepherd's dog and the house dog."

Such panegyric exceeded that of even the Egyptians and Greeks. But the priests who accompanied Cyrus and his troops into Egypt were accused there as well of being responsible for the evil treatment and reputation of the Persian dogs. Historian Josephus says that, following the death of Cambyses, their imposed Persian king, the Egyptians slaughtered the Mazda and thereafter were well treated by the succeeding Persian ruler, who adopted the Egyptian practice of punishing humans for any mistreatment of dogs.

The true blame for the purposeful, albeit repugnant, actions of the dogs introduced into world trade and employment, mostly by the Persians, may properly lie at the feet of the Assyrian king Sennerachib. This ruler established his merchants in the Hittite capital, where they traded woven cloth and rich tapestries for war chariots, armor, and war dogs. That Sennerachib used such dogs in the hunt and in battle is shown by the bas-reliefs in the library of his grandson Ashurbanipal, discovered in Nineveh by the Turkish archaeologist Homudz Rassam in 1852. Sennerachib prized his canines but taught them to perform incredibly repulsive actions, even boasting of it, as disclosed by a clay tablet also found in his grandson's library.

Following the sack of Babylon in 689 B.C., Sennerachib declared to his scribes: "I tore out the tongues of those whose mouths uttered blasphemies against my god Ashur and plotted against me, the god-fearing prince. I defeated them . . . .Others I smashed alive with the very same statues they used to kill my own grandfather . . . . As a burial service for his soul I fed their corpses, cut into small pieces, to the dogs . . . pigs . . . vultures. I removed corpses the pestilence had felled . . . after the dogs and pigs had fed on them . . . filling the streets of Babylon . . . ."

A happier memory of early dogs is bequeathed to us by the Nabeteans, who came out of Egypt with an Arabic culture enhanced by the Egyptian adoration of animals. They would take their Aramaic language to the Middle East (where it would become the common tongue, continuing into the Christian era), and they would accord the dog a role in their religion as they created their society at Petra, in ancient Edom, and in the surrounding desert (now Israel). In Petra they carved elaborate house and temple fronts from the pink cliffside rock and developed an advanced civilization.

The Nabeteans worshiped Mithras, the bull, as their chief god, and provided the dog as his bodyguard. The absorbing history of the Nabeteans is related by Nelson Glueck in *Dieties and Dolphins*. (The dolphin, also a part of Nabetean religion, perhaps memorializes a seagoing past.[3]) As director of the American School of Oriental Research in Jerusalem, Glueck supervised the digs at sites in Israel. On several stella found there, Mithras is shown under attack by enemies, usually snake gods among them. In each case Mithras is protected by dogs, just as Anubis, the Egyptian guide and protector, cared for the souls of the dead. Citing a sketch showing such a canine seemingly at the throat of Mithras—hardly an appropriate act by a protector—Glueck explains that "he is in the fray in order to consume the blood or life force" of the god, a mission similar to that of Anubis in various Egyptian death scenes. The Nabetean stella also picture Artargartis, their fertility goddess, on her throne and in the field, with dogs at her feet. At sea the goddess appears to be protected by dolphins.

THE DOG IN EARLY GREEK CULTURE

The quest for canine roots in early civilization brings us to still another nation that would hold dogs in high repute as guides for souls of the dead, healers of the sick, hunters, and guardians of farms and towns. The ancient Greek word for hunter translates literally as "dog leader." Oppian's book, perhaps the first on canine history, is entitled *Cynegetics*—"Art of Hunting with Dogs." Beyond religious and metaphysical attributions to their dogs, the Greeks paid them the highest possible mundane compliment, making their consistent behavior the model for the highest of Greek aspirations—to become chosen guardians of the state.

The story of the Greeks begins on the island of Crete, the American historian Will Durant tells us. Surely, the ancient architectural glories found there, restored in the 1890s by Sir Arthur Evans, match in grandeur the best of Egypt and Anatolia and the beauty of Ephesus. The settlers came by ship, first Minoan vessels from Anatolia, later the cedar-hulled craft from the port of Byblos. From Anatolia, Greece imported iron work, wool, many tools, and weapons. From Egypt came grain, Greyhounds, gold, and the gems of Nubia and Yemen.

From the sea came Hittites, Mycenaens, Dorians, and other brigands who would destroy the original tree-trunk fortifications and raze the homes and palaces of Crete in 1400 B.C. By that time Crete had become a repository of world culture destined to rise again. Historian Arnold Toynbee writes that

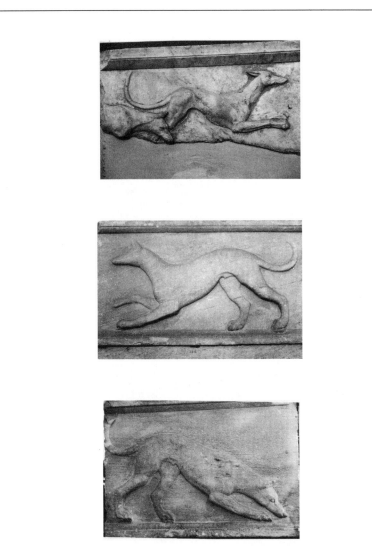

The ancient Greeks loved hunting. Royalty and the upper levels of Hellenic society often maintained their own preserves that could accommodate hundreds of dogs. Plebians, by comparison, formed hunting parties and employed dogs, nets, and spears to course game. These renderings of typical Greek coursing hounds, from shrines at Salamis and Thespiae, bear unmistakable similarity to Egypt's Pharaoh Hound. As Greece and Egypt were trad-ing partners, we can safely assume the fleet, red hounds easily found their way from one great civilization to the other, affecting the Greek gene pool. (Courtesy the National Museum of Greece; Photos by Sabine Callaris)

On the marble base for an ancient kouros *(statue) is a representation of two young men training a dog against a cat—or perhaps simply amusing themselves.* (Courtesy the National Museum of Greece; Photo by Sabine Callaris)

This statue of a house dog bears a bemused expression. (Courtesy the National Museum of Greece; Photo by Sabine Callaris)

archaeologists testify that the oldest remains of a truly advanced human habitation are found there. There were various routes for the African migrant, he notes: those who returned south, like the Dinkas; those who went north (Anatolia and Europe) to become Neolithic agriculturalists; those "who made the Egyptian and

A child's toy from the Museum of the Agora. (Photo by Sabine Callaris)

Sumeric civilizations"; and those who did not take the easier land route but went by sea—the Minoans who settled Crete.

The traveler to modern Crete sees the Minoan culture as restored, along with the world's finest artifacts of the ancient world reached by Minoan and Phoenician mariners. The homes, storage houses, palaces, theaters, temples, and frescoed walls (the technique of painting on wet plaster evidently invented here) eloquently tell the story of their civilization in artifacts of surpassing beauty.

As shown in a mural in the National Museum in Athens, dogs were early imports, used in the hunting of wild boar. In this image, the canines seemingly fly in their eagerness; their leader, a hunter, stands with his spear poised; the boar flees in raging fear and anger. The bulls and Mastiffs portrayed here are evidently from Anatolia, the graceful hounds are from Egypt, and the smaller hunting dogs depicted may be Laconian hounds brought in by invading Dorians. Dogs are not shown in the Cretians' favorite sport, bullfighting, Anatolian style: The single fighter, man or woman, grasps the horns and alone takes down the bull. In 1400 B.C. Mycenaen Greeks from the mainland had infiltrated Crete, and Dorians from the northern mainland would follow. The story of the dogs would be mostly told by the art on Greek jars and Egyptian pottery. No war dogs protected Crete.

Some early Greek colonists living in Egypt by permission of the pharaohs (when Crete and Phoenicia were major trading partners with Egypt) departed for home following the defeat of the Minoans by Mycenae and the ultimate

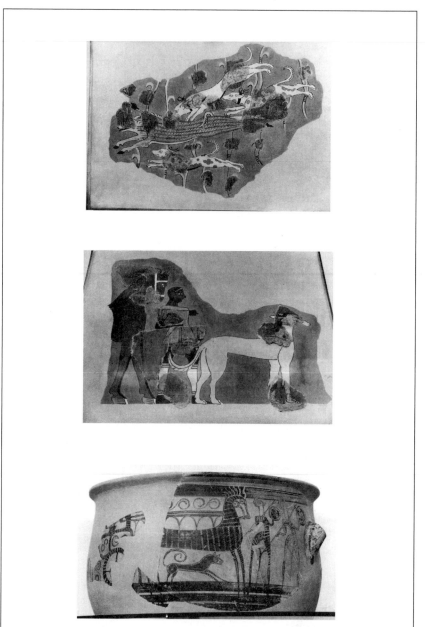

Boar hunting was a popular sport in ancient Greece. The pottery bowl and fragments of frescoes shown here, from the Palace of Tyrins, show some of the dangers and joys in which the Greeks took pleasure. (Photos by Sabine Callaris)

conquest of all Greece by the Dorians. They settled along the Aegean Sea, taking with them some Hyksos, who also had remained in Egypt after their invasion, to help build a new Greek nation. Others went on to the plains of Argos with their dogs. As they extended toward the Gulf of Corinth, one of their cities would be called Thebes, after the Egyptian center of religion. Other Greeks from Crete, as well as Anatolian peoples, joined them, bringing dogs and livestock to the mainland settlements. Some of the immigrants, especially the Minoans, were seafaring and would help to establish Greek colonies in Italy.

The Egyptians and Anatolians brought to Greece much of their art, crafts and learning, the smelting of iron, and also a Semetic form of the alphabet created at Ugarit, plus Egyptian religious cults. Crete provided skills in weaving and smelting, ship building and trading. Settlers from Phrygia, famed for its sensual music of the flute, helped make Greece a nation of music lovers. Phoenicia remained friendly, bringing to the Greeks its skills in the manufacture of pottery and glass and the smelting of tin and copper to make bronze; from all this would come abundant trade opportunities. Greek olives and their oil were in great demand, as were the legendary Molossians. The dogs from Egypt and Anatolia were required by the Greeks to safeguard the peaceful pursuits of their culture. Greyhounds were so popular among the Greeks that the Romans would call them Grecian hounds. Their Molossians, bred and trained at Epirus, on the border of Macedonia, had served well in the Dorian invasion. The demand for these dogs would rival that for Greyhounds in world trade. With all this burgeoning commerce, the new Greece was soon absorbed with trade and the threat of menacing competition from Asia, Africa, and a nearer neighbor, Italy.

From 307 to 272 B.C., the dashing, romantic young Pyrrus reigned as king of Epirus and Molossia, in the mountains of northern Greece (now southern Albania). Here also his countrymen bred and trained the known world's finest war dogs.

Pyrrus demonstrated such great hunting and leadership skills that he was requested in 281 B.C. to lead allied forces to the relief of Greek settlers in Italy who were threatened by the Romans. Pyrrhus crossed the Adriatic Sea with 25,000 infantry, 3,000 horses, many Molossian dogs, and twenty elephants. He defeated the Romans at Heracleia in a "Pyrrhic victory." His losses were so great he could not follow up his battlefield win and was forced to reach a treaty with the Romans. Plutarch tells us that when an aide nevertheless complimented him on his triumph, Pyrrhus answered, "Another such triumph will ruin me."

The exquisite pottery of Greece, like its sculpture, eloquently describes its culture and the life of its people. Portrayed on this covered bowl is Paris, the hero shepherd boy, in Elysium with the fair Helen of Troy. Paris's hunting hound also looks upon Helen with an expression of open admiration. (Photo by Sabine Callaris)

This Greek artifact portrays shepherds attending their hard-working stock dogs. (Photo by Sabine Callaris)

The accomplishments of Pyrrus in Italy continued on into other wars until he was ignominiously killed at Argos following many heroic exploits. He had removed his helmet after a battle and an aged woman, who declared that he had killed her son, threw a tile at him, striking him on the head. Pyrrus fell dead.

The Molossian dogs forged a more enduring reputation, as did the Laconian Hounds trained for war by the Spartans. Aristotle, in his treaties on animals, praises the Molossians and the Laconians and suggests, "Dogs that are born of a mixed breed between these two kinds are remarkable for courage and endurance of hard labor." Some modern writers refer to the hybrid as the "Cretian Hounds." The Molossians in time would become recognized as superior war dogs and were used as such by the Romans, though some may have been the mixed breed recommended by Aristotle. Molossian Mastiffs were in great demand as war dogs and household guardians for generations to come. Equally popular into modern times were the giant Mastiffs of the Persians, Hittites, and northern Greeks. These dogs were said to have originated in Tibet and had been brought into Greece as the spoils of war following the defeat of Xerxes in 480 B.C. in the battle of Salamis.

In Greece such dogs guarded the temple of Asclepius, god of healing, and were assigned within the temple to help patients by licking their wounds and bruises and generally comforting them. According to legend, such dogs saved the city of Corinth from attack. Forty-nine of the Mastiff guardians were slain by the enemy, but the last dog alive gave the alarm. The people he saved built a monument to all courageous Mastiffs. The Molossians on duty at the temple of Minerva were said to be able to distinguish Greeks from the barbarians who often sought to enter. The barbarians, even in disguise, were effectively barred.

Later the people of Corinth placed a marble dog over the grave of their cynic philosopher Diogenes, who insisted in his lifetime that he not only lived like a dog, he was a dog (cynegetics in Greek meaning the art of hunting with dogs). Diogenes reputedly carried a lantern or a candle in search of an honest man, and was himself known for his honesty—he had gone bankrupt as a banker. Unfortunately, in time *cynic* came to mean "one having the qualities of a surly dog." Diogenes possessed all the virtues of the well-bred dog and was said to have been the most famous man in Greece in his time, but his style was sometimes a bit rough. When Alexander the Great came upon Diogenes lying in the sun and stated, "I am Alexander the great king," Diogenes replied, "I am the philosopher Diogenes the dog." Replied the royal warrior, who was near to conquering the world, "If

A Greek hunting scene of the late fifth century B.C. (Photo by Sabine Callaris)

This graceful amphora portrays a grouping of Greek spearmen and their hounds. (Photo by Sabine Callaris)

I were not Alexander I would be Diogenes." When Diogenes died in 323 B.C. at age ninety, his hometown of Snipe, which had expelled him as a young man, raised a monument to his memory.

The hounds of Greece were a natural choice to pursue the hare, as the amusing scene on this two-handled cup shows. (Photo by Sabine Callaris)

A hare and a small house dog decorate this interesting piece of ancient Greek pottery. (Photo by Sabine Callaris)

ARGOS, COMPANION TO ODYSSEUS

The Greeks duly honored their dogs, but the canine best remembered in their history survives for sentimental reasons. He was Argos, the companion and pet of their great hero Odysseus. Homer celebrates the adventures of Odysseus in his epic poem *The Odyssey*, relating fantastic deeds in the Trojan War and its aftermath and closing with the tender story of the reunion of the great warrior with faithful Argos.

Following the fall of Troy, on the Turkish coast (a city once thought mythical but identified as an historic reality by German archaeologist Heinrich Schliemann in 1871), the Greek hero Odysseus, having helped to restore "the fair Helen" to her husband Menelaus, king of Sparta, began a long homeward journey. He would be caught up in the toils of Calypso on a fairyland isle and with Circe, who could turn men into swine, but he finally escaped again, after twenty years' absence from home. At fifty he remained an athletic man who yearned for his wife, Penelope, his son Telemachus, and Argos, his favorite hound, vowing to return to his palace and farm at Ithaca.

In majestic cadences, Homer tells the story. Odysseus is warned by the goddess Athena of difficulties at home. Wife Penelope is discouraging young suitors seeking to win her and Ithaca by marriage. She has fended off her suitors for nearly twenty years by pretending she will make a choice when she finishes a web she is weaving. Her artifice is wearing thin. Odysseus, grateful and humble, disguises himself as a beggar and accepts the guidance of Athena home. He will not be welcomed, Athena warns, and the young suitors may seek to kill him, and after twenty years his own son may not recognize him, nor may Penelope. As it happens, his swineherd, Eumaeus, seeks to run him off the property as a vagrant but then, hoping to gain news of his missing master, he takes in the lowly beggar. Meantime Penelope is nearing the completion of her web. The goddess Athena arrives to advise action. The dogs discern her and bark. She speaks to Odysseus, but Eumaeus and those with him neither see nor hear her. Homer reminds his readers that the gods decide who may see and who may hear them—the dogs evidently qualified.

Odysseus, still in rags, walks with Eumaeus in the barnyard. In the distance, on a manure heap, a dog is sleeping. In approximate translation of poetry into prose, Homer continues the story:

"As Odysseus and Eumaeus talk, the sleeping dog raises his head and pricks up his ears, a showing of joy. It is Argos, who Odysseus had bred before leaving for Troy. In olden days Argos was taken out by the young men when they were hunting wild goats, or deer, or hares . . . but now he was neglected and slept on the heaps of manure in front of the stable . . . and he was full of fleas. When Odysseus saw the dog on the other side of the yard, Argos dropped his ears and wagged his tail. He knew his master. Odysseus turns, brushes tears from his eyes without Eumaeus seeing it, and says, 'Eumaeus, what a noble hound that is . . . his build is splendid. Is he as fine a fellow as he looks, or is he only one of the dogs that come begging around a table, and are kept mainly for show?'

"'This hound,' answers Eumaeus, 'belonged to him who has died in a far country. If he were what he was when Odysseus left for Troy, he would show you what he can do. There was not a wild beast in the forest that could get away from him when he was once in its tracks. But now he has fallen upon evil times, there is no one to care for him.'"

Argos was now content to die. He had seen his master.

The world would praise Homer for his poetry. Aristotle—philosopher, naturalist, and author of an enduring treatise on animals—indirectly presented his praise to Homer for so effectively creating Argos, the hero's dog. "Most critics consider that Homer did well in representing the dog of Odysseus as having died in his twentieth year," he wrote. For twenty long years Argos was faithful to his master. It was true, large dogs could and did live a score of years. They also could see and hear the gods. They were faithful. Homer knew it. So did Aristotle.

THE ANCIENT BODYGUARD OF CHOICE

The rise of Greek power was accompanied by the rise of the canine as an essential partner of man in achieving domination in a rugged, fiercely competitive world. The dog, faithful and obedient, was the only creature living that could be totally trusted and remain near at all times, even if for a royal personage. Among those living in constant danger were potential heirs to a throne, to noble status, or to any other extraordinary good fortune. In the Persian royal line, scores of young men and women were slain by members of their own families in the contention for power. Most royal families and noble lines in Egypt, Greece, and Rome suffered in the same manner. The queens of Byzantium sometimes had their own sons killed or blinded, and the kings did so more regularly. Under those circumstances it was quite logical for those at risk to want a dependable, strong guard dog with them at all times.

Such dogs were beyond price and often accompanied their adored owners to the grave. Such dogs were considered more valuable than slaves in ordinary commerce and became the most acceptable gifts of royalty to one another. In the close association of man and animal in war, only the horse might rate as high. Some dogs were not for sale at any price. The Greeks, like most people of their time, regarded the faithful dog as a member of the family.

The stele of the Ilissos is a shrine to the memory of a young huntsman. The monument includes the young man's favorite dog and other figures in postures of remorse. (Courtesy of the National Museum of Greece; Photo by Sabine Callaris)

The Dog's Place in Greek Ritual

Even so, the Greeks venerated dogs less than the Egyptians did but included them in rites reminiscent of Anubis. The philosopher Pythagoras not only suggested that dogs should be used in last rites for the dying but also taught belief in metempsychosis—that the human could migrate to another body, human or animal. The human soul could be best guided by a dog, he said, especially if the mouth of the living dog was placed near to the mouth of a dying person. This idea was adopted by the Greek Orphic cult that also marked the resurrection of the divine Dionysus, son of their god Dionysus Zagreus, following his death to redeem all mankind from sin. After death, according to Orphic believers, the soul would go to Hades for judgment. The gates there were guarded by the fearsome three-headed dog god, Cerberus. Orphic theology thus was close to that of the Anubis cult in Egypt.

Historian Durant suggests that Pythagoreans took their diet, dress, and theory of transmigration from the ancient Orphic belief. Pythagoras then provided an

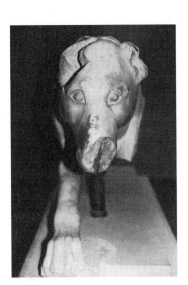

Even in its partially shattered state, the expression on the face of this sculpted dog recovered from a site near the Acropolis commands a head-on glare capable of stunning any adversary. (Courtesy Museum of the Acropolis, Athens; Photo by Sabine Callaris)

This young hunter and his dog celebrate the end of a successful hunt. (Courtesy the National Museum of Greece; Photo by Sabine Callaris)

Egyptian insight to Orphism after he studied the cult of Anubis in Egypt, where he refined his own concept of an afterlife. "Some Orphic practices would have been highly repugnant to Christians," Durant would write. "Nevertheless, there were in Orphism idealist trends that culminated in the morals and monasticism of Christianity."[4]

The teachings of Pythagoras influenced not only Greeks, but spread widely, even to India. The legend of his own dramatic conviction to belief in the transmigration of souls originated in Egypt. There, it was said, when he was in the holy city of Thebes, Pythagoras heard the yelping of an abused dog, an unusual incident in Egypt. He ran to the rescue of the animal, saying that in its cries he recognized the voice of a dead friend. He later often related the experience to his students, though without fixing the scene in Egypt.

THE DOG'S INFLUENCE ON GREEK PHILOSOPHY AND EQUALITY

Socrates, the great Greek philosopher, swore by the dog, as did many fellow Greeks. Plato was said to have accepted some Orphic beliefs, though not all. He preserves in his *Republic* a Socratic dialogue on the subject of human behavior and that of dogs, relative to requirements for the creation of an ideal state. The dialogue took place in the home of Plato's friend Cephalus at Piraeus.

Socrates pays his high tribute to the dog in opening, suggesting that the most qualified guardian of the perfect state, the Republic, must possess the qualities of a well-bred dog. The dialogue is with Glaucon and Adeimantus following a discussion of the various human components of the idealized state, "arising . . . out of the needs of mankind." One by one the essential citizens are chosen; Socrates probes for the true requirement in each classification, and they come to the guardian. "And the higher the duties of the guardian," says Socrates, "the more time, and skill, and art, and application will be needed by him?"

"No doubt," Glaucon replies.

"Will he not also require a natural aptitude for his calling?"

"Certainly."

"And the selection will be no easy matter . . . but we must be brave and do our best."

It has become clear that the ideal guardian of the state must possess the virtues of a well-bred dog—referred to earlier as "our friend, the dog"—that are mentioned in the dialogue: loyalty, reliability, affection, judgment, and aggression. The ultimate role of the guardian is likened to "the divine shepherd of the human flock." The guardian "must love truth and judge between good and evil . . . he must take into the world an adamantine faith in truth and right and be undazzled by the desire of wealth or other allurements of evil."

"What are the duties and rights of women?" Socrates asks after the guardians of the ideal state have been discussed and described. Are dogs divided into hes and shes, or do they share equally in the hunting and in keeping watch and in other duties of dogs? Or do we entrust the males to the entire and exclusive care of the flocks while we leave the females at home, since the males are greater in strength?

"No, they are alike," he is told. "The only difference between them is that males are stronger and females are weaker."

"Then, if the women are to have the same duties as the men, they must have the same nurture and education?"

The philosophers agree, they should indeed, but they also agree they will be laughed out of serious consideration if they pursue such a line. Yet they fast and conclude: "You agree then that men and women are to have a common way of life—they [the guardians] are to watch over their citizens, in common [in peace and war] they are to keep watch together, and hunt together like dogs, and in all things, as far as they are able, women are to share with the men?"

It was agreed. However the Greeks, themselves creators of the Athenian democracy, continued to exclude women and slaves from their own ideal government. Not until two thousand years later in lands where humans, arriving with their dogs, were given a second chance were female rights at last recognized. Remote New Zealand, realized only in the mind of Claudius Ptolemy some 2,000 years ago, granted the right of women to vote in a national election in 1893, closely followed by Australia. The women of the United States received their vote franchise by the 19th Amendment to the Constitution in August 1920, about 2,500 years after Plato, in his "Republic V," made clear that females in his ideal state could and should match the males in leadership virtues to be found in the well-bred dog. Greek women won their right to vote in 1974.

THE HUNTING DOGS OF GREECE

Aristotle predicted that the Greeks would breed the world's best dog. Such a canine, shown on an ancient Greek jar, has been identified as a Laconian-Molossian but obviously is a likeness of Anubis. The hybrid mentioned by Aristotle did not attain the popularity of the Laconian Hound or the Molossian Mastiff. The Laconian, bred by the Spartans for war, also was used in hunting large game. The historian Denison B. Hull describes the Laconian as "a small, wiry animal, something like a Beagle, though its ears stood up straight . . . . It was said to have been bred by crossing a fox with a dog."[5] The Greek hunter also had dogs more likely to have challenged lions, such as "the giant Molossian from Epirus, the ancestor of the modern Mastiff . . . and the St. Bernard," according to Hull. "The Molossian could take down the biggest game in Europe, such as the aurochs, the huge wild bull and the ancestor of modern cattle. The beast stood six feet high at the shoulder and had enormous horns with sharp points." Another canine hunter named by Hull is the Cretian hound, "probably a cross between the first two." Greek legend credited all dogs to the mythological Lailapys, the bronze dog created and brought to life by the god Hephaistos. Several gods owned the animal before it was taken to Grecian Thebes to conquer the huge Teumessian fox that was destroying the crops and flocks. Lailapys and the fox were at stalemate when Zeus stepped in and turned both animals to stone.

The Greeks hunted by driving animals into nets, Hull writes. An iron-tipped spear was used to kill the wild boar, though he could destroy man and dog alike. Hull describes a javelin, five feet long with a leather loop attached twelve to eight inches behind the point of balance: "By twisting this loop around the shaft and putting two fingers through it, the hunter could give his javelin a spin like a rifle bullet." Bows and arrows were available but the Greeks, preferring their spears and dogs, did not often use them.

Hunting was not merely a sport, not entirely devoted to providing food, Hull writes, but more a training course for war. The dogs lived well. "They ate bread soaked in the broth from the master's meat or in milk, and were sometimes given the roasted liver of an ox. And every day, four times at least, they were taken for a walk. If they led a dog's life, it was a good life."

The Celts, living north along the Danube, made miserable the lives of Macedonians and some of the Greeks by their endless raids on their southern neighbors. Earlier arriving from Anatolia, these groups of herdsmen, traders, iron miners, and smelters found a region of iron and salt near what is now Salzburg. "The men who forged iron and men who wielded the weapons came together," writes historian C. D. Darlington. They invented the iron horseshoe, which enabled their horsemen to ride down most enemies. They had brought shepherd dogs with them from Asia Minor and undoubtedly took from the Macedonians some of their Mastiffs and Molossians. They created a solid agricultural base along the Danube and were able to take Rome in A.D. 387. They also killed King Phillip of Macedonia, and their legends assert that they once encountered both Phillip the Great and his son Alexander and put them down. The Celts raided Greek Delphi, and advanced along the coast to Byzantium (then a Greek colony), and back into Anatolia, their probable ancient homeland, where they founded a colony, Galatia.

The Ayrian Celts would conquer most of the barbarian tribes of northern and central Europe, bringing them their language and many skills, including the manufacture of some of the world's finest weapons. They established in Europe a common culture, including customs, mythological beliefs, and religious practices. "To the west they brought the iron age," says Darlington, "They appear everywhere as promoters of true progress in Europe." Even their dogs were praised. Xenophon, a Greek writing in the fifth century B.C., advises, "Don't take the first dog that comes along for hunting the wild boar, and for hunting hare, the Celtic dogs are preferable to all others." Gordon Childe in his *Pre-History of European Society* writes of the Celts, "In Europe their expansion marks the moment when the pre-history of our continent begins to diverge from that of Africa or the Pacific."[6] The Celts endlessly challenged Rome, breaking through the Roman walls and taking from Roman legions control of parts of Spain and the British Isles. Wherever they went, the Celts took their dogs, breeds of their own as well as those from Greece and Anatolia, among them the Welsh Corgi, believed by some to be the most like the Mesolithic wild dog. The forces of William the Conqueror attacking England in 1066 would eventually meet the Celts and their war dogs, who would fight all comers. Tim Newark, in his *Celtic Warriors* , provides a history of the warfare, describing one encounter in which the enemy defeated its Celtic foes in a battle lasting but a single day. However, two more days were needed to put down the Celtic war dogs that continued to fight fiercely in defense of the bodies of their wounded and slain masters, and to keep the enemy from taking the horses and supplies.[7]

The "barbarian" Celts and Germans who did the most to harass the legions of the Roman Empire in the West spoke different languages but pursued the same ends. They were checked and defeated but never gave up the struggle, fighting as Gauls and Belgai against Caesar, and as Welsh, Irish, and Scots against the Normans and English. They brought a superior culture, craft skills, and weapons, as well as their fighting dogs, to most of the barbarian tribes of Europe before the Romans arrived. But their discipline, unity, and political skills did not match that of the Roman Republic.

5

THE DOGS OF WAR

⟨ɯɯɯ⟩

The Latins and the Etruscans of Magna Gracia ended their long, fierce quarrels, subdued other tribes along the Tiber and the Tyrrhenian Coast, and completed the construction of Rome on seven hills beyond the marshes of the Tiber delta in about the seventh century B.C. They created a city, a republic, and an empire that would dominate the world for almost 1,000 years and ensure long and profitable employment for the domestic dogs of the Western world.

THE LEGEND OF ROMULUS AND REMUS

Legend, reported in some detail by Plutarch and others, said that Rome was founded by brothers Romulus and Remus. In one version they were lost in a shipwreck, then unexpectedly saved. In another account, they were born to the virgin daughter of the king of Alba, who ordered his servant Teratius to destroy them. Teratius instead hid them where a cowherd later found them being suckled by a she-wolf.

Plutarch relates both accounts, omitting the possibility that the cowherd's dog probably was the initial finder of the infants. Some later writers have suggested that the animal suckling human babes may have been a hybrid wolf-dog, common in many areas of the world. Plutarch continues the legend: The boys became separated later in life. Romulus, rising to leadership among the Latin tribes, learned that Remus—whose name was near to *ruma*, meaning "beast's breast," Plutarch noted—was living in virtual captivity, and later rescued him. But Remus was killed soon thereafter, possibly by Romulus, in a quarrel over building plans for Rome. Romulus buried his brother with honors. The legend,

---

77

however dubious, is said to demonstrate the sense of protection and trust pastoral people felt in their hybrid dogs, who cared for their sheep and children. Or, possibly, their faith in wolves. The ancient Egyptians did not share the Roman trust in wolves. An Egyptian papyrus illustrating a satirical children's story, according to Egyptologist Adolph Erman, shows Epuat the wolf god herding sheep while a cat herded ducks, both leering animals obviously contemplating a tasty meal.

Archaeological findings indicate that an individual named Romulus began the construction of Rome with the assistance of Etruscan builders, whose ruins and tombs a few miles from Rome demonstrate their high culture and skill in urban development. The early Romans would borrow much, good and bad, from the Etruscans, including their belief in divination from the livers of birds, the use of slave gladiators who fought to the death in public combat, and similar exhibitions by fighting dogs. Erected on seven low hills on the Tiber—a site rejected by the Etruscans when they first built their town of Veii, twelve miles farther beyond the marshes—the Rome created under the direction of Romulus would be possibly the most exposed city site ever seen in a world beset with warfare, piracy, vendetta, and general crime. "Only from the sea was Rome protected," naturalist C. D. Darlington observes, adding that the location was on two trade routes, one used by those taking salt from the mouth of the Tiber, another passing to the Greek colonies to the south. Wandering peoples arrived in the new town from the southern routes: Greeks and skilled craftsmen from Anatolia on the north, and some from the Greek islands via the salt route. The growing city became largely populated by former enemies—Etruscans, Sabini, Alba Longa, and strangers from other places. Not all of these contributed to the welfare of the great city, to say the least. According to Plutarch, Rome was overrun with vagrants, vandals, and fleeing slaves, the latter soon put to work as Roman slaves. Rome required perpetual vigilance inside and outside its walls. "It was a miracle that they survived at all as an independent state," Darlington writes.

Rome had a great need of dogs. The Wolf Spitz, possibly the animal involved in the Romulus-Remus legend, was on the scene and available. The Italian historian Gino Pugnetti, in his book *Cani,* says the Great Spitz has left fossil remains "tens of thousands of years old" in Africa, Asia, and northern Europe.[1] The Greek and Etruscan colonies may have also supplied Mastiffs and Molossians. The Egyptian Greyhound was popular in Rome as it was in earlier societies. It became known in Europe first as the Phoenician Hound and later as the Italian Greyhound (not to be confused with the Toy-sized dog of the same breed, which it is un-doubtedly behind). There was a sufficiency of dogs, though not, in the beginning, war dogs.

Romulus began the political organization of Rome by creating a senate of 100 leaders of the participating clans. The governing Patrician-military class would own all the land in Rome's 500 square miles and would control the priesthood. The arriving traders, craftsmen, scribes, and other professionals constituted a plebian class, who enabled the city to function in an orderly way. They had free-dom of religion but would struggle long to win their right to vote and later to own property. In time the Patricians consorted with lower-class women, and plebians married above their class, providing a further genetic mix in an already heterogeneous society. Each ally of Rome was allowed by compact to intermarry with Roman citizens if they agreed not to intermarry with other allies participat-ing in the government of Rome. Humans at last, by law, were permitted the genetic benefits long provided to their animals, especially their dogs.

Romulus created an army of 6,000 men and 300 horses, settled an affair of rape and seduction with the Sabines, conquered the Albans, and continued to or-ganize his government along Etruscan lines. Then the Roman republic took up the struggle against Carthage that Greece had been forced to abandon by its own political division and weakness following the death of Alexander the Great.

Etruscans would provide Rome with a relatively high culture, which included veneration of dogs in the Egyptian and Greek tradition. Since the Etruscans cre-mated their dead, placing the ashes in ceramic urns, it is not known whether they observed the Egyptian custom of interring their canines with humans. But their tomb art shows that dogs participated in the funerary games and ceremonies honoring the Etruscan dead. A strange tomb fresco startles: An Egyptian Grey-hound is shown attacking a blindfolded man with a club while being held on a leash by a masked antagonist. Ellen MacNamara, in her book *Everyday Life of the Etruscans*, tells us that the scene depicts an incidence "of human sacrifices in the life of Hercules, the Greek hero who became a god. Other Etruscan art seems less morbid, scenes of dancing, banqueting after a hunt, hunting dogs getting their share, sketches of children playing with their canine pets."[2]

MacNamara also describes the strange hunting proceedings of Etruscan nobles: "In Etruria, where wild pigs and stags are caught in the usual manner of hunters, it is said that success is greater if music is used as an aid. The music is soft and sweet, not the brassy noises of drums and horn used to frighten game in some early civilizations. As an experienced piper begins his sweet strains, nets and traps are set. The piper's sweet sounds waft up to the mountains through gorges and thickets into all retreats and breeding grounds of game. At first the animals are terrified . . . later they abandon their young and flee their lairs . . . [finally] these wild beasts of the Tyrennian forests are gradually attracted. Once they approach the vicinity of the piper, men and dogs drive them into the nets and traps."

In tomb mosaics, hunters and their attendants are shown carrying game into pavilions where the hunters recline on couches, devouring the feast but also sharing with their dogs under the tables. Other paintings show hunters equipped with spears and mounted on horses, riding with packs of hounds through game preserves in their rugged country. In the Greek manner, the commoners walked, or ran with their dogs, keeping their limited packs on leash until the lead dog picked up the scent. The Etruscans produced weapons more sophisticated than ordinary spears but preferred to give their game—deer, wild boars, and hares—a sporting chance.

When the Gauls invaded Italy in the fifth century and sacked Rome, the Etruscans and their civilization fell, to become lost from history for more than a thousand years. While they endured they provided a strong Greek influence toward learning and moderation. They brought into Greece from Anatolia a knowledge of iron smelting, and into Italy a Greek alphabet and knowledge of basic architecture. They showed greater respect for the dead than did most Asian migrants. They maintained their own temple at Delphi and taught the Dorians and the Romans the use of ships.

However much Etruscans contributed to the culture and construction of Rome, it was Romulus who would be remembered for persuading his former enemies to join him in the creation of a new city-state; twelve tribes entered the confederation. They improved the salt road to Rome, where dogs carried much of the cargo from the new port built at the mouth of the Tiber, beginning a worldwide transport system. Dogs were not only beasts of burden along with pack mules and horses, but eventually they also guarded the roads and strategic checkpoints. Rome would need to rely for its defense on a small militia as well as shepherd dogs trained for guard duties, plus Mastiffs imported by the Etruscans from their Phoenician sources. Rome created a seaport and a navy under Etruscan guidance and prepared itself for a place in the export trade as well as warfare and colonization.

Alexander the Great died at age thirty-four, after marching his troops and Molossian dogs around the southwestern Mediterranean coast to attack Asian and African allies and vassals of the doomed Persian Empire, and thus to control the world. He marched because he lacked sea power. Rome now used its growing might to establish its dominance over other Italian city-states and began the construction of a navy, with the aid of Greek and Anatolian workers. The Greek shipwrights and iron workers from the mountains of Anatolia built seaworthy ships and modern weapons of iron and bronze. Some of the Greek colonies also loaned Rome naval vessels with which to attack the Phoenicians, weakened by their loss of ships and timber supplies during Alexander's conquests.

The first of the Punic wars was fought and won by Rome. Hannibal of Carthage, elected governor of Carthaginian Spain by the army, seeking to avenge the defeat of Carthage twenty years earlier, in 218 B.C. marched on Rome via France and across the Alps. His incredible army included, in addition to infantry, horses, and war dogs, a vast herd of African elephants. Hannibal devastated the towns and farms of the Po Valley after winning many battles, but ultimately lost the war. What Rome's Wolf Spitz shepherd dogs did against Hannibal is not recorded. Rome had taken control of Sicily earlier, and now it took Spain. Since Hannibal had allied himself with Macedonia, the war dogs bred and developed in neighboring Molossia and Epirus came under Roman control. Rome admired and copied most things Greek; thus they at some point also acquired the famous Greek Molossians.

The Romans used Molossians, Laconians, Greyhounds, and Mastiffs in their progress to world dominance, equipping the giant fighters with collars studded with forged iron knives and hooks. The Molossian became a favored fighting dog. Polybius, the Greek historian captured by the Romans in the second century A.D., specialized in military history and wrote of the work of Roman war dogs. They attacked the enemy, defended the camps, guarded captured enemy fighters, and carried burdens and secret messages through enemy lines (sometimes swallowing the message in a copper pellet that, with luck, would later be recovered). He credits a Roman general with fitting dogs with blankets and pots of Greek fire, and incendiary composition used as a weapon, which enabled them to create panic among mounted adversaries when they "seared the bellies of the horses."

Rome was destined to become one of the world's first successful empires. From the beginning it did not appear to have such a prospect. Because it was exposed, Rome required many troops and dogs for its security. Its power would come from the strength of the individual citizen, skillfully involved in the militia, represented in the government, and genetically provided with intelligence and endurance. Rome would adopt and absorb the Hellenic culture of Greece, Egypt, and the ancient Middle East. And like Egyptians and Greeks, the Romans would demonstrate a special affection for these useful guardians of their state and properties, the dogs.

The Romans wrote appreciatively of their canine partners, which also were pictured in mosaics, on vases and jars, and in sculpture and paintings. Early writers specialized: Varro discussed the sheepdog Columelle, the hunter of small game; Lucretius in *On the Nature of Things* analyzed the natural ability of the canine: "The onward reaching power of scent in dogs leads them whithersoever the cloven hoof of wild beasts has carried them in their courses." Thus he identified the genetic sense that would make the canine man's most useful partner.

Cicero, Rome's great statesman and orator, praised dogs as faithful friends. "Such fidelity of dogs protecting what is committed to their charge, such affectionate attachment to their masters, such jealousy of strangers, such incredible acuteness of nose in following a track, such keenness in hunting—what else do they evince but that these animals were created for the use of man." The Latin poet Ovid sings lyrically of hunting with Greyhounds; Virgil, poet of pastoral pleasures, writes of the hunters' dogs, "their nostrils infected for the stag's hot chase," and of the valiant sheepdogs whose owners often clipped their ears and tails to keep them from suffering greater injury in combat with wolves and foxes. In his *Georgics,* Virgil poetically praises "the swift Spartan hounds and fierce Molossian . . . . Never with these to watch, dread nightly the fierce and ravening wolves . . . or Spanish desperadoes in the rear." And of hunting dogs: "And oft the shy wild asses thou wilt chase, with hounds, too, hunt the hare; Oft from his wildwood the wallowing deer uprouse; and the bear and scare him with their baying. And o'er the mountain urge into toils some antlered monster to their chiming cry."

Rome grew as a city on trade routes from the civilized southern Mediterranean and the Red Sea to the beckoning barbarian West, both shores and hinterland. The populace shared a Greek culture influenced by the early civilizations in Babylon and Egypt and that of Rome's own partners, the Etruscans, who, like the Egyptians, had great respect for the dead, as their decorated tombs unearthed in the twentieth century disclose. Fewer dogs wandered at large in Italy and Greece than did those among civilizations showing less veneration for the dead. In the Roman Empire, most animals had their work to do.

Patrician families could afford to keep a Molossian as an estate guard and might also have a smaller dog, such as a Basenji, as a house guardian. Also much in demand would be a sight hound that could also be used for hunting and to add a touch of dignity to any noble house. The Romans developed their own breeds of large dogs and took them to northern and central Europe to work as sheepdogs. The Kuvasz, originally from Anatolia, and the Maremma, Abruzzese, and Tatra, credited to Tunisia, are all examples of breeds that show the genetic influence of those Roman dogs. Of course, the Molossian must also be included, its descendants having been used as mountain rescue dogs, and passing this attribute to one of their descendants, the Saint Bernard of Alpine celebrity.

The Romans appeared to respect their dogs in the manner of the Egyptians, though without any religious recognition. However, they also took from the Etruscans their appalling practice of using dogs in the circus and fighting pits along with slaves and social undesirables. Dogs guarded the training schools of the gladiators and were sometimes sent into the arena in contests of mortal combat with bears, tigers, lions, or one another. The favorite fighting dog of the Romans, historian Pugnetti writes, was the *Iperean Molossys,* often victorious in combat with wild animals. In England, Pugnetti suggests, such games began in Roman times. The animal of choice for battle there, known as *Pugnaces Brittanica,* was later exported by British breeders. An indigenous British breed, the Bulldog, originally fought bulls, as the German *Bullenbeiser,* the forerunner of the Boxer, would do later. Both shared the Molossian bloodline.

❧

"Rome conquered the world against its will," the historian Livy would write. Rome also gave to the world its system of laws and government, to one day be copied in far away America, plus its philosophy, received originally from Greece and Egypt, and it extended the faith it sometimes repressed at home, Christianity. The teachings of Jesus of Nazareth were carried throughout the Empire by many civil servants and tradesmen—learned Christian clerics, scribes, and other bureaucrats. Wherever the Romans went, their civil servants and their trained dogs proved their worth, the latter as guardians of livestock and caravans. Dogs also protected storehouses and arsenals, as public and private property was always at risk, especially in occupied territories and even in the camps of the

Roman legions. The rulers of new kingdoms and their nobles in the hinterlands kept guard dogs in their castles and private apartments, the canines performing the work they first learned in the palaces of ancient Nineveh. When Byzantium became the capital of the Eastern Roman Empire and Christianity was sanctioned by Constantine and his successors, dogs also guarded churches, shrines, and other holy places, including monasteries.

By this time dogs may have come close to outnumbering people, since many early societies condoned infanticide. Among the emerging Arabs, the practice was limited to female infants. In the latter days of the Roman conquests, as trading increased, the Middle East and Western world were coincidentally swept by plagues, further reducing populations not lost in famines and wars. Abandoned dogs became more in evidence, running wild, foraging for food, and generally besmirching their reputation as loyal friends of humankind. But the wars went on, herds and flocks were moved into areas where predatory animals continued to take their toll, and the need for large shepherd, guardian, and war dogs continued.

THE FAMILY OF BREEDS GROWS

Historian Pugnetti credits the Tibetan Mastiff as the progenitor of most modern large breeds, suggesting it was introduced into Europe by the Phoenicians, known to have brought them to England. Assuredly the Mastiff, whether of Molossian, Tibetan, or Persian origin, was introduced by the Romans to most of the western world and, via Spain, even to the Americas. Pugnetti describes the British version as "a blood-thirsty fighter" but adds that "careful breeders" produced a strain to guard sheep and isolated towns. Another Mastiff offshoot, the Bullmastiff, widely used in military and police work, has been taken to South Africa (where its ancestors continue to exist as big-game hunters) to serve as guard dogs, especially in the diamond mines. The Great Dane was also introduced to the barbarian tribes of Europe and the British Isles. Said to have originated in Greece but later bred, as the name Deutsche Dogge suggests, in Germany, the Dane is a cross between Mastiff-like dogs and "Irish Greyhounds," according to Pugnetti. The breed remains one of the largest of all the domestic dog breeds.

The Bergamasco, Pugnetti suggests, was brought to Europe by the Phoenicians 2,000 years ago to join the Maremma sheepdog of northern Italy. Longhaired and white, Maremmas could be seen easily while they watched over the flocks and are "comfortable in the cold and a terrible enemy of the wolf," he writes. Wolves, it seems, sometimes confused the Maremmas with sheep, moving ever closer until a safe retreat was too late.

The Roman legions took their dogs into Gaul and the rest of central and northern Europe, and eventually to the British Isles. The Celts and Basques earlier migrated into the Baltic states and the mountains of Spain and France; the Celts and their dogs reached as far west as the British Isles. Neolithic peoples probably brought some kinds of domesticated animal with them as hunting companions much earlier than fossil finds so far have indicated. Francois Bourliere of the University of Paris reports that the earliest domesticated dog thus far discovered is in the Starr Carr site in Yorkshire, England, the bones dating to 7,500 B.C. He adds that earlier finds have been reported in Scandinavia and in Russia, but there exists a lack of real evidence that dogs were in those regions at that time.

Frederick Zeuner of the University of London suggests that all dogs probably originated farther south. The Celts came from the shores of the Caspian Sea and passed through the steppes and heavy forests of Paleoartic regions to reach the Danube and ultimately areas that became Germany, France, and the British Isles. They created settlements and brought in their dogs across the land. When the Roman conquerors reached England, they came upon a Celtic populace in the north that was difficult to subdue. The Celts and their dogs fought valiantly. The canine partners of humans continued to hold their own in cold, damp lands of northern and central Europe. The barbarians, as the people were called by the Greeks and Romans, depended on hunting as well as on their cultivated livestock for food. Lakes and streams provided fishing, but forests had to be cleared before extensive use of land for crops was possible.

Predators still remained a threat to livestock as well as to humans themselves. Tribes sought arable land that could be improved for agricultural purposes by hard labor and also made secure against hazards normally encountered. Families and tribes continued to fight one another, as did mountain shepherds in earlier times. They also competed for trade opportunities, the leaders among the victors becoming chiefs of tribes, owners of ships, and, ultimately, rulers of land and sea. A feudal society arose as the decline of Rome persisted. "The birthplace of Western society was an outlying world where the urban culture of Hellenism failed to strike root," British historian Toynbee would write. "The Romans created a super-structure of Hellenic civilization in Europe and England, defending it with walls and troops, but such protection largely vanished when Rome fell."

The Roman Empire crashed in the fifth century A.D. Militant Muslims took over North Africa and Spain, including seaports and what remained of Phoenician shipping after defeats by Greece and Rome. The capital of the Eastern Roman Empire, Constantinople, survived as a trade center and the eastern outpost of an increasingly powerful Christian church. Rome itself, sacked by Vandals and other barbarians, survived though the Arab threat would continue. Pope Leo X would save Rome from destruction at the hands of the infamous Atilla the Hun in the mid fifth century.

The need for dogs increased with the demise of the Roman enforced peace. In addition to serving the Roman legions, dogs protected flocks and herds in wild, underdeveloped areas and against tribal strife and vandalism that existed under the Roman peace. In the ensuing disorganization following the fall of Rome, Arab traders took full advantage of the changing political climate to maintain and expand their silk, spice, slave, gem, and date trade with Europe and sent camel caravans into an ever-widening sphere of commerce, deep into Africa and to China.

THE GROWING IMPORTANCE OF CHINA

Early domestic dogs pictured in Chinese hunting scenes appear similar to breeds originating in Egypt and Persia that would have probably come through the caravan route. Chinese contacts with the West began early, but seemingly were limited to Persian and Arab trade caravans that reached India and Tibet.

The early Paleolithic people entering China brought goats, sheep, and dogs through the valley of the Kansu, "the only route possible" according to Darlington, and were followed in later years by Persian horsemen and smelters of ores. It took migrants a thousand years to reach the Yellow River, where organized Chinese agriculture began. Those left behind hunted wild asses and sheep in the highlands, eventually domesticating them. Nordic-type dogs were used, probably brought from Persia, to work with the flocks. Eventually western migrants, craftsmen able to make weapons of bronze and iron, won dominance over the agriculturalists along the Yellow River.

Fascinating accounts of the partnership of man and dogs in ancient China were told in the late thirteenth century by Marco Polo, the Venetian merchant-traveler, on his return from Tibet and Cathay in A.D. 1275, where he served four years in the court of Kublai Khan. Polo earlier accompanied his father on a trade venture into the remote, forbidding land that was almost unknown to people of the Western world. Polo's accounts of marvels in the land of the great Khan, grandson of the founder of the Mongol dynasty, were dismissed by many who read them in his book, *The Travels of Marco Polo the Venetian*.[3] He was denounced as a fraud by scholars and public authorities, but his reports for the most part have been found to be true, including his dog stories.

Polo entered China from the northwest, on a route that extended from the Black Sea, which he reached by ship from Venice, through a harsh region of steppes and deserts to the plain of Pamir on his way to Yanjin (Beijing), the city captured by Ghengis Khan and made his capital in A.D. 1221. On the heights bordering Pamir, Polo saw huge sheep, "as large as the wild asses," and the big dogs that guarded them. These were evidently the dogs the Persians bred from the Mastiffs brought from early civilizations in Mesopotamia. (The conformation of Assyrian Mastiff dogs on bas-reliefs and sculpted heads in Nineveh appear similar to the Chinese and Tibetan guard dogs depicted in the art of the Han dynasty [200 B.C.], though some details differ.) Polo said he joined in the hunting of fierce tigers near Chintigui. "In this country are found the largest and fiercest dogs," he wrote. "They are so courageous and powerful that a man with two dogs and armed with a bow and arrow can overmatch a tiger. Thus attended should he meet a tiger, he sets on it his intrepid dogs, who instantly attack. The animal seeks a tree at a slow pace, he has too much pride to show fear. During this deliberate movement the dogs fasten themselves upon him and the man plies him with arrows until, weakened, he is taken.

"In Tabeth," Polo continued, "they have dogs the size of asses, strong enough to hunt all sorts of wild beasts, and particularly the wild oxen, called *beyamini*, and are particularly wild and fierce." Polo had been with noble lords who hunted with dogs in Italy and India, he said, "but nothing to equal the style and grandeur of Kublai Khan, the Tartar conqueror." The Great Khan, he said, had four wives, twenty-four sons, and 10,000 hunting hounds, plus 200,000 Mongolian horses. The horses were in great part used in a post-road mail system, which the ruler was successfully establishing in his immediate kingdom; Polo judged it to be the swiftest and most efficient in the world. Two brothers managed Khan's hunting dogs, commanding a force of attendants that numbered 10,000 men. The animals and attendants were in two groups of 5,000 liveried men each. One group of attendants, in red uniforms, cared for 5,000 dogs; the other division, uniformed in blue, cared for the other 5,000. Paintings of the dogs in *Les Livres de Graunt*

Cann, reproduced from Persian originals, show the Khan hounds to look very much like large wild African dogs or large Chow Chows.

The Chow Chow, in ancient China, was given the duty of guarding temples from evil spirits. Also known as the Tartar dog or the Chinese Spitz, it has been bred for many centuries as an edible dog as well as a hunter and working dog. The Chinese call the breed *hsiung kou* (bear dog), primarily for its appearance, though it may also have been used to hunt bears. The Chow Chow served Chinese emperors and nobles much like the Greyhound served the pharaohs of Egypt.

THE TARTARS

The Tartars of the northern steppes required many dogs as well as horses, as they were herdsmen and horsemen who drove their animals to fresh grasslands in areas from Manchuria to the Carpathian Mountains. Their ancestors are credited by Darlington with "probably inventing" the bow. They lived on the flesh and milk of their horses, cows, and yaks, and the flesh of sheep, goats, and dogs. Also known as fierce fighters, they menaced the Chinese for 3,000 years and also attacked the Russians in Asia. With their kinsmen the Huns, Mongols, and Turks, they pushed westward the people who would populate central Europe. They may indeed have bred the first of the Chintigui dogs, whose feats of aggression astounded even Marco Polo. The Tartars too valued their valiant dogs. Estimating time in a cycle of twelve years, they designated each quarter cycle by the name of a deity—first, the lion; second, the ox; third, the dragon; and fourth, the dog— a practice followed in part by the Chinese into the present time.

The dangers found on the Chinese roads and trails in the early thirteenth century exceeded even those of tiger hunting, Polo found. The Tartars attacked caravans and took prisoners to be sold as slaves. Within China, robbers, thieves, and armed men who also seized travelers for sale as slaves or to be held for possible ransom were more feared than the Tartars. Khan's forces dealt harshly with such brigands when they were caught. "People who harbor such designs always carry poisons with them, to avoid being exposed to torture," Polo wrote. "But their rulers, who are aware of this practice, are provided with the dung of dogs, which they oblige the accused to swallow, as it occasions their vomiting up the poison."

CHARLEMAGNE

Charlemagne, king of the Franks from A.D. 768 to his death in 814, was the grandson of Charles Martel. The latter accepted Christianity from missionaries sent from Rome and had a vision of re-establishing the fallen Roman Empire. Charlemagne conquered most of Europe, except Spain (held by the Arabs), Scandinavia, northern Italy, and England; he crowned himself emperor of the West in A.D. 800 after making a compact with Pope Leo III. He called his realm the Holy Roman Empire, though Voltaire would sneer, "It was not holy, Roman nor an empire." Still, Charlemagne kept some order among the feudal lords in Europe and was responsible for the creation of schools and the spread of learning and the Christian religion in his realm, though he himself was nearly illiterate. Monasteries and towns were built, and artisans and craftsmen were welcomed from abroad.

Charlemagne, a great hunter and warrior himself, kept the Roman status of dogs alive long after the serfs and peasants of his lands could not afford the protection or companionship of a dog. The end of shepherd kingdoms, the invention of new weapons such as the long bow, and the use of gunpowder decreased the requirements of dogs for war, as did the curtailment of hunting. The farmers and herdsmen were mostly serfs, with few if any rights. Lords of the manor owned dogs, but fewer were required where dangerous animals were less threatening and the serf and his family could be worked to exhaustion planting, herding, and doing the work of dogs for the benefit of the noble who owned them. Not more than 10 percent of the populations lived in towns where officials, wealthy merchants, and some master craftsmen owned property. Hunting gave way to agriculture and Charlemagne's loyal domains, where royalty and nobility still had hundreds, even thousands, of dogs for their grand hunting adventures.

Dogs, no longer kept for work, often returned to the wild. Some followed owners who fled to the forests, though most canines ran in savage packs, not only in pastoral areas but even in small towns and cities, feeding on garbage and carrion as they had done in earlier times and continued to do in some parts of the Middle East. With the spread of plague and famine through the Western world, dogs were believed to eat the flesh of the dead. They were feared as evil, supernatural beings, and so the images of werewolves and monsters were created in folklore. Ancient legends of *Cynocephales*, dog-faced monsters, were revived and depicted even by monks in their manuscripts. The prevalent religions—the East-ern and Western Christian churches based in Constantinople and Rome, as well as Judaism and Islam—had long regarded dogs as representative of pagan beliefs. Dogs were suspected of carrying deadly diseases, such as the plagues then sweeping much of the known world. In China, dogs continued to hunt and herd, but in the Western world, their numbers declined in proportion to the heavily declining human population.

By the end of the first millennium A.D., in more settled areas, the lives of dogs began to improve. Some monasteries continued to harbor them, and kings and nobles continued to give their hunting and herding breeds more attention and care than they provided their serfs. There were saints who cared for animals and were honored by the church: Cosmas, Damian, Eustace, and Hubert among them. The monasteries sheltered scholars and scribes who learned something of Eastern cultures and probably gained a new appreciation for canines in the course of transcribing manuscripts in which dogs were praised by ancient Greeks and Romans. Returning Crusaders found Islamic warrior chiefs in the East still using dogs in war and peace, despite some prejudice of their faith against them. The status of dogs improved as secular governments in the West made peace with Pope Gregory VII in Rome and as Constantinople was preoccupied with Muslim at-tacks in the East. There again was a demand for shepherd dogs, Greyhounds, and Mastiffs. Dog breeding became an activity encouraged by royalty and in some monasteries, and by the year A.D. 1000, the nobility had come to regard their hunting rights and privileges with even greater proprietorship, and took great interest in the quality of their dogs.

The rise of local, regional, and international trade at the beginning of the eleventh century signaled a rise of new opportunity for people and animals alike. The horse would continue to be the chief means of transport on land, and the dog the favorite guardian of all types of commercial activity. Dog breeding re-vived, not only for sports and pastoral pursuits but again in fields of shipping and protection, as merchants were once more moving about, heading for new cities and fairs that were the beginnings of cities. The invading Muslims and Norsemen had been kept at bay, the Mediterranean was again an open sea, and entrepre-neurs were looking for colonial opportunities on distant shores while extending trade to the Far East. A network of trade routes developed, and dogs were still required to guard the caravans that used those routes. Plagues and wars would continue to obstruct the trading, but world commerce was growing, prosperity was increasing, and wealth was burgeoning. The canine population got back more of its long-lost duties, and the breeding of specialized dog breeds increased.

The basic commodities exchanged in trade were still limited. Ann Freemantle in *Age of Faith* lists some of the exchanges: "Cloth woven in Flanders from wool imported from England. For the rest, early West-to-East trade dealt in such basic commodities as grain, flax, fish, salt and wines . . . from the north and south came furs, fish, honey, and hemp."[4] Italy traded textiles and glassware to the East for spices and silk. Craftsmen too were exchanged by their own free will: Turkish civil servants went to China and Egypt, and from Egypt and Anatolia, masons and iron workers journeyed to Europe. Towns became wealthy and relatively secure. They not only could welcome skilled bureaucrats, artisans, and the masons who would build grand cathedrals and high walls, but also serfs who sought a better life.

Once again the cities required dogs, as did monasteries and cathedral schools, and canines were again used as workers, guardians, playmates for children, drawers of carts, and, of course, hunters and shepherds. Ownership of dogs, singly or in great number, became a mark of security and success. Royal and noble patronage of dogs extended worldwide. In the palaces and country manors dogs were again as pervasive as they had been in Rome and Thebes. Most portraits of kings, nobles, patriarchs, and the wealthy included a dog or two. Merchants in group portraits posed with dogs. Noble women appeared with lap dogs, house dogs, and cats. Saint Eustace was shown riding with hounds and Pointers.

THE RENAISSANCE

Jacob Bronowski places the beginning of the Renaissance in Spain in the twelfth century (though the classical part of the movement is usually ascribed to Italy) by the Toledo school of Translators, "where the ancient texts were turned from Greek (which Europe had forgotten) through Arabic and Hebrew into Latin." The American educator Will Durant, in *The Renaissance,* would credit Petrarch, Boccaccio, and Dante with providing great impetus, if not the beginning of the era, in the early fourteenth century. It was in Italy that French and English scholars near that time found the Pierian spring of knowledge and inspiration.

The Dark Ages ended slowly, especially for dogs, as the era of enlightenment began. Whether the origin was in Spain, Italy, in the widely scattered schools and universities founded by Christians in the Western world, or among the Jews who did seminal work at Alexandria and Toledo, a passion for learning appeared in widely scattered parts of the Western and Eastern worlds. Erasmus of Rotterdam, Martin Luther, and John Wycliffe, the Oxford University don, all sought to instill a yearning for education in the lives of ordinary people. These celebrated scholars would take the message of learning, reform, and freedom to the people. Erasmus's books became the most widely read of his time (the early sixteenth century), bringing him great celebrity. Since the Bible was available only in ancient languages at that time, Erasmus traveled widely to be consulted by popes, patriarchs, kings, and nobles, giving his account of social conditions after the disasters of the earlier century. His writing sought to guide common folk into education to enable them to read the words of Jesus Christ for themselves. His reports on progress were often bleak. Ninety percent of the population lived on farms and in villages, with little access to schools or reading. A few cities became local trade centers, but did not match the 200,000 population of the seaport city of Naples; Paris, with its university and 150,000 citizens; or London, the new capital of England, with its 50,000 residents.

Erasmus, visiting London, found the streets malodorous, packed with garbage and ravaged by dogs; the narrow streets of smaller places were worse. Excepting the war dogs, most canines had been left on their own during the years of war, pestilence, disorder, and destitution. Only the rich could afford them. Humans took the sheep along country lanes to their pastures, as they could not find other work. There was no end to filth or disease. It has been estimated that more than 50 percent of children died in their first year. Few homes had soap or salt or hot water. J. R. Hale, in his book *Renaissance Europe,* details the life of the people, destitute and plague-ridden, with little hope beyond that of heaven promised by the squabbling churchmen. Most dogs survived by running wild.[5]

Conditions could also be bad for royalty and nobles, at times. Louis XI of France was so terrified of assassination that he isolated himself in his castle, surrounded it with fortifications and archers, and dismissed most of his attendants for fear they might try to poison him. From Spain he ordered Mastiffs, good at guarding and fighting, as were those that centuries earlier had come from Rome as war dogs. Explorer Vasco Balboa, on his return from Central America where he led a Spanish expedition, would boast of the efficient way his Spanish Mastiffs killed American Indians.

The wars went on. The aristocrats continued their hunting. A knight traveling about Europe, taking employment where he found it, complained of the inhospitality of the dogs—he was set upon by them at every door. Pope Leo X was severely criticized for his addiction to hunting with his horses and dogs. However, conditions continued to improve, and often peace would prevail for as long as twenty years.

A network of trade routes developed, from Cadiz, Spain, to Tashkent and Khotan along the silk and spice routes to China. Dogs were widely used as guardians. The plagues and wars would continue to obstruct the traveling merchants, though robbers were a greater terror. Through it all world commerce increased: The wealthy sought spices, gold and gems, silk and other costly textiles. A fashion craze began. The towns became wealthy and more secure, importing craftsmen and tradesmen. Even escaping serfs were sometimes given work in the growing towns, as well as clerics of the church who became employed in trade and government.

Once again towns and cities required dogs to guard their gates, officials, traders, and even the professional people required to move from place to place within the walls. Tapestries, paintings, mosaics, and pottery again reflected dogs in every aspect of contemporary society. These works of art continued to show families with dogs in attendance, nobles hunting with packs of dogs, and merchants gathered with their own dogs. Ownership of dogs, singly or in great numbers, became a mark of security and success. Royal and noble patronage of specialized breeds extended worldwide. Members of royal families recorded their experiences with hunting dogs, among them the German emperor Frederick II (1220–1250), who, at an early age, dictated a book on dogs and falconry; and Edmund, Duke of York, fifth son of Edward III, who wrote *The Master of the Game* on the training of coursing hounds. The great poet Geoffery Chaucer issued his timeless good advice in *Troilus and Cressida:* "sleeping dogs . . . just let them sleep."

6

THE WORKING DOGS

⚭

In the 1960s, Fernand Mery of France withdrew from his work in medicine and biology and as president of the Academie Veterinaire de France to prepare a book answering a series of questions about his beloved friend and companion, "a cross-bred dog." "Why are we so fond of them?" he asks. "What do we know of their obscure origins? Of the secret of evolution?" The result was *Le Chien,* a fascinating compendium of information answering most possible questions about dogs and their behavior.[1] Mery concludes in part that our love of dogs relates to their emotional resemblance to ourselves, reacting as we react "to pleasure, pain, and joy." He also provides continuing proof that canines as effectively influence our behavior as we do theirs, generally for the good of all concerned.

Mery's historic record and views seem verified when we see the scores of paintings of classical artists of the Middle Ages and Renaissance that show the quintessence of humankind posing with their favorite dog or dogs, obviously hoping to further enhance their own unique virtues by their close association with a canine. Royalty, nobility, priest and pagan, commoner and common scoundrel, all through the ages evidence a hope that they may be considered as good as their dog considers them. And the canine has rarely been known to refuse man the favor of its company. The universally popular name Fido, from the Latin meaning faithful, points to a prime virtue of most canines. The use of the name traces back to the Midddle Ages, an era when many dogs were given better treatment than most of the human population. In the day of the rediscovery of Plato, humans seemed to desire to resemble, or to at least be associated with, the well-bred dog.

We have joined our own dog Kiwi in a somewhat similar association, look-ing back through the windows of time—books, pictures, and records—for the answers to one of the questions posed but not answered directly by Mery: When and where did the partnership of man and dog begin? Mery, like Konrad Lorenz, leaves no doubt that the association began in prehistory. Both scientists were well experienced with animals and in the fields of medicine and biology. Each suggests that dogs learned to appreciate human beings by following them into the hunt, lurking about their camps and villages, and sharing their food. They do not doubt that the association was voluntary and mutually beneficial. Like Jacob Bronowski, Mery attributes the absence of dogs in most European caves and rock shelters to the artist's absorption with the magic of prehistoric times. The painter, alone in the hidden shelter, creates his obscure drawing to appeal to the divinities; he is portraying his fantasy, his conquest over the boar, bison, and stag. He is praying perhaps, dimly understanding that the picture itself is the magic.

Even Neolithic man, possessing credible weapons for the big-game hunt, needed assistance. His Paleolithic predecessor more urgently required help. Early Stone Age man stalked game with a club or a stone, nothing more, as Bronowski has noted. Mery, referencing Lorenz, suggests that early dog and man came together by slow, gradual association, and credits Lorenz with first noticing the conditions of earliest possible bonding. Lorenz researched the Baltic Sea areas and found the bonding already in place. When and where did the close, trusting asso-ciation begin?

Recent archaeological discoveries place the beginning of civilized mankind in a time frame of two million years, and placed the likely geographic beginning at Africa, since that is where most fossil finds have been made. Also Africa, least affected by the great glacial movements that might alter the development of a human race, was most congenial to the preservation of their fossil bones and artifacts. Close rivals for such precedence have been found in the Middle East and China, but the primal site remains Africa, where *Homo habilis,* the tool maker and hunter, was migrating about the continent, following the vast, wandering herds that he depended on for food supply 400,000 years ago.

At the Natural History Museum in London, scientists working with paleoanthropologist Christopher Stringer have created a model of migrations of early man after studying and analyzing fossil finds in hundreds of areas, now sum-marized as the "Out of Africa" theory.

The model begins about a million years ago, and shows small groups of migrants leaving Africa for Asia, which itself becomes a secondary base for dispersion. Here small groups or tribes spread throughout an area to become known as "the Fertile Crescent" where first signs of "anatomically modern people" in settlements have appeared. Mery refers to cave dwellers along the Niger River in northern Africa who left drawings of the hunter with his spear and his dogs, and a naked bowman with his dogs pictured in a Teneri rock shelter in Algeria.

So we have evidence that the man and dog began their mutually beneficial partnership while still in Africa. Lorenz presents his deduced beginning of the association of those humans with animals that would become the first domesticated dogs. It is an assumed adoption of puppies by Stone Age women who may have lost a child or otherwise required a suckling infant to ease the painful pressure of milk. Similar situations have been solved in this way among primitive women of the Arctic in modern times. The pup stayed to become a "child" in a Paleolithic family, its behavior not much different from that of a pup growing up in a pack of wild dogs or wolves. Also the bonding of wild dogs and human hunters had begun where the two species—socially similar, family-oriented, earthbound, and migratory—associated in the search for food: in Africa. Dogs and humans would hunt together, walk halfway around the globe together, and, some 80,000 years later, sail together from England to New Zealand to complete the circle.

⚭

We have followed the African nomads and their dogs on the long trail north and west, over some 70,000 years. Man changed, rising to the status of *Homo sapiens,* or Neanderthal, the wild creature who walked erect and created and used tools. His companionship with canines was a personal and fruitful one. During the long marches and wandering in search of food and comfort, man observed that some dogs worked better than others. A few, especially the bitches, were happier to perform guard duties as needed. Other canines that gave evidence of keen scenting powers or exceptional vision were considered of great value. They understood the signals and commands of man who increasingly demanded alert, obedient response in the hunt and in battle. So humans kept the preferred animals and began a process of selective breeding.

At the same time, humans were gathering wild grains and roots on the march, discovering that seeds spilled on the earth took on new life when rains came and the sun warmed them; at such times a pause in the wandering seemed wise. There were stops along the Nile Valley and at a green oases in the desert, as at Faiyum in northern Africa and Jericho in Palestine, and some Paleolithic migrants went on to the Indus Valley of Asia. The settler became a planter. He used his hunting dogs to capture and hold alive the animals he once killed, and in time, he successfully domesticated horses. The dogs learned to contain wild livestock, to protect them from predators, and to keep them out of growing crops. They learned to respect the ownership rights of humans over all other domesticated animals.

"It took at least two million years for man to change from the little dark creature with the stone in his hands, *Australepithicus* in Central Africa, to the modern *Homo sapiens,*" writes Bronowski. "The largest single step of man is the change from nomad to village agriculture. . . . What made that possible? An act of will by men . . . [and] a strange and secret act of nature . . . [and] . . . at the end of the Ice Age . . . a hybrid wheat appeared. . . ." The herdsman and the hunter had the good sense to plant the best of the wild wheat naturally crossed with goat grass. "Agriculture is one part of the biological evolution; the domestication and harnessing of the village animals is the other," Bronowski continues. "The sequence of domestication is orderly. First comes the dog."

That larger step into farming would drastically change the lives of both humankind and dogs. We have seen them advancing in responsibilities and into specialized work in Egypt and Mesopotamia. Their role had changed in the course of hunting. The Berbers wandering the desert lands needed an animal that could sight, outrun, and wear down big game. They created the Greyhound, the Saluki, and the Sloughi. The Egyptians, pausing to plant farms at the end of the desert, bred a number of types, including those of the Berber tribes, as well as the red wolfhound and smaller dogs useful in hunting and herding.

⌒♒♒∽

The dog's roles now changed increasingly as farm villages became towns and cities. Dogs first learned not to harm livestock and not to even taste the parcels of meat they were required to deliver. They also learned to contain and protect their charges. Some dogs became beasts of burden, and when the wheel was developed, they pulled carts. They worked as draft animals in the streets of Egyptian towns, along the mountain trails, and from the seashore to inland towns, transporting fish, flour, and artifacts. By the Middle Ages, big dogs would pull small, light chariots in Egypt or gigs carrying an artisan and his tools in central

Europe, averaging, it was said, thirty miles a day. They also pulled a kind of travois (fashioned of poles strapped to the dog's shoulders, the ends dragging on the earth), as well as sleds and toboggans.

The big dogs operated crude machinery: the treadmill that lifted water in Egypt and ground grain in Anatolia, the pumps and presses in Greece and later in Scotland. The demand for such dogs continued, and new types were bred worldwide. The basic stock continued to be the giant canines from the highlands of Iran, Afghanistan, and Tibet; dogs from India, noted by Herodotus to have been in the armies of Cyrus the Great of Persia; and those brought from India later by the soldiers of Alexander the Great.

The dog's basic duties now changed. Fewer war dogs were required since more effective weapons were developed. Fighting dogs performed in the pits and circuses of Rome, or were still trained by the military to act as messengers and guards or to sniff out the enemy. Fewer carried burdens in the cities, instead bringing supplies to the sick and wounded and protecting travelers from animal and human predators.

The widespread assumption that wolves were the primary progenitors of the big dogs, if not all dogs, would seem to be disproved by Lorenz, who credits many smaller dogs and even the Great Dane to Aureus, or jackal, beginnings. The wolf actually was the most feared enemy of early man, as they existed widely in great numbers. In the north, the wolf was tamed and undoubtedly was a leading progenitor of domesticated canines. The record in Egypt, however, where dogs made a strong beginning in domestic service to man, shows the wolf to have been much distrusted, as has been noted by Egyptologist Adolph Erman.

Supporters of the wolf theory assert that the behavior patterns of dog and wolf are similar, each having similar social and hunting patterns, with one exception: The wolf is not known to hunt with man. Wolves can be tamed and domesticated; however, they appear to lack a dog's sense of responsibility in a relationship with humankind. The wolf, a most admirable animal, is a loner outside his family and pack. Lorenz points out that wolfish zig-zag movements in responding to human beings indicate his doubt. The domestic dog appears to instinctively accept responsibility, without doubt or question.

Whatever may be the beginning of the association of humankind and canines, we have found a path of the global migration of the man/dog partnership. In time the world pedestrian trek would be complete, the famous Captain James Cook in his ship *Endeavor* closing the last gap from Plymouth, England, to New Zealand

and Botany Bay, Australia, on a voyage that lasted from 1768–73, with two hounds and a few sheep aboard, the working dogs the winners.

☙❧

The contributions of dogs grew as civilizations developed and populations increased. Food supplies were assured for many people after the early farmers of Mesopotamia and Egypt learned how to control and manage the rivers with dikes and canals, and leather pails, carried by dogs. One of the earliest inventions of mankind, the plow, could best be used with animal assistance. Big dogs helped to capture and contain wild oxen and asses that could be trained as draft animals. Dogs didn't work well as draft animals, but they successfully transported burdens strapped to their backs and on travois, sleds, and small carts, along narrow, difficult trails. They excelled in guarding and herd duties and efficiently protected livestock in new frontier lands of the Fertile Crescent. But, as the Hebraic scriptures tell us, man was not content there. Many continued on as nomadic hunters. Among those who settled to herd or farm, there was fighting for land and water rights, as related in the story of Cain and Abel and the legends and histories of the Middle East. "Wild men of the mountains," shepherd tribes and their dogs, swept down upon the farms and towns. Prisoners were taken, men, women and dogs, who were condemned to lives of slavery. Warlords created kingdoms and empires.

As the slave trade expanded, and those affording them increased their flocks, their lands, and their power to wage war, the productive partnership of man and dog endured. Slave power was cheaper and more versatile, but slaves usually had to be guarded and sometimes recaptured. In the time of the Roman Empire and the Dark Ages to follow, as tribal warlords beyond the reach of the Roman legions sought to keep their power, slavery spread; some dogs lost their place in the homes and religions of the Middle East. Many canines not needed as shepherds or guards merely served to amuse royalty, nobility, and sometimes the common people by fighting bears, running down helpless hares, killing one another in the amphitheaters of Rome and its provinces, and baiting bulls and bears in the fighting pits. A world trade in canines flourished, with large shepherd dogs and stock-guarding types much sought after.

The brutalization of humans in slavery accompanied the dispersion of the canines. The capture and enslavement of people increased as populations grew. Slave workers replaced dogs in some instances. Their cost was little more than that of dogs, and they lived longer and were more versatile. Primitive slaves could be taught to dig canals, build walls, and plant and harvest crops. Arab slave traders dominated the commerce in humans, ranging through Africa and extending their trade by sea to Asian coasts, in time reaching the Indian Ocean. They returned from China with tea, silk, paper, and rare dogs: the Chow Chow, used for hunting and as food; "sleeve dogs," used in the Orient to warm one's hands; and the sacred temple dog, the Lhasa Apso, smuggled from Tibet.

Hunting and fighting dogs, as well as rare and unusual breeds, appealed to Western royalty and wealthy persons as lions and leopards did to the kings of Egypt and the Middle East in earlier times. Those who could afford the sport of pack hunting would appoint titled court favorites as masters of the hounds, responsible for creating hunting packs numbering into hundreds and even thousands of dogs.

The distribution of canines about the world for purposes other than herding sheep, guard duty, and as war dogs occurred when large packs began being developed for the hunt. The Greek dogs, including the Molossian and Sparta's Laconian Hound, continued to enjoy favor. The ruling classes developed enormous wealth and wanted dogs for such aristocratic sports as riding to a pack of hounds, using falcons, by coursing, or by sending dogs after hares with the *liam,* or slip lead, in the Greek style. The noble lords themselves would in time undertake the maintenance of excellent breeding stock and the development of new strains.

The Arabs introduced the sport of riding to hounds on their fast ponies, accompanied by packs of lean, fast dogs. Pastoral people from Neolithic days, they had been herdsmen and farmers in northern Africa, until the pastures died and the deserts spread. They were relatively isolated from world trade until the rise of Mecca as a commercial and religious center following the development of camel transportation and the domestication of the horse. Power and wealth came with the spread of Islam in the seventh century A.D. The Islamic Qur'an, like the Hebrew scriptures, had little good to say for canines. But the prized Arab dogs continued to herd sheep and to protect the caravans along trade routes to Mecca, including those on *hajj* to the Holy City, a feat required of all faithful Muslims. In the tents of the sheiks could be found such dogs, among them the handsome Saluki, its name meaning "noble."

Ann Robbins, in her history of the Greyhound, credits the Arabs with increasing the speed of their "gaze hounds" by the careful kind of training they also gave to their horses.[2] Historian Mary Crosby, in *World Encyclopedia of Dogs,* tell us that the Saluki was venerated by the proud sheiks who refused to sell them, but would award them to foreign rulers and powerful friends they wished to honor and influence. Crosby writes that an Arab noble, upon entering the home of a distinguished family, first bows to the Saluki before acknowledging his human hosts.[3] The Saluki often lived in the sheik's tent, where the puppies were cared for by the women.

⚬☙

Arab wealth and power grew, and the Islamic religion spread worldwide. A century after the death of founder Mohammed, the Muslim forces he had united were creating an empire that reached from Persia to Spain. The horse and the camel, used well by the Arab forces, provided a new kind of military power. The dogs of war would turn to other tasks. The Roman military would continue to carry the fighting Mastiffs about the world, beginning in Carthage and Spain, while Celts and Spanish Iberians from Africa are credited with supplying big dogs for herding and guard duties.

A scene of lion hunters and their dogs (circa A.D. 235). (Courtesy the Borgheses Collection, Rome; Photo by Sabine Callaris)

The Persians were likely first to introduce the Mastiff to southwest Asia. The bas-relief portrayals of such dogs on the walls of the Nineveh library and Theban tomb art in Egypt show huge, powerful fighting dogs that may have originated in Tibet, where Persian merchants traded. The Mastiff is shown as a war dog in Assyria, a guardian of tombs in Nippur, and a hunting and war dog in Egypt. It continued in demand by warlords, merchants, and others who needed such dogs and could afford them. There was endless warfare as empires rose and fell, from the time of Sargon II to that of Alexander and Julius Caesar; the commerce in war dogs and guard dogs flourished.

In Egypt, a general trade in canines developed. In particular demand were small dogs bred to live in the house as companions to and guardians of children. Popular among them was the Basenji and various types of stock dogs. The house dogs drew carts, carried burdens on their backs, and delivered messages. A wall painting in a Theban tomb shows a water-lifting invention, still in use some 4,000 years later, operated by a man who was assisted by a dog. Since water was a scarce, precious commodity, the dog evidently was also required for protection of the operator and his lift.

The seagoing Phoenicians, the Minoans, and the Egyptians themselves (via their Nile river boats and Red Sea ships) sold to the Mediterranean nations their own canines as well as breeds from Persia, Afghanistan and Tibet.

Rarest of all Greek hunting dogs was the Indian Hound, used by Cyrus of Persia and Alexander the Great as a war dog, according to Herodotus, and described by Aristotle as a cross between the Indian tiger and Greyhound dog. A bitch in heat was tied and left in a lonely spot in tiger country, the great naturalist and philosopher explained. If the male tiger did not kill and eat the unfortunate female, as often happened, he coupled with her. The proof, Aristotle insisted, was in the brindled, tawny appearance of the pups. (EDITOR'S NOTE: Of course, we know that such a mating is biologically impossibile. Aristotle's "proof," the brindled, tawny appearance of the puppies, is a characteristic color of many dog breeds, including a number of sight hounds.) Whatever the genealogy of the Indian Hound, if such a breed ever existed, it has been lost, whereas miniaturized versions of the huge Greek Molossians can still be found guarding villages and herding sheep in the Greek mountains.

The Greeks were ardent hunters, though they did so more to protect their herds and flocks from dangerous wild animals than to supply their tables with food. Oppian's *Cynegetics,* on the art of hunting with dogs, is probably the earliest book written on canine behavior and training. Denison Hull, a Chicago architect, trainer of foxhounds, and translator of Xenophon's works from ancient Greek, describes the hunting practices of the Greeks: First, the Greeks required an excuse for the need to hunt; it was rarely done for sport alone. "A dangerous lion . . . that ought to be destroyed before it carried off the slave's children, or killed sheep or goats, needed to be killed." A line of nets would be set for it, and the hounds brought out to track it down and drive it into one of the nets, where the men could spear it in relative safety. Sometimes the beast that was ravaging crops was a wild boar. It would be tracked to its lair by strong hounds and run into a net, where the most experienced man would lead the attack with a spear (and sometimes got himself killed). Often there were reports of large hares (there were no rabbits in Greece), and the keen-nosed Laconian Hounds would be brought out to pursue them. Again, the game would be run into nets by the dogs. "After praying to Artemis and Apollo, the keeper of hounds would slip the hound with keenest nose," Hull writes, "the hounds giving tongue across the fields." [4]

The hunters would use javelins rather than bows and arrows. The preference was a long, heavy spear, especially when a boar or ox was the game. Greek hunting style was widely copied. St. Hubert, writing a guide to this kind of sport, describes the Greek practice as slipping the *liam,* or leash. "Suit-hounds," probably the Berber Sloughi or similar hounds, were held back by the huntsman, who "slipped the liam" for the lead dog scenting prey, who gave the signal "with his sonorous voice." St. Hubert, later canonized for his work with animals, evidently went far back in developing his famed hunting hounds.

Coursing became the sport of kings and nobles. Charlemagne appointed one of his highest officers (said to have been a son of his court favorite, Count Orlando) as the officer of his Greyhound kennel to regulate the coursing rules for his court and country. King Canute of Denmark, after invading England, assured the purity of the sport by decreeing "no meane person may keepe any greihounds"; the punishment for the killing of a Greyhound was death for the offender. Raphael Holinshed, the historian whose work inspired Shakespeare, tells the story of the rivalry of Picts and Scots for prized Deerhounds. Pict nobles invited to hunt with the Scottish king Cranlint concluded that the king's dogs were better than their own. King Cranlint generously agreed to provide them with some of his fine hounds, but held back the best. The Picts learned of the subterfuge, and they stole the king's best hound. In the ensuing battle, 60 Scots and nearly 100 Picts were slain, according to the story.

The Romans taught the British and continental Europeans about enjoying leisure, especially with their dogs. William the Conqueror, who also brought social refinements to England, kept his canines hard at work in providing him with recreation and entertainment business. Riding to hounds, racing, stag hunting, and sport in general that required horses and dogs became proper and elitist in a rigid society of the Western world, freed finally from the menace of the marauding Arabs and Vikings. British commoners were allowed to have a dog or two when they could afford such a luxury, and were permitted to watch the upper-class "sport" of canines fighting in the pits.

European royalty and nobility, prospering as world commerce increased, were much interested in importing of small "curiosity" breeds as well as Mastiffs and Greyhounds, though all qualified as appropriate gifts for heads of state, titled nobility, and the hierarchy of various religions. In a war-ravaged society, even monarchs required protective dogs for personal safety and comfort. A king could not trust members of his own family. Witness the fact that, in Persia, scores of fratricidal events occurred. Even in religion-dominated Byzantium, King Basil allegedly murdered his brother to gain the throne, and a queen was accused of blinding her own son to preclude his attempt to dethrone her. Dogs were faithful and could readily be accommodated into the bed chamber. They continued to be the best guarantee of royal safety.

Arab traders whose ships plied the eastern waters when they, for a few centuries, controlled the traffic of the Mediterranean had a major part in introducing foreign breeds to Europe. Thus the Saluki, the Afghan Hound, and the Borzoi came to grace the palaces and manor houses of Europe. The aristocracy also required thousands of canines for their principal recreation—hunting, racing, and dog fighting. Nobles themselves would, in time, undertake the maintenance of excellent breeding stock and the development of new strains. Queens also took a personal interest in hunting and other sports involving dogs. King Henry VIII dispatched to the queen of France his royal gift of "hobbies [falcons], Greyhounds, hounds, and great dogs," and she graciously responded that he had made her "the gladdest woman in the world."

"Dogs with specialized abilities or dogs with curiosity values have always been valuable trade commodities," writes historian Mary Crosby. "They were also exchanged between courts of ruling powers as tokens of friendship and esteem. Wars and movements of armies also contributed to the spread of breeds." The only exception appears to be in the Egyptian trade, where the Basenji seemingly disappeared from Asia and Africa and did not reach Europe until modern times. In the early nineteenth century, the Basenji was rediscovered in what was then the

Belgian Congo, and the breed is now esteemed throughout the world as an elegant, fastidious house dog.

The Great Dane also has had a somewhat mysterious evolution. The hunting Mastiffs shown in Assyrian bas-reliefs are said by some to be similar to the Great Dane, and thus assumed to have come from Greece. So the Great Dane of today would be descended from the Molossian, which in turn most likely originated in Tibet or India from dogs arriving with early Stone Age people of Central Asia. Gratius Faliscus, in A.D. 200, wrote of such Mastiffs fighting in Rome, from where they were taken by Celts to Denmark and Germany, and later to England by the Roman army. Germany's Landgraffen popularized the Great Dane as an excellent boarhound; Landgraff Phillip of Hesse wrote that his dogs killed 2,522 wild boars in the 1559 season. Duke Henry of Braunschweig had perhaps the largest pack. He appeared at the Obserwesser hunt with 600 male Great Danes. Such canines are said to be the progenitors of the modern Great Dane.[5]

When the Belgae tribe of Celts traveled south into central Europe, they took with them their bronze and iron weapons and armor, giant ale mugs crafted of metal, their looms and sheep, and their dogs. They had fought the Macedonians, Molossians and Dorian Greeks, and probably acquired their giant Mastiffs in the process. Possibly they took dogs north earlier from Anatolia where they had learned the secrets of metallurgy. Celtic art discovered in the peat bogs of Denmark indicate that they had arrived south of the Adriatic to settle in central Europe about 100 B.C. on their way to the British Isles. One of the finest pieces of Celtic work in metals—a huge bronze cauldron plated in silver, found near Gundesrun, Denmark—depicts the stag-horned god Cernnos surrounded by animals, including a large, rugged Mastiff. Depictions of canines have been found in Denmark and Britain dating to 7,500 B.C.; thus it appears that Lapps and invading Romans also brought in big war dogs that worked as shepherds and guardians on land and as guard dogs aboard ships and canal boats.

Some 600 years later, Hubert, the son of the duke of Guienne and a local lord among the Belgae in the vicinity of the Ardennes forest on the Franco-Belgian border, would develop some of the most famous of all canine breeds. His black-and-white hunting hounds were behind the Bloodhound, a breed that would become a major factor in law enforcement and detection work throughout the world.

Hubert was known in his youth as something of a roisterer as well as an avid hunter. His redeeming grace, however, was his love of animals, especially dogs and horses. According to legend, young Hubert and his friends thoughtlessly went hunting on a Good Friday. Hubert, about to down a fleeing stag, saw a the vision of a cross suspended between its antlers. He spared the stag, and soon thereafter took Holy Orders. In time he became a bishop of the Catholic Church and established an abbey at Liege, a town destined to become a major center of trade. Hubert also created a center for the breeding and training of fine Mastiffs in the nearby Ardennes forest.

The Vision of Saint Hubert, *by Albrecht Durer, recalls the pivotal incident from the life of the patron saint of hunters.* (Copyright © The British Museum)

The young Bishop of Liege and his successors would continue to breed hounds capable of discovering and pursuing game by smell. Known as the St. Hubert Hound following the death and canonization of the bishop, the breed became widely known in the Low Countries of central Europe, and its descendant, the aforementioned Bloodhound, achieved fame in Victorian times throughout the world.

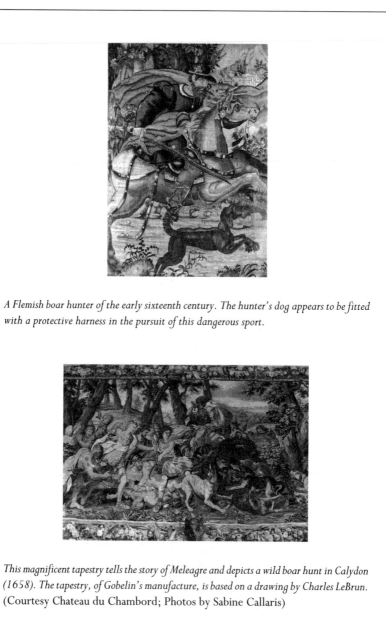

A Flemish boar hunter of the early sixteenth century. The hunter's dog appears to be fitted with a protective harness in the pursuit of this dangerous sport.

This magnificent tapestry tells the story of Meleagre and depicts a wild boar hunt in Calydon (1658). The tapestry, of Gobelin's manufacture, is based on a drawing by Charles LeBrun. (Courtesy Chateau du Chambord; Photos by Sabine Callaris)

The fame of the hounds spread, and William the Conqueror of Normandy used such dogs in France to support his troops as well as to run down opponents of the family regime. When William took forces to England in 1066 and earned the sobriquet of Conqueror, his St. Hubert Hounds guarded and defended his bases and followed remaining dissenters to the end of any trail. Often the end was not violent, historian Crosby tells us. Bloodhounds, despite their fierce demeanor, were actually very docile at times. They sometimes greeted joyfully the humans they were pursuing. But woe to any captive that might attempt to get away!

The St. Hubert Hounds were used as intended in much of Europe and in England. Crosby cites their merits in this field as stated in an ancient *Guide to Dogs* clearly based on *St. Hubert's Guide,* published several centuries after his death in 727: "To find out the hart or stag where his harbour is, you must be provided with a Bloodhound, Draughthound, or Sluithound, which must be led with a Liam."

The new place of canines in the church and monasteries was symbolized by a famous fresco, painted in 1355 by the Italian artist Andrea de Firenze in the church of Santa Maria Novelle in Florence, that was said to depict the papal view of the order of the church and society at the time. The pope is the central figure, at his right the representatives of the church hierarchy: a cardinal, a bishop, and an abbot, and lesser deputies, including monks, friars and nuns; on his left, the Holy Roman Emperor and his officers and vassals; as well as the common people. Before them are sheep, symbolic of the Christian flock, and black-and-white dogs, representing the order of Dominicans, said to be from *Domini Canes,* Latin for "hounds of the Lord."[6] The order was founded by St. Dominic in the twelfth century; his priests adopted the convenient double entendre of the *Domini,* by which they became known thereafter.

It was a Christian vision enlightening the world, made possible when Pope Leo III placed a temporal crown on Charlemagne in St. Peter's in Rome on Christmas Day, A.D. 800. Charlemagne, ruler of the Franks and Germans, would do his work well. He appointed a master of hounds as an opening gesture and led his military and dogs against the pagans—Moors and Asiatic Avars. He tamed the Celts and created a Christian empire from the Baltic to the Mediterranean, with the Eastern Christian church also reluctantly tolerating his dominion. Charlemagne's favorite recreation was hunting with dogs that he was said to value as much as he did his many mistresses. He had embraced Christianity and concluded that clerics were the most honest and dependable persons available to become his civil clerks, so he employed them to manage his growing empire. They collected taxes and enforced laws with the help of trained canines. The Dominican

The royal hound stands triumphant over the felled stag in this Versailles sculpture created during the reign of Louis XV.

In another Versailles sculpture, an unfortunate hunting dog is about to be dispatched by a raging lion.

"Hounds of the Lord" performed their religious tasks equally well, training and providing needed clerks in the schools that they established, caring for their parish duties, and converting and suppressing heretics.

Prospering aristocrats continued to use their dogs to protect their lands and homes. Villages and towns also benefited from the presence of guard dogs, and the canines held their place in growing new and old forms of recreation. Following the Battle of Tours, in which Charles Martel turned back the Muslim cavalry, the use of horses was introduced into Europe. The vassals, pledged to supply their kings with mounted warriors, also could use their horses with coursing. The sport of coursing, introduced by the Romans, grew more popular as Greyhounds supplied by Phoenician traders became available; its interest surpassed that of hunting large game as forests were cleared and manor lords acquired more land. The Greyhound could outrun any other canine breed and snap up the hare without missing its stride, and so became a major factor in coursing meets and later in the Greyhound racing that is still practiced around the globe.

Stag hunting with packs of large, strong hounds also continued to hold favor in most of continental Europe and the British Isles. As larger game grew scarce, the fox replaced the stag in the chase. Foxhounds came into favor, and the fox hunt became an aristocratic exercise. England became the leading exporter of such animals to other parts of the world. Beagles soon followed, though hunting with the Beagle was not a high social event. The Beagle hunter, like the coon hunter in America, was less interested in the social implications of a sport requiring horses than he was in watching the dogs work.

The rare British sport of otter hunting required a special breed of hound able to take on the apparently playful otter in its own element, water. The otter, a tough, agile creature with sharp teeth and punishing jaws, proved a formidable opponent. King Henry II of England himself was the first Master of Otterhounds over his pack. Queen Elizabeth I also had such a pack and "was probably the first lady Master of Hounds," according to historian Crosby. The otters fought on their own grounds and in the water, forcing the dogs to swim for hours before engaging in a hard, enervating struggle. There appears to be no record of the export of Otterhounds, a breed that resembles a "rough-coated Bloodhound."

꩜

Herding, hunting, and fighting had been the main work of the dogs until the end of the Roman "peace" that endured nearly 900 years. Mastiffs were widely used for fighting, and as guard dogs over the camps and strongholds of the Empire. Islamic warriors had taken away some of the outer provinces, and the Celts, with their Mastiffs from Greece and Anatolia, had broken wide passages through the Roman walls, taking over lands that would become centers of an oncoming feudal society of local lords arising from their ownership of land, flocks, herds,

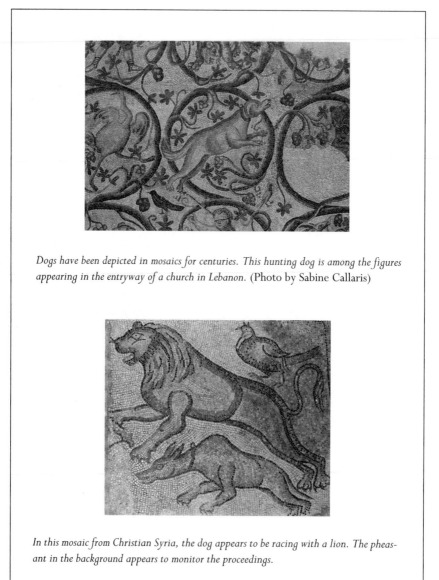

Dogs have been depicted in mosaics for centuries. This hunting dog is among the figures appearing in the entryway of a church in Lebanon. (Photo by Sabine Callaris)

In this mosaic from Christian Syria, the dog appears to be racing with a lion. The pheasant in the background appears to monitor the proceedings.

horses, and dogs. Some of the new lands were well covered with forest, requiring the large Mastiffs for protection from bears and wolves as well as for the hunting of big game. The end of the Roman occupation permitted tribes and clans to resume their ancient enmities with each other, and ever-present outlaws who raided the towns, herds, and flocks left unguarded.

The dogs fought and exterminated large predators, such as bears and wolves, in most of continental Europe and the British Isles by the mid sixteenth century, but wealthy landowners required Mastiffs to discourage poachers and thieves. Some former war dogs continued to wear their spiked, iron collars. The ideal poachers' dogs, it was said, were those trained to help in taking game and sheep but who refused to indicate loyalty to any poaching suspect if they themselves were captured. The leading requirement for big dogs was ferocity in the pits, fighting badgers, wolves, and bears as high stakes were wagered by the sport's wealthy patrons. The reputations of the British canines in this area were well known, and thus the dogs were sent to Rome itself to fight, and later to France, Germany, and Spain for breeding purposes, as presents to the royal houses.

This sculpture from Tuscany depicts a saddened, desolate Greyhound.

Thousands of dogs were used for show and play; thirty kinds of sporting hounds and forty breeds of working dogs were listed in commercial shipping manifests,. Terriers, racing dogs, and exotic canines such as the Chow Chow and the tiny Maltese (a favorite of ladies of fashion) entered the world market of working dogs.

Among the most famous of the working dogs in Victorian England were the Bloodhound and the Saint Bernard. Queen Victoria was said herself to care for and bathe her eclectic pack of canines, bestowed upon her by almost every major monarch. Much later King George VI purchased a Pembroke Welsh Corgi puppy as a pet for his young daughters Elizabeth and Margaret; these wonderful cattle dogs have been in residence in Buckingham Palace ever since.

When a monk named Bernard de Menthon entered the Alpine reaches of Switzerland to convert the Celts to Christianity in the twelfth century, he found a high level of civilization. The Celtic tribes were skillful workers in metals; they lived in villages, built forts that would become models for those in southern Europe, and stored their grain in heated pits; they used their dogs to draw carts and sleds. The good monk Bernard converted many to Catholicism and established a hospice for his monks where it was much needed, high in a major Alpine pass. The monks of Saint Bernard Hospice used dogs to help them with their work, following trails, carrying burdens, and rescuing snowbound travelers. In 300 years, the famous Saint Bernard descendants of the Molossians that the Celts had obtained in their travels had become widely known for their deeds of rescue; it became the work of specially trained dogs in 1750.

The Mastiffs of most European countries were known for their strength and ability to pull carts and sleds in early days, but the Saint Bernard could follow a trail in deep snow, find a lost hiker half frozen and buried, and return the victim

This marble carving for a sarcophagus in France shows Selene, the Greek moon goddess, tending to her beloved Endymion, who was granted eternal sleep to remain forever young. In this group, a small dog keeps a close watch on the proceedings.

to the hospice. Nearly 3,000 humans had been saved at the time a dog named Barry, a veteran of the rescue corps, was credited with bringing in 40 lost persons in the course of his life. He was said to have been killed with an ice ax in his forty-first rescue attempt by a panic-stricken hiker who, caught in a blizzard, thought Barry was a bear coming at him. Actually, Barry died in his bed—of old age, as befits a hero. His mounted remains may be viewed in the Museum at Bern.

7

CANINE ROOTS IN BRITAIN

ᏯᎥᎥᎥᎡ

The earliest dog owners in Britain are said to have been Cro-Magnon people, well advanced in Stone Age culture, tall, strong individuals whose fossils were discovered in Wales in the nineteenth century. They evidently walked onto the British island from Holland or Belgium in a glacial age when forests grew on land now covered by the North Sea, about 8000 B.C. The skeletons of dogs and their owners found at Starr Carr, fixing the time of the earliest domestic dogs in Britain for many years, were carbon-dated at 7500 B.C. The Mastiffs that accompanied the cultured Celts are depicted on their owners' artifacts found in many parts of Europe. Mastiffs would dominate all other canines in Great Britain, and from them would come the Bulldog, long a symbol of the national character. The Bullmastiff, also a descendant of the Mastiff in combination with the Bulldog, was developed as a guardian of the home and property and is a well-bred canine measuring up to the ancient standards of Socrates and Plato for human behavior.

Jacquetta and Christopher Hawkes, in their *Prehistoric Man in Britain,*[1] credit the Tardenosians, "probably originating in North Africa," with bringing the first canines to Britain, possibly by the way of northern France and Belgium. Such dogs were undoubtedly used for the hunt. They may have walked through the forests of what is now North Sea bottom, after the Tardenosians abandoned the desiccated areas of North Africa. The Celts with their Mastiffs arrived in relatively modern times, fighting their way down from the north. British prehistorian Frederick Zeuner suggests that the ancestors of dogs in Britain may have been domesticated in the Russian Crimea about 12,000 years ago.

The Celts in their wide migrations east and west learned iron work in early times, perhaps from the Hittites, or they may have developed such skills on their own when they discovered iron in the Austrian Alps. They wandered often and far while fighting their way from the Baltic, moving south against any force in their path. Often they invaded lands in which they proposed to settle, but some moved on. It was the Celts, armed with their excellent iron and bronze weapons, who stopped the terrible Asiatic Tartars advancing on the west from Russia. There they learned the uses of the horse. That they and other tribes also had their protection dogs with them is indicated by historian Edward Gibbon in his discussion of Roman troubles on its eastern flank. He refers to "the wild people in the plains of Russia, Luthuania, and Poland" (some being the Tartars) as invaders of lands the Romans believed they had already conquered, lands peopled by tribes "whose nature was fixed between the faithful dog and the rapacious wolf."

Ten thousand years ago, the Slavs, Celts, Huns, and other primitives established themselves in that Baltic region where historian Konrad Lorenz has found evidence that southern migrants entered with their Aureus dogs. He assumed that those canines may have hybridized with northern wolves of the Baltic sea region. Gibbon's comment suggests that humans at that point did not yet trust the wolf. Some hybridizing, however, may have occurred.

The wandering, warlike Celts must have been among those who created the ideal Mastiff, based on figures in their metal work—canines who helped them to fight the Romans from Asia Minor to Ireland and Wales, where they finally established a culture that endures today. Celts arriving in Britain brought their Druid priests, their dogs, their secrets of metallurgy, their legends, and their agricultural and pastoral skills. When Caesar invaded the British Isles in August, 55 B.C., he discovered that an old enemy was there to meet his human and canine army. Of the latter, the Celts had their own superior breed, Molossian descendants, which they discovered and won to themselves in Macedonia.

Throughout years of tribal strife and resistance to Roman rule, the Celts, Angles, and Saxons, who had arrived in Britain from the mainland, found a common goal. They were united in resisting the Romans, but continued their intertribal strife as they absorbed Rome's culture, borrowed from Greece in good part. The Romans sent in their military engineers to create roads and fortifications, and began building the city of London and other ports and towns. But the "barbarians," mostly Celtic, also continued to break through the Roman walls and attack the new towns as they had done in the Roman provinces of Europe. When not in revolt against Rome, the Celts and their war dogs were in action against invading Vikings from the north and the Angles and Saxons who were establishing themselves in the south.

The Roman force numbered fewer than 40,000 men based in port towns and in forts along the Roman walls. Order was maintained much of the time since Rome's former European enemies had learned to respect its military rule. "There was law; there was order; there was peace; there was warmth; there was food, and a long-established custom of life," Winston Churchill would write. "The population was free from barbarism . . . the use of Roman utensils and even of Roman speech steadily grew."[2]

Churchill himself was a splendid exemplary of the Platonic dictum that a nation's guardian should have the virtues of a well-bred dog. Some wags have suggested that he even resembled the British national emblem, the Bulldog. He was exceptional in most ways, but shared the general British feeling for pets. Churchill was "dog's best friend," his American biographer, Will Manchester, writes. In his country home at Chartwell, here were generally four dogs, all belonging to his children. He composed a poem to daughter Mary's pet "Pug" when it became ill. "Kiss Puggywug and give him a hug . . . wrap him up tenderly all in a rug," he advised. Pug recovered to play with Mary and Sir Winston's cat, Tango.

A good life for dogs began in England. It was marred, however, by some Roman practices that would worsen after the military departed during the collapse of the Empire. The Romans allowed their conquered people freedom of religion, ultimately introducing Christianity into the islands. Even the abominations of the Druids, who engaged in human sacrifice, were tolerated. But the Roman army stopped short of attacking the Celts in their strongholds in Scotland and Ireland. The legions also introduced Roman pit fighting and games with fighting dogs. Nevertheless, in A.D. 367, the Saxons, Picts, and Scots united to rebel against the invader. Rome had taken troops from Britain to quell uprisings elsewhere. A struggle for the islands developed, with the Picts (Celts) from Scotland up against British adherents to Rome in the south, who were backed by the Angles, Saxons, and Jutes. There was incessant fighting and a confusion of goals, the kind of strife in which war dogs were required. Merchant ships from Phoenicia, Greece, and Italy brought in weapons, war dogs, and sporting dogs needed for pack hunting, racing, and bullfighting. During this time the Celts were solidifying their hold on Ireland and land behind the Welsh mountains and fending off the thrusts from Scandinavian invaders to the north.

The Dark Ages following the fall of Rome in 456 were dismal for both dog and man in the British Isles. The Romans had spread afar their addiction to animal combat: They supplied fighting dogs to their provinces and brought back provincial champions, several from Britain, who fought well in Roman amphitheaters. Bullfighting was a natural sport for any army that worshiped Mithras, depicted as the bull, god of male fertility in many religions. Worship of the bull was not limited to men, however. In Crete, one of the most liberal early civilizations, ancient frescoes show young women joining young men in the bull-tossing festivals. Dogs took the place of humans and fought bulls, bears, other wild animals—and one another—to the death. Such exhibitions were popular in Spain, Germany, France, and especially England. Canines were bred to seize and nip young bulls, guiding them to market or to slaughter, or for fighting in the bullring. Called butcher's dogs in England and Bullenbeisers in Germany, they developed into the modern Bulldog and Boxer, respectively, that in modern times serve as police dogs, guardians, and guide and war dogs.

Historian Josephine Z. Rine attributes the beginning of the "sport" of bullbaiting to the Moors in Spain, where they were in control during the Arabian caliphates. But the Berbers and Moors may have been preceded by the Romans and the Celts. Rome invaded Spain in 206 B.C., taking along its Mastiffs; the Celts arrived a century or more earlier. The Arabian, Berber, and Moor forces entered Spain and France in A.D. 705–715 and were stopped by Charles Martel at Poitiers. Probably all such forces brought in Mastiffs, and the Berbers surely brought their Greyhounds. The dogs fighting in the bullring in Spain were smooth Mastiffs, Rine writes. They seized the bull's ear, lowering the animal's head to give the rest of the dog team opportunity to attack. Rine credits the British with developing the broad-jawed Mastiff that could seize the bull by the nose as well as the ear. The dog that stubbornly held on, its jaws clamped on the bull's nostrils, became the earliest version of the modern Bulldog. "Sooner or later the bull did get his head up and frequently tossed the dog thirty feet in the air," she writes. "At this point, men stood around with blankets stretched between them to catch the dog as he fell."[3] But the Bulldog never gave up.

Bullbaiting became Britain's most popular sport. In 1189, the time of King John, the cruel exhibitions had government support, organized under the supervision of Lord Warren of Stamford. As a public diversion, bullbaiting endured until 1845, when it was outlawed by an act of Parliament.

But the whole of civilized Europe was emerging from the Dark Ages, and dog keeping was much in vogue.

Much of the nobility followed the early example of Charlemagne's establishment of his royal kennels under the supervision of a royal court officer, the master of hounds. Dogs were important again in the Holy Roman Empire, and especially in the British Isles. The breeding and training of hunting dogs became an aristocratic avocation. Kings and queens would personally handle their canines. The commoners watched dog fighting in the pits, and those who could afford it had their own protection dogs. Serfs belonged to the land under the laws of Charlemagne and later those of William the Conqueror. Serfs ranked about equal with dogs, or perhaps a bit lower, under the feudal system initiated and perpetuated by William in England.

Land ownership determined the wealth of each aristocrat. They took the produce of the fields and owned the flocks, herds, and dogs. The breeding, training, and exploitation of canines was in the hands of the nobility, who themselves had hundreds, even thousands, on their vast estates. By the time the Romans departed Britain in the fifth century A.D., the Vikings, Angles, Saxons, and Jutes had taken over much land and established colonies, despite the fierce opposition of the Celts, who used fighting dogs in both Scotland and Ireland.

The raids would continue for 400 years, the Danes proving themselves especially successful in establishing permanent settlements. They were at last checked by Alfred, the young brother of Ethelred, the Saxon Earl of Mercia, who would succeed his brother as Alfred the Great. Alfred was the kind of hero who inspired legends celebrating his wisdom and valor. He led his troops to victory and had the loyalty of local nobility and peasantry. He gave his people a Book of Laws, encouraged the spread of Christianity, and established a dynasty. By 918, when Alfred the Great had been dead seventeen years, his son Edward at last ruled all of England.

The Danes, however, continued to hold lands and power in the north. They continued their attacks on London and the rest of England, being opposed, following the death of Edward, mostly by peasant militia and their dogs, who defended lines along the Humber. Alfred's weak royal successors sought to maintain their armies with mercenaries and by bribing enemy commanders, a policy that failed. In 1016 Edmund Ironsides, the firebrand descendant of Arthur, revolted against the futile policies of the past maintained by his father, King Ethelred, and undertook, at the age of twenty, to restore the glorious example of Arthur the Great. Two years later, both Ethelred and his fighting son were dead, after Edmund had driven the Danes from London. The loss of Edmund Ironsides led the dispirited English to accept a Danish peace offer from King Canute, ruler of the Danes and three other Scandinavian kingdoms. It was agreed that Canute would acquire his fifth realm and become the temporal and spiritual ruler of England.

Canute then chose to live in England, newest of his five kingdoms, because he liked the English lifestyle and was especially fond of riding to hounds. He did not, however, share the British/Celtic love and respect for dogs. One of his early acts was to issue a decree requiring all owners of hounds running free within ten English miles of his hunting preserves to cut their canines' tendon hocks to prevent them from chasing game. This cruel practice persisted in Europe for several centuries. Nor did Canute want to be called a dog, a pejorative used freely by the English. Churchill credits Canute as a man possessing some good sense, but also an ill-governed temper.

King Canute died in 1036, leaving two sons—"ignorant and boorish Vikings," according to Churchill. Alfred, a descendant of Arthur the Great, was living in exile in Normandy, and he undertook to sail to England to seize the throne but was captured and blinded. The crown continued in contention until William of Normandy settled the issue in 1066 at the famous Battle of Hastings.

Churchill and other historians make no mention of the role of the Norman war dogs in the Battle of Hastings, though they probably were on duty, as was the custom of the time. William brought his dogs and later used them in rounding up defiant resistance groups and quelling revolts in outer provinces. It was British breeders, probably working for the Conqueror, who developed the English Bloodhound near the end of his reign. "William brought in the St. Hubert dog from France," adds David Taylor in his *Ultimate Dog Book*. "From the St. Hubert, the Bloodhound, the now-extinct Talbot, and the old English Stag-hound were derived." The St. Hubert, says Taylor, originated in the eighth century in the Ardennes forest of Belgium, "where the patron saint of hunting kept a large pack of them."[4] English kings would continue to use dogs in war, but not in large numbers. The army of Henry VIII had a specialist corps of 400 soldiers in charge of such dogs, according to a chronicler, "all of them garnished with good iyron collars."

The dark reign of the Stuart king Charles I demonstrated that royalty had little concern for the common people, and his rule ended in civil war. There were sixty-nine royal forests and 781 royal parks established, but these were not for the benefit of the overworked ordinary folk. "Dog tenures" were granted for the care and maintenance of the royal hounds. Severe punishment was imposed on poachers caught in the reserved hunting grounds. It was said that the poachers themselves used dogs in their illicit operations; Greyhound-like dogs called "lurchers" were trained to chew their way out of snares and never betray their owners by identifying them if caught. Those privileged to hunt were proud of their well-trained animals of excellent breeding that could command profitable sums overseas. A good English Greyhound would bring the same price as a slave or a serf. The Bloodhound was used in hunting as well as police work. Their excellent sense of smell enabled them to find game and locate humans, and they were expert in bringing down the stag. Ireland became known for its peerless staghounds, Scotland and Wales for sheepdogs, and England for its Bulldogs and Greyhounds. Elizabeth I, daughter of Henry VIII, was an enthusiastic hunter. An artist depicted her standing on a forest platform, past which the beaters would drive the animals within gun range. The queen's Toy dogs and sight hounds stayed at home when she hunted the stag.

༄

Many large, strong dogs were required for police work demanded by English kings. The Normans under William the Conqueror introduced their laws and methods, but William also retained the English system of shires and reeves. The Shire Reeves, later known as sheriffs, enforced laws, aided tax collectors, and generally constituted the first line of law and order in the kingdom. "In England," Churchill wrote, "the king is everywhere—in Northumberland as in Middlesex; a crime anywhere is a breach of his peace; if he wants to know anything he tells his officer, the sheriff, to impanel a jury and find out, or, in later days, to send some respectable persons to Winchester to tell him." The sheriffs and their deputies had able assistants in finding people—their dogs. The laws, however, favored nobility and wealth, and especially noble hunters. Peasants who illegally "slew the hart or hind should be made blind," a bitter minstrel sang, and, of the king in the days of William the Conqueror, "He preserves the harts and bears . . . and loves the stags so much . . . as if he were their father."

Under the system there was a time of peace now and then, and an increase of prosperity, during which hunting, bullfighting, minstrel appearances, and country dances provided amusement for all. Writing was taught in many of the monasteries and cathedral schools, and books appeared, some on the care of domesticated animals, especially dogs. Ownership of fine animals continued to be a noble avocation. Nobles often personally trained and looked after the animals. The English, Irish, Scots, and Welsh produced special breeds for sport and herding, and other breeders provided the working dogs required by the growing numbers of traders, shopkeepers, and craftsmen. Dog dealers and shippers sold Pointers, Setters, and Retrievers. Small Terriers began to emerge and over time branched into distinct breeds. These dogs caught and destroyed the rodents that infested homes, shops, and storehouses, as well as the larger predators that were the bane of farmers through their toll on livestock.

Small dogs were favorites of some royal persons. Louis XIII of France always carried his favorite Toy dog (possibly a Papillon) in a basket into his throne room, where he petted and played with it while hearing petitions from his subjects. Queens often were pictured with their children and dogs. Mary, Queen of Scots, was allowed to have her English Toy spaniel share her last days and to accompany her to the scaffold, where the dog was hidden among her garments. Henry VIII, annoyed that his hunting dogs were allowed the freedom of the palace and forgetting his previous order permitting it, banned all dogs "except some small spanyells for ladies and others." When his emissary, the Earl of Wilshire, went to Rome to petition the pope to annul Henry's marriage, he took along his dog. Legend says the dog bit the pope's toe. The petition, in any case, was denied. Dr. Johannes Caius, physician to Henry's children, wrote a treatise called *Of Englishe Dogges*. In it, he mentions the "Spanyell Comforter, 'warm little dogges to asswage the sickness of the stomach.'"

Queen Elizabeth, like her bitter rival Mary, loved dogs, not only for her personal amusement but also for coursing. She authorized the Duke of Norfolk to organize the sport, creating a system of laws and regulations. In 1599 she dispatched her court favorite, the Earl of Essex, with an army of 22,000 men, including a force of Bloodhounds, to put down the Irish rebellion. Such dogs had long been used against individual Irish, Scot, and Welsh dissenters by sheriffs and their deputies, but the Essex force of 800 hounds and their handlers may have been the first use of official war dogs at home. Essex left under a cloud; according to Michael Creighton in his book, *The Age of Elizabeth,* he had quarreled with the queen, who "gave him a box on the ear." But he was partially forgiven by the time he departed as "Lord Deputy of Ireland."[5] His expedition was a failure. Essex, disliking his mission, did not attack the main base of the rebels in Ulster; his men sickened, and his dogs saw little action.

Shane O'Neill, leader of the Irish Celts, had united forces in Ulster and used his men and dogs to harass Essex. Then O'Neill outflanked Essex in diplomacy, arranging an audience with Elizabeth that produced a fitful alliance and a temporary peace. O'Neill went back to Ulster after promising Elizabeth that he would "clear the robbers [Scots] out of eastern Ulster." Essex, in disgrace, was ordered back to England and executed. Sir Henry Sidney was named new Lord Deputy of Ireland. Shane O'Neill made an alliance with France. Then O'Neill's forces attacked his enemies the O'Donnells, his former Scot allies who now objected to his pact with Elizabeth. O'Neill was invited to a "peace party" with the O'Donnells where he and his bodyguards were killed. A few days later O'Neill's head was presented to Lord Deputy Henry, according to Tim Newark's *Celtic Warriors*. Hugh, son of Shane, took over the cause of Elizabeth. "Celtic warriors had succeeded in destroying the one Irish warlord who could have kept at least one part of Ireland wholly Gaelic," writes Newark. The war dogs were long kept busy in Ireland.

⁂

In years of economic distress and plagues, dogs, like the human populace, suffered severely. Many ran at large, foraging in competition with the poor in the countryside and city streets. The filth of the towns, especially London, the capital, was execrable. Rosamond Bayne-Powell, in her *Eighteenth-Century Life*, describes the scene: "There was, of course, no drainage, and heaps of dust and filth occupied every open space within and without the city. Pigs browsed upon these dumps, and the refuse was occasionally sold to market gardeners." Dogs also visited the garbage heaps; bullocks and horses were driven through uncleaned streets; the stench was abominable. Bayne-Powell lists the ten worst London nuisances, "ordure, rubbish and driving of bullocks in the streets, and the prevalence of mad dogs," topping her list.[6] Lord Tryconnel, speaking in the House of Lords, began by saying, "London . . . abounds with such heaps of filth as a savage would look upon with amazement." Sir Walter Besant records that in the plague of 1543, when canines were thought to be spreading disease, "all dogs except watchdogs were to be killed," adding, "It [the plague] proved happily of short duration."

Thomas B. Macaulay, in his *History of England,* reports that in the rural areas during the time of plagues and hunger, angry citizens killed deer and wild boar kept for the pleasure of the king and nobility, using their own dogs to do the job. "There were great massacres of foxes to which the peasantry thronged with all the dogs that could be mustered . . . no quarter was given . . . to shoot a female with a cub was a feat that merited the warmest gratitude of the neighborhood . . . huge bustards and wild cats were hunted by the people from the British channel to Yorkshire . . . , " Macaulay recorded. "The last boar that roamed our island was slain in Scotland. The last wolf was killed in 1685." The people in their destitution and anger finally had spoken with their deeds.

Many working dogs, besides watchdogs, continued to be employed in the city during the difficult times. Some pulled mail carts and the carts of knife sharpeners, bakers, and butchers. Dog carts brought fish from Southampton to London. A few shopkeepers, prospering despite the generally poor conditions, had their own coaches or were carried about in sedan chairs. Some had dogs attending them, as did women in public, if the family could afford a dog or two. For the shopkeeper a dog's protection was important. He went to work early, kept his shop open until quite late, and traveled home wearily through mostly darkened streets. Wealthy merchants had canine protectors, since they would carry home the day's trading proceeds they dared not leave in the shop. The ordinary poor didn't have dogs; they could never afford them.

Conditions in rural areas began to improve. Cottage industries, such as carding, spinning and weaving of wool, cobbling shoes, and the manufacture of common items of clothing and household needs, grew as English traders and shippers found world markets for such products. "During the first half of the eighteenth century . . . England basked in a last Indian Summer of village industry and the overseas trade of merchant adventurers," historian Jacob Bronowski writes. Craftsmen, the millwright, the watchmaker, the canal builder, the blacksmith were beginning the Industrial Revolution, and the problem of getting the goods to market was great. Dogs helped guard the cargoes on roads and trails and on the growing numbers of canal boats sailing to the ports and markets where other dogs guarded the warehouses. The cobbler and tinker traveled about with their dogs as did other independent workers. Millwright James Brindley of Staffordshire bettered the quality of life by improving the grinding of flints used in the pottery industry, then by improving use of water power generally and constructing canals to carry goods and supplies to markets and port towns. His canal connecting Manchester, a source of coal, to Liverpool created a vast industrial and shipping center contributing to British commercial growth. Prosperity of a new kind came to the common people. They worked hard, they lived a bit better, and, most important, many enjoyed the companionship and security provided by their dogs.

Fine English canines, like fine English woolens, were wanted everywhere in world trade. The Germans sought breeding stock but also developed their own famous breeds. Francis I of France had his agents purchase hunting and fighting dogs in England, as did Phillip I of Spain, a country that long had exported its own fighting Mastiffs. Henry Tudor, king of England, following his victory over Richard III, set aside an entire island, to become known as the Island of Dogs, for the breeding, care, and training of the animals. In time England would export many breeds, including Bulldogs, various gun dogs, Toys, and Terriers. From England and Scotland would come a variety of fine sheepdogs, including the beloved Collie. Queen Victoria, after visiting Balmoral Castle in Scotland, brought back some of the beautiful longhaired Rough Collies to Windsor Castle, giving the breed worldwide publicity. From Ireland came a number of breeds that found long term support around the world: The beautiful Irish Setter, so well known for his glowing red coat; the Irish Wolfhound, tallest of all breeds; and several others added a special dimension to the growing family of dog breeds.

The ports of London and Liverpool grew enormously as British ships took leadership in world trade. The British East India Company and similar firms were active in Africa, India, Russia, and the Levant, as well as in the new American colonies, from Hudson's Bay to the West Indies. Exports included textiles, especially high quality woolens, cotton fabrics, druggets (carpeting), and manufactured articles made in thousands of cottage factories. The leading imports in the late 1600s were liquors and wines, indigo, sugar, silk, coffee, tea, cotton, and linen. Dogs were not on the commercial lists, nor were slaves, but there was a heavy commerce in both.

The popularity of canines in England probably exceeded that of any country but Egypt, even in the Middle and Dark Ages when strays ran wild. Despite the many varieties produced at home, many breeds were imported, including various Toy dogs, Mastiffs, Greyhounds, and Dalmatians, used as coach dogs.

"There is this day among us a newe kinde of dogge brought out of France, speckled all over with white and black," a London journal reported in the days of Queen Elizabeth. Named for the province of Dalmatia in Yugoslavia, where it arrived a few thousand years after the first such spotted dogs appeared in Egypt, the Dalmatian's natural affinity for horses made it a fashionable addition to the livery of a fine carriage. Later, in America, Dalmatians became associated with fire companies because of the association with horses and still stand proudly on some metropolitan fire trucks long after the horses were replaced by the modern internal combustion engine.

Irish-bred coursing hounds were also popular throughout England. Lord Lurgan in 1868 would take his celebrated Greyhound, Master McGrath, who had won all but one of the thirty-six races he had run, to Windsor Castle at the command of Queen Victoria, herself an ardent dog fancier, so she could see him herself.

British writers would extol the work and exemplary behavior of dogs. Sir Walter Scott would celebrate in poetry the fame of Snowball, a racing Greyhound that won forty coursing meets, as well as praising the St. Hubert hounds in verse in his *Lady of the Lake.* John Ruskin wrote of *My Dog Dash;* Lord Byron penned an epitaph to the Newfoundland Boastswain: "in life the firmest friend, first to welcome, foremost to defend." Sir Thomas More, in his *Sermon on the Lord's Prayer,* provided an addendum, "Whosoever loveth me loveth my hound." It remained, however, for a French count, Gaston Phoebus, author of a popular book on hunting called *The Noble Art of Venerie,* to most effectively demonstrate his love of dogs. When he traveled to England, he was said to have brought with him most of his 1,600 dogs.

It has been written that dogs lost much of their sterling reputation during the Dark Ages and much of their usefulness to society following the Industrial Revolution of the late eighteenth century. The former comment is like saying that slaves caused the evils of slavery. Unwanted animals ran at large during the Middle Ages, competing with poor people for food. During the plagues, some dogs may have even consumed human flesh, as has been alleged in the Middle East throughout history. Whether domesticated dogs ever consumed human flesh is debatable. Charles Darwin asserted that dogs do not eat carrion, the flesh of humans. As for lost usefulness, with the arrival of the Industrial Revolution, it is doubtful there was any decline in the population of working dogs. The military use of dogs had declined, except in the Americas where they were used to subjugate Indians. In most livestock-producing areas, the growing demand for meat products in urban areas increased the need for working stock dogs.

The invention of the steam engine created a source of power more efficient than that of humans or animals. Ponies and dogs were no longer needed to run treadmills, so the use of water power, wind power, and dog power diminished when steam was made to turn wheels. Conversely, the use of dogs to guard shops, factories, and homes grew, along with the use of more stock dogs for handling larger numbers of food animals. In the end, the increased invention and construction begun with the more efficient harnessing of water power in the early days of the Revolution would make the world a better place for humankind and domesticated animals alike. With the boons though came long hours of hard labor in factories and mines, the increased slaughter of food animals, the perils of vivisection, and cruel games and sports involving dogs.

◯◯◯◯◯

Another revolution was also under way at the same time, in the thought of humankind. It would change for the better the interrelationship between humans and their canine partners.

In 1859 a British naturalist, Charles Darwin, published a book on which he had been working for ten years and which he had researched for much of his adult life. Called *The Origin of Species,* it would shake the world with controversy not yet ended. Darwin was shocked at the bitter reaction to his work, especially that of the religious community. He had once studied for the ministry himself and himself believed in God. He had not anticipated that his theory of the evolution of mankind, simplified by some critics to a "man descended from monkeys" doctrine, would lead to vicious attacks. One cartoonist's view published in a London newspaper showed Darwin's head on the body of an ape. Bishop Wilberforce of Oxford, debating Darwin's theory much simplified to "survival of the fittest," demanded of his learned opponent supporting Darwin's view, "By whom, sir, do you claim descent—from the monkeys, your father, or your mother?" The controversy and philosophical turmoil goes on.

More than a century after Darwin published his book, C. D. Darlington in his own classic *The Evolution of Man and Society* provides in the opening paragraph his estimate of Darwin: "For his argument in *Origin of Species* Darwin mobilized the whole of available knowledge of the past and present behavior of plants and animals. Only then could civilized man, or some of them, be persuaded to make the deeply repugnant assumption of a hereditary continuity with the rest of the living world . . . Darwin's methods are still those we have today."

Darwin, a gentle man, created a massive controversy, and his work attracted countless foes. He also became, in subsequent writings, the best friend of dogs the literate world has ever known. His defense of canines was not intended as such; he never assumed that dogs had enemies, since he lived and labored in England. He mentions dogs in various works, even suggesting that they can attain the same intellectual and metaphysical levels as primitive peoples or very young children. In 1832 Darwin was given the unpaid post of naturalist aboard the British Admiralty survey ship *Beagle,* assigned to map the southern coasts of South America. His visits included Patagonia, at the extreme southern tip of the continent, where primitives much like those of extreme southern Africa went about almost naked yet in extreme cold. They hunted with dogs similar to the wild dogs of Africa, an anomaly previously noted by earlier European visitors. The hunters of Tierra del Fuego were mostly dark-skinned, though they lived in a climate characterized by ice and snow. No link between Fuegians and South African Bushmen was offered by Darwin, except as to their marriage customs, but other visitors linked the dark Fuegians to the Hottentots of the Cape of Good Hope, suggesting a possible South African ancestry. Darwin was interested in biological, social, and religious aspects. He likened Fuegian religious beliefs, and that of other very primitive peoples, to the typical responses of dogs. "The feeling of religious devotion is a highly complex one," he wrote in *The Origin of Species,* "consisting of love, complete submission to an exalted and mysterious superior, a strong sense of dependence, fear, reverence, gratitude . . . . No being would experience so complex an emotion until he advanced in his intellectual and moral faculties to at least a moderately high level. Nevertheless, we see some distant approach to this state of mind in the deep love of a dog for his master, associated with complete submission, some fear, and perhaps some other feelings." Darwin adds, "Professor Braubach goes so far as to maintain that a dog looks on his master as a god."

Darwin went a long way himself in explaining the popularity of the dog, its emotional attitudes providing humans with ego-enhancing affection—"human love returned with interest," he commented—and other virtues. And he also insisted that dogs do have a conscience and an appreciation of "spiritual or living essences" equal to that of primitive humans: "The tendency in savages to imagine that natural objects and agencies are animated by spiritual or living essences is perhaps illustrated by a little fact I once observed," he wrote. He then described the distractions to his own dog by the strange behavior of fabric mysteriously disturbed by wind and air currents. His dog, "full grown and very sensible," noted the inexplicable movement of the fabric—inexplicable because no living thing was in it—and growled fiercely and barked at the disturbance. "I think he reasons by himself in a rapid and unconscious manner that the movement without any apparent cause indicated the presence of some strange living agent . . . ." Darwin might have reminded his readers that the highly civilized deducted and reasoned in a similar way. Odysseus, visited by the goddess Athena, indeed saw her and spoke with her, and the dogs present barked at her, but his swineherd who was talking with him did not see the goddess. "The gods allow only whom they wish to see them," Odysseus reasoned. (As a pup, Kiwi, our Australian Cattle Dog, slept without fear during episodes of thunder and lighting—though Mitzi, our Boxer, would run and hide. But Kiwi would awake in panic when a strong wind blew, immediately seeking close human protection. She evidently found the wind, arising from no obvious cause, inexplicable and fearsome. Now, as an adult, whenever there is lightning, thunder, and wind, she also prudently hides.)

Darwin also recalled that Professor Braubach maintained that dogs possess some power of self-command, effecting restraint from stealing food from the master not from fear but from moral sense. And Darwin listed other virtues, such as sympathy and conscience, writing, "I agree with [American naturalist Louis] Agassiz that dogs possess something very like a conscience. They have been accepted as the very type of fidelity and obedience." In fact, the most popular name for a dog in many countries at the time was Fido, from the Latin meaning fidelity.

Returning to scientific fact and observation, Darwin records that in Tierra del Fuego the natives prized their dogs even above humans in some situations, allowing the elderly women of the tribe to expire on the ice in time of famine or imminent danger, though their dogs were never thus sacrificed.

☾༄☽

Darwin firmly believed that naturally acquired characteristics could be inherited a century before genetic principles, DNA, and RNA were discovered. He suggested that the best way to study unusual human traits would be to study dogs: "Many instincts are so wonderful that their development may appear to the reader a difficulty sufficient to overthrow my whole theory." He differentiates instincts and habits and adds, "If we suppose any habitual action to become inherited—and it can be shown that this does sometimes happen—then . . . the distinction between instinct and habit becomes so close as not to be distinguished." He finds good examples among dogs.

It cannot be doubted that breeds of Pointers (I have myself seen a striking instance) will sometimes point and even back other dogs the very first time they are taken out; retrieving is certainly in some degree inherited by retrievers; and a tendency to run around, instead of at, a flock of sheep by shepherd dogs. I cannot see but that these actions, performed without experience by the young, and in nearly the same manner by each individual, performed with eager delight by each breed, and without the end being known—for the young Pointer can no more know that he points to aid his master, than the white butterfly knows why she lays her eggs on the head of a cabbage—I cannot see they differ essentially from true instincts.

If we were to behold one kind of wolf, when young and without any training as soon as it scented its prey, stand motionless like a statue, then slowly crawl forward with a peculiar gait; and another kind of wolf rushing round, rather than at, a herd of deer, and driving them to a distant point, we should assuredly call these actions instinctive. Domestic instincts, as they may be called, are far less fixed than natural instincts, but they have been acted on by far less rigorous selection, and have been transmitted for an incomparably shorter period, under less fixed conditions of life.

Masters of flocks and professional hunters know that animal instincts make it easier for the trainer to establish habitual patterns to make the animal a better partner in any venture. Sheepdogs, as Ruth Moore points out in *Evolution,* are naturally very bright, which follows since dogs, horses, and humans have the same type of brain and all have worked together for thousands of years. Large sheepdogs have the size and strength to fend off jackals and wolves; smaller dogs, such as the Australian Cattle Dog that does an instinctive backward flip to avoid the hooves of cattle and horses, lend themselves to quick training for that specialized work. (Our Kiwi rounded up horses and did a back-flip to avoid a colt's kick the first time she dashed into a pasture, and she herded ducks near our pond the first time she saw them.)

Darwin suggests that the breeding of dogs can improve their abstract qualities: courage, tolerance, obstinacy. "How strongly these domestic instincts, habits, and dispositions are inherited, and how curiously they become mingled, is well shown when different breeds are crossed. Thus it is known that a cross with a Bulldog has affected for many generations the courage and obstinacy of Greyhounds; and a cross with a Greyhound has given a whole family of shepherd dogs a tendency to hunt hares. These domestic instincts, when thus tested by crossing, resemble natural instincts . . . ." He then notes an instance of a domestic dog descending from a wolf grandfather, "showing a trace of his wild parentage in only one way, by not coming in a straight line when called." The domestic and wild instincts of animals become mingled, as Darwin suggests, and endure a long time. (Kiwi, without a Dingo in the family for generations, stalks game by standing like a statue, slowly approaching, then leaping at prey, and, though definitely not crossed with a Greyhound, she loves to hunt rabbits.)

Darwin asserts that dogs are descended from wolves and jackals and notes that the greatest advances in domestication of plants and animals occurred in Paleolithic times in Egypt and during the time of lake habitations of Switzerland, "where much diversity of breeds" may be found. He states that even the rudest of civilizations have tamed and domesticated the dog, adding, "I here state, looking to the domestic dogs of the whole world, I have found, after laborious collection of all known facts, that several wild species of *Canidae* have been tamed, and that their blood, in some cases mingled together, flows in our domestic breeds." Darwin elsewhere named wolves and jackals as ancestors of dogs; in *The Origin of Species* he writes of "several wild species of *Canidae*." Seemingly, Darwin anticipated the findings of earliest evidence of humankind in southern and equatorial Africa, where the wild canine species would be "the African wild dog."

In *The Descent of Man,* Darwin again extensively discusses dogs, referring to studies of other works and his own experiences with "my terrier" and obviously other dogs kept at the Darwin estate near London. In a section comparing "mental powers of Man and the Lower Animals," he suggests that in some instances dogs reared wolves, teaching them to become dogs in their behavior, but he concludes that wolves and jackals were the actual ancestors. "Our domestic dogs," he writes, "are descended from wolves and jackals, though they may not have gained in cunning, and may have lost in wariness and suspicion, yet they have progressed in certain moral qualities, such as in affection, trust-worthiness, temper, and probably in general intelligence."

He directly examines Aristotle's assertion that a dog cannot think in abstractions, charging that the error is being reasserted in modern times. "Greatest stress seems to be laid on the supposed entire absence in animals of the power of abstraction . . . . But when a dog sees another dog at a distance, it is often clear that he perceives it is a dog in the abstract: for when he gets nearer his whole manner suddenly changes if the animal is a friend." Like man, Darwin deduced the dog "refers what he perceives with his senses to a mental concept . . . . When I say to my terrier, in an eager voice (and I have made the trial many times), 'Hi, hi, where is it?' she at once takes it for a sign that something is to be hunted—looks quickly all around and then rushes into the nearest thicket for any game . . . up a tree for a squirrel. Now, do not these actions show that she had a general idea or concept that some animal is to be discovered and hunted?"

(Kiwi, sleeping nearby as this is written, responds to a variety of words—*squirrel, rabbit, cat, kitty,* names of dogs, names of people—and scurries to search. If it is remarked that there are dogs or other animals she knows on the television screen, Kiwi now dashes to the porch to confirm. Early on she discovered that pictures of animals on television are not the real image she has envisaged in her mind. As a pup she would go to the tube to watch the pictured animal, but no more. She knows that the animal there isn't real.)

Darwin, discussing the ability of primitive humans to think abstractly, points out that dogs have visions in their dreams. He suggests a dog has the power of thinking in abstraction to the same extent as the average child. Again he refers to his dog: "When (after five years) my voice awakened a train of old associations in the mind of the dog, he must have retained his mental individuality, although every atom of his brain had probably undergone change more than once during five years. This dog might have brought forward the argument lately advanced to crush all evolutionists, and said 'I abide amid all mental moods and all material changes . . .' It is a remarkable fact that the dog, since being domesticated, has learned to bark in at least four or five distinct tones. Although barking is a new art, undoubtedly the parent species of the dog expressed their feelings by cries of various kinds." The scientist Darwin then describes various types of barks and their meaning. He concedes however that the dog's communication does not match that of articulate man: "That which distinguishes man from lower animals is not the understanding of articulate sounds, for, as everyone knows, dogs understand many words and sentences. In this respect they are at the same stage of development as infants, between the ages of ten and twelve months, who understand words and short sentences but cannot communicate a single word." He suggests that "dogs understand some cries of birds and other animals that humans do not understand."

Darwin also suggests that a dog and a savage may use a similar mental process in solving problems, such as finding water, using examples he has derived from desert lands. He proposes that dogs have vivid imaginations, as do humans, and vivid dreams, to which any dog owner can attest. "Only a few persons now dispute that animals possess some power of reasoning," Darwin writes. "The more a naturalist studies the habits of a particular animal, the more he attributes to reason and the less to unlearned instincts."

It appears to me that dogs are capable of deductive reasoning. Kiwi, playing with Queenie, a Greyhound, in the animal-rich household of our children, Mike and wife Cyndi, sees that Queenie runs swiftly and always wins the race for a biscuit, covering a circular course through brush and obstacles with long, graceful strides and leaps. After two such experiences, Kiwi simply cut across at 180 degrees but still lost the race. A third time she awaited Queenie's arrival around the circle, then dashed out to meet her in a joint finish, thus winning a biscuit too, for good thinking. Kiwi and Bud, an English Springer Spaniel, improved their hunting of squirrels by enclosing the prey in a parenthetic attack so they closed in before the squirrel reached a tree. They shared the kill, a big fox squirrel. This doesn't always work. Most times the squirrel still wins. But deduction and imagination seems to be guiding them.

Darwin also credits dogs with possessing moral values, such as his own dog, friendly with a cat and pausing to give the cat a sympathetic lick as it lay ill in a basket. He praises the dog who always will fly at anyone who strikes his master "as he certainly will," and testifies that almost any pet dog will demonstrate great sympathy for master or mistress with their tongues if he or she appears injured or distressed. He adds that they enjoy their work, stating that "a young shepherd dog delights in driving and running around a flock of sheep, but not in worrying them."

In his discussion of the ability of dogs to find water, Darwin assumes that the animal and the savage would try in the same manner, by trial and error, by seeking hollows where water might be found until one or the other succeeded. Darwin cites the work of Arctic sled dogs to support his belief in their deductive reasoning. When they enter on thin ice, they strive to disperse to lessen the danger. "Dogs rise to command when a situation requires and the dog is free to act on his own," he writes. He insists that dogs hide bones with thoughts for the future, not merely to protect them from others fond of bones, and that they do not steal bones from the table. He deplores but does not condemn the use of dogs in vivisection, adding sadly: "In the agony of death, the dog has been known to caress his master, and everyone has heard of the dog suffering under vivisection, who licked the hand of the operator; this man, unless the operation was fully justified by an increase of our knowledge, or unless he had a heart of stone, must have felt remorse to the last hour or his life."

⌒₩₩₩ↄ

Adam Smith, the dour dean and great moral philosopher, economist, and professor at the University of Glasgow, in his *Wealth of Nations* did not go along with Darwin in some of his conclusions about dogs, particularly the notion that the dog buries his bone in anticipation of future needs, nor that a dog sometimes shares his bone with another. "No one ever saw a dog make a fair and deliberate exchange of one bone for another with another dog," he writes. He rules out mothers of puppies, obviously, but of course sharing is not trading. We may admit that Smith's conditions "fair and deliberate" never have been met. Adam Smith uses the example of two Greyhounds chasing a hare as "seeming to cooperate" in the capture of their prey, adding, "This, however, is not the effect of any contract but of the accidental concurrence of their passions in the same object at the same time." (However, it should be noted that wild dogs share the kill.) Smith continues: "When an animal wants to obtain something from a man or another animal, it has no other means of persuasion but to gain the favor of those whose services it requires. A puppy fawns upon its dam, and the spaniel endeavors by a thousand attractions to engage the attention of its master who is at dinner."

Probably Adam Smith did like dogs after all.

8

FERAL CONNECTIONS

CELLO

In 1927, near the village of Choukoutien, China, a quarrying project for a railroad crossing the Hopei plain some forty miles from Beijing exposed a series of caves among the gray limestone hills. They attracted the attention of David Black, a Canadian biologist who was teaching anatomy at Peking Union Medical College. Black theorized that ancient man may have inhabited some of the exposed caves. He was perhaps inspired by the work of Raymond Dart, professor of anatomy in South Africa, who had written of his fossil find, *Australopithecus,* in an item that was reprinted in newspapers worldwide in February 1925. The news was startling: Dart had found the fossil skull of a creature proclaimed to be the "missing link" between man and ape, which might designate southern Africa as the birthplace of the human race. By 1929, Black and his associates at the medical school had found in the Choukoutien caves hundreds of chipped stone tools and fossil bones including a partial skull discovered in one of the caves by his Chinese associate W. C. Pei.

China was in a state of unrest at the time; irregular soldiers and outright bandits roamed the Peking hills. A find of any sort might have been confiscated or stolen from anyone suspected of treasure hunting. The scientists worked in secrecy, but in December 1929 they revealed their dramatic discovery to a visiting American scientist, Roy Chapman Andrews, who disclosed it to the world. "There it was," Andrews wrote, "the skull of an individual who had lived half a million years ago . . . one of the most important discoveries in the whole history of human evolution." Again the news spread worldwide. Africa's claim to being "the navel of the world," as naturalist J. Bronowski termed it, was challenged by Asia.

Three years later other fossils had been discovered in the Choukoutien caves. The skulls were compared with that of *Pithecanthropis,* recently uncovered in Java, and Dart's African find and the three skulls were found to be much alike. They were dated at something less than Andrews's estimate for *Sinanthropis Pekinensi* (Chinese man of Peking)— between 300,000 and 400,000 years old. The African *Australopithecus* was still the eldest of the ancient trio. In plain English they became known as Peking Man, Java Man, and Southern Ape, the last still having priority as a "missing link." The early descendants of all three may have been progenitors of *Homo erectus* and later *Homo habilis,* who would walk from Africa into Eurasia between the Red Sea and the Mediterranean to the Euphrates River. From there he would turn north to the Black and Caspian Seas, east to the Indus River, through India, and across China and Mongolia. Ultimately *Homo habilis* would arrive at Siberia's Lake Bakail and the Sea of Okhotsk and go on to the Bering Strait and a land bridge to North America.

Some of the fossil bones found in the Choukoutien caves were those of canines, later designated as "unharmed Dingo bones." A few of those fossils were indeed harmed, however—they had been gnawed, not in a violent way but by a creature, probably human, intently chewing on them. Cannibalism too had occurred within the caves, humans consuming the flesh of their own kind. Some of the dogs had not been harmed. Had some dogs, instead of human beings or other animals, been the objects of worship and favor? It was recalled that dogs in the Canary Islands were first worshiped and then eaten, but no one could be sure about those Chinese canines. Scientists would learn that dogs were and still are food sources in Asia. The canines in the Choukoutien caves were evidently sacred animals, such as the Chow Chows later shown in Chinese pottery. The approach of global conflict stopped the digging. Japanese invaders entered China, World War II began in Europe, and there were other distractions. The fossil bones of Peking Man disappeared. But the records of Black and his fellow scientists fully confirm that primitive humankind was in China at least 300,000 years ago. In 1990, anthropologists Li Tianyuan and Dennis Etler discovered 350,000-year old fossils there, establishing a possible claim to priority for China, a claim not yet accepted by "Out of Africa" adherents.[1] The early migrants were hunters with their dogs; China's farming communities along the Yellow River were not settled until 4,000 B.C. Others from the Peking area followed a path north through central Mongolia toward Lake Baikal in Siberia. They were the ever-wandering hunters.

China gave the world many interesting new canines following the arrival of Neolithic people there about 30,000 years ago. Modern civilization developed faster in China than in Europe, since it was created in part by experienced migrants from Africa and the Middle East. Many newcomers to China moved into the north, while those in Europe traveled south. Northern China thus in the beginning received relatively peaceful nomads satisfied to remain in the tundra country. The early arrivals from Anatolia and Persia learned to make bronze weapons and tools and to spin and weave wool, and they brought in not only domesticated dogs, but the domesticated ass, sheep, and goats, able to live in the cold, arid climate. Since Peking Man had been in China thousands of years earlier, they may have domesticated on their own the horses, swine, and perhaps the huge sheep arriving from North America across the Bering land bridge. Naturalist C. D. Darlington suggests that some late Stone Age migrants into China had "five thousand years'" experience living in "coherent, stratified societies," but he adds that those semi-civilized people passed through even earlier Stone Age tribes of the north.

It was Paleolithic (early Stone Age) people who moved on to the Pacific coast, passing through central Asia and northern China without experiencing the agricultural civilizations extending along the Yellow and Yangtse Rivers. The Paleolithic hunter had no wish to become civilized. He was a wanderer and was content with what he found, moving about with his family and his dogs. Later, some of his kind would stop in central Asia, as in Africa, to plant seeds (in China adding rice to the menu) and tame some animals, adding the native pig and mountain sheep; he would breed large dogs, crossing them with the northern wolves; and in central Asia, some hunters would capture and train horses. They would become the fierce warlords who would conquer southern China and turn back to take over Russia, and to threaten most of western Asia and Europe. These Tartars, Mongols, and Huns terrorized Eurasia.

At the same time, Neanderthal hunters continued to walk north, perhaps pausing in wonder when they reached the shores of Lake Baikal, above Mongolia, the world's oldest, largest, and deepest freshwater lake, near Irkutsk, Siberia. Neanderthal "tool kits" have been found where migrants paused, near the warm thermal springs in a scenic area matching that of the Grand Canyon in North America. The finds have been dated at 30,000 to 50,000 years ago, the artifacts rivaling those found in Africa, Mesopotamia, and North America.

The humans who crossed the Bering Strait land bridge may have walked around Lake Baikal or found still other routes to the shores of the Bering Sea. Fossil discoveries in North America show that they passed through glacial openings inland and along the Pacific coast. Early stone tool kits indicate that the first to arrive in North America had not advanced beyond the Paleolithic stage of hunter and dog working as partners. No arrowheads from the time period were unearthed. In the next 30,000 years, however, migrants crossed over who carried pottery, bows and arrows, sledges, the forerunners of modern sled dogs, and even the more sophisticated dogs of China, some such breeds or their likenesses to be found at fossil sites in Mexico.

꩜

Migratory routes southwest out of Asia provide another picture. Digs along the Malay peninsula, on the islands of Indonesia, and in Australia and Tasmania tell us that those hunters took nothing along but late Stone Age tool kits and dogs, the only domesticated animals to accompany them. Some did bring a new invention probably from Central Asia, the bow and arrow, and may have had sight hounds and Northern-type dogs from central Asia. In his book *The Prehistory of Australia,* naturalist D. J. Mulvaney estimates the time of human and Dingo arrival in Australia at 20,000 to 30,000 years ago, based on fossils and tool kits found in sites at Cape York, where primitive men and dogs walked across from New Guinea or landed from dugout canoes.[2]

The precise replica of that early Stone Age man can be found hunting today along the Herbert River in Queensland, Australia, Mulvaney tells us. "He marches out of the Stone Age with his primitive spear, his dog beside him. Called the Dingo, it is said to be the oldest living race of dog." The Dingo, or wild dog, has stayed with us at least half way around the globe, the wolf being a welcome addition as the going to the north got rougher.

꩜

Perhaps prior to continuing further, we should define specifically the domestic canine that joined man as a globe trotter, and to inquire whether the Dingo and the wolf meet our definition.

"*Domesticate:* to tame, to reclaim from wild state; to habituate to home life, to convert to the advantage and purpose of man." And we can add in modern times: "to control by selective breeding, to direct, for human benefit, genetic pattern." Studies are now under way in the United States relating specifically to canines, their genes, and DNA. Meantime the Dingo, with some lapses, appears to fulfill the basic requirements.

The sex life of our canine friend and partner, and the parameters of its entire existence, have been largely controlled by humankind for at least 80,000 years, and it has yielded to that control with great affection and fidelity and yet maintained a basic, natural behavior. Selective breeding, hybridization, and mutations continue to leave dogs with innate instincts, generally controlled. Our own dog Kiwi, with a touch of Dingo blood, plays with cats but also likes to chase them. Hunter, the family Weimaraner, herds white rats for granddaughter Julie and allows the furry pets, dressed in tiny ballet skirts, to ride on his back, while still retaining his dignity. And Bud, an English Springer Spaniel in the family group, permits the cats to sleep between his paws but also rules the household animals, including Queenie, the acquiescent Greyhound.

Hundreds of dog breeds have been created in recent centuries, mostly to fill the special work requirements of humankind. Some breeds were developed for the comfort and delight of children and the elderly or those interested in developing unusual canine forms. We continue to follow the ancestral descent of all dogs serving humankind in the creation and spread of civilization. The relationship has flourished into modern times in its original state among numerous Paleolithic peoples.

The trail has been somewhat obscure, but the evidence of Paleolithic artifacts has marked the way, both the main, purposeful course of the hunters following the herds and the variations, as the ice retreated and then again expanded. The most recent warming periods reached three peaks, estimated at 72,000, 115,000, and 24,000 years ago. The last of the pedestrian migrations that included humans and dogs as partners occurred when Asians crossed the Bering land bridge or walked island stepping stones to New Guinea and Australia.

Those primitive hunters almost without exception made early use of canines as they wandered in search of game. Evidence of very early man living with canines has been found in China, central Asia, and Java. Evidence of Paleolithic man also has been discovered in the southwestern United States in comparatively modern times. Artifacts of late Stone Age humans (Neolithic) have been found in New Mexico and California, dating between 30,000 and 70,000 B.C.

Anthropologist Louis Leakey himself came to visit archaeological digs in California and to appraise the results. "This can be the oldest site of its kind," he announced after visiting the Calico Hills in the Mojave Desert in 1963. He summoned a conference of geologists and archaeologists to discuss the finds. Among them was Jeffrey Goodman, possessor of doctorates in geology, engineering, business, and archaeology, who had directed some of the American digs and would, a few years later, publish a book proclaiming the finds to be of worldwide significance: "Anatomically modern humans" had left "tool kits" in the southwestern United States preceding in time those found in Africa and Eurasia! The discoveries of primitive tools and weapons at Calico Hills and Santa Rosa in California; at Folsom, New Mexico; and at other sites in the United States, Mexico, and Central America provided proof that early humankind in the Americas "were the first *Homo sapiens* in the world to have migrated to the Old World," rather than the reverse. Goodman in fact asserted that humankind did not walk from Asia into America by way of a Berengia land bridge, since conditions of climate and environment generally would never have permitted it.

After providing his reasons in his book *American Genesis,* Goodman issued a challenge: His own theory could be proved wrong "only if earlier dates for *Homo sapiens* were found in other parts of the world with a tool kit that demonstrated sapient knowledge."[3]

The American finds, demonstrating that late Stone Age people had indeed come to America long before they arrived with their canines in a time once fixed at 15,000 B.C., could not be denied. However, Goodman's assertion that those "Paleo-Indians" may have carried their original culture to Asia and Europe has created extensive controversy. Few agree that American Paleo-Indian culture has ever captured Europe. The American finds, the Leakey endorsement, and Goodman's persuasive reports on the California discoveries have support however, and his challenge is backed by some new fossil and tool finds by other American archaeologists, among them Richard "Scotty" McNeish.[4]

McNeish's "incontrovertible proof," reports *Science* somewhat skeptically, "consists of hundreds of objects collected recently at Pendejo Cave at Fort Bliss, New Mexico." McNeish fixes the time by carbon-dating at 30,000 years. The fossils consist of buffalo bones and an animal toe bone with a projectile point in it. No human fossils are included, but human fingerprints (or outlines) appear in the clay. Ancient artifacts have been found in Pennsylvania, Alabama, Tennessee, and the Carolinas, providing support to the claims of early arrival in eastern North America by archaic Cherokee, Delaware, Iroquois, and other Native American tribes.

Do new discoveries of Paleolithic man in what is now the southwestern United Stated force reconsideration of the global precedence of humankind? The seeming brash challenge to the "Bering Strait–Out of Africa" theory may in some ways have been met by new discoveries in Israel, Turkey, and Faiyum Oasis in Egypt. Fossil bones of "anatomically modern humans" dating to 92,000 B.C. have been found in Galilee, and bones of the woolly mammoth, evidently killed by human hunters who assembled the bones to create shelters, have been discovered in Russia. Paleolithic man undoubtedly reached the Americas, Australia, and New Zealand thousands of years earlier than previously believed. However, Goodman's position relative to the Bering Strait land bridge is also countered by fossil finds along the probable line of march, at Lake Baikal and in the Yukon.

ᧁᎻᎻᎾ

Had the man/dog partnership dissolved, as sometimes seemed the case during the Middle Ages? The contrary was true in the north. Life was even more difficult there, but the hunter was determined to make his way. He had the advantage of fire; he could subsist on a level above the animals and maintain his mastery of the environment. He knew how to build housing: crude huts of bark, skins, or woolly mammoth bones, and snow and ice igloos (though it is said that not more than one-fourth of all Arctic dwellers ever saw such an igloo). The dwellers in the far north, whether in Afghanistan, Siberia, Tibet, or China, and those in the most southerly region of the Americas, Tierra del Fuego, developed an extreme ability to cope with ice and snow, to take advantage of the few months that were somewhat warm, and to use to the limit the few plants available and every part of the fish or beast they caught. In all instances dogs were and continue to be in close association with humankind. The Lapps used dogs to help with the herding of the reindeer and invented skis to enable man to better do his part. The Aleuts invented boats to enable them to take the large fish of the Arctic seas and kept dogs with them on the ice, in the boat, and in the home.

Dogs adapted well to Arctic conditions. They grew thick, double coats and were tireless at drawing heavy sleds over ice and carts over tundra. They could bring down musk ox and tundra wolves weighing 175 pounds. Providing they were fed, they served man faithfully, and they ran down what existed of Arctic game if permitted. In later years, Robert Scott, who was racing to be the first to the North Pole, failed to use dogs because "they ate too much." He tried Siberian ponies instead and lost the race to Robert Peary, who, with 133 dogs, reached the pole in 1909 with his crew of twenty-four men.

⌘

The hunters coming out of Africa were differing peoples who chose varying migration patterns. Darlington and others show that mankind changed during thousands of years of development in Africa, from the dark pigment of the tribes that for the most part remained in the equatorial region to the olive hues of many of the Caucasoids and the pale skins of Berber mountain dwellers. Some northern Africans resembled the Bushmen, or Caucasoids, and also had Mongolian features, olive skin, and folded eyelids. The various Paleolithic people left their records in the caves and rock shelters of northern Africa, as well as fossil and artifact finds in Algeria, showing them hunting with dogs. Some of these hunters evidently departed for Asia early into the Pleistocene age and moved north into central Asia and China. The possible route, at least that of the later migrations, was via Arabia, Anatolia, and what is now Russia. Others from North Africa may have reached a similar site via Persia and Afghanistan, and still others by way of northern Europe and Scandinavia. Who might have taken such routes?

Africans with Mongolian attributes evidently reached central Asia in time to qualify as Peking Man; the dog skeletons found in their burial places have been loosely designated as Dingo. The human skulls are similar to those found in Java, on the way to Australia, where Dingos still hunt with Aborigines (not greatly dissimilar from African Bushmen) or with Feugians at the southern tip of South America, near the rim of Anarctica. The Mongolians of northern China may have bred the Chow Chow attributed to them. Konrad Lorenz suggests that the red coat of the Chow Chow indicates its part-Aureus ancestry: It may carry some of the genes of the red hound of Egypt.

But there were other routes from Africa to China. In an earlier time, trade routes of the civilized Middle East included Persia, Afghanistan, and Tibet. A third route, via the Americas and Australia, passes through northern Europe and reaches northern Asia by way of Denmark and the rest of Scandinavia, or Denmark and the Baltic shores and thence to central Asia. The bones of Mastiffs are found along this route, as well as the artifacts of some of the most skilled and diverse of all Paleolithic hunters, the Lapps. On most of their travels the Lapps were accompanied by the Samoyed people and their dogs. The Lapps migrated into central Asia at an early time, and then into Denmark and in Sweden, where some still dwell.

We now know, based on recent fossil finds and modern dating methods, something of the gypsy habits of the Paleolithic hunters from their limited record cut in stone or painted on rock shelter walls in Algeria. The rock art establishes a time frame for the hunters who first migrated from North Africa about 70,000 years ago. They were migrants with Mongolian features, and others resembled the tribes of the Caucasus Mountains. They too, accompanied by their dogs, may have crossed Arabia, Persia, Afghanistan, and on to Tibet. Some proceeded north following the reindeer from northern Europe to the northern extremity of what is now Sweden—Lapps, Samoyeds, Basques, and Finns. They are the likely creators of the typically northern dogs that would become man's sturdiest and most reliable supporters on earth's most difficult terrain, the tundra and ice of the far north and far south.

Such hybridization could occur anywhere on any of the routes. The interchange of populations and trade in the Middle East, Persia, Afghanistan, Tibet, and India began about the time of settlement in Mesopotamia of herders and planters from Africa. Persia lay across the trade routes to the Orient. Humankind, trade and religions crossed. Many Medes and Persians, in the time of Zoroastrianism, held believed in one God, and they also held the dog in veneration as the proper guide to conduct souls to their ultimate fate, as did Egyptians and peoples in other parts of the Middle East. Goods (including dogs) and ideas were exchanged, so it was believed in Babylon and Nineveh that the great Mastiffs acquired from the Persians originated in Tibet. But dogs may have been taken from Africa into central Asia and northern Europe by people calling themselves Lapps, Celts, and Basques. We need to inquire further before choosing an answer.

Darlington establishes the Lapp tribes, whose close neighbors were the Samoyeds, Vogula, Ostyaka, Chukchis, and Finns, as coming from central Asia into the Scandinavian peninsula in Neolithic times as fishermen and cultivators. The Lapps have also been placed in Denmark, across the entry to the Baltic Sea, Sweden, and Norway, where they remained until they were pushed out by Germanic tribes. Many of the Lapps picked up the trail of the plentiful reindeer in northern Europe, and followed the herds north with their dogs as the most recent glacial warming peaked, about 30,000 years ago, into Sweden where they still live as a pastoral people. Some Lapps and Samoyeds went farther into the extreme north of Russia. As they traveled, the Samoyeds created the tough sled and hunting dogs that still bear their tribal names. David Taylor, in his *Ultimate Dog Book,* refers to the Samoyed, now a well-bred snow-white favorite, as "this glamorous creature that will turn heads and make friends wherever it goes."[5] It has become a universally admired show dog though it began as a hard-working sled dog of the far north.

The Lapps, Finns, and Samoyeds arrived in the Baltic Sea area in early times, bringing their own breeds of dogs. Konrad Lorenz has found in those canines a common trait: All were southern Aureus dogs at that point. The cross breeding of northern large wolves and Aureus hunting dogs probably began in northern Europe, continuing in Asia. About 20,000 years ago, Lapps and others had departed the Baltic and may have reached lands along the three great Asian rivers, the Ob, the Yenisei, and the Lena, and the area around Lake Baikal in Siberia. All are on a possible route of "Out of Africa" migrants who eventually, as Asians, would cross the Bering Strait bridge into the Americas.

The Finnish Spitz and the Norwegian Elkhound may have both descended from Lapp dogs, brought from central Asia. In Sweden the Lapps were followed by the Svears, who gave Sweden its name, and Goths and Germanic tribes who interbred, creating the warlike, seafaring Vikings. The Norwegian Elkhound is considered to be pure Scandinavian but probably was first bred by the Lapps. Olav Wallo, in his *The New Complete Norwegian Elkhound,* says that the Elkhound came from Danish "swamp dogs" bred by "gypsies."[6] The Lapps, who were the world's foremost gypsies before Europe was well settled, brought big dogs into Denmark, where their central Asian artifacts have been found in the Danish "kitchen middens." The Elkhound, protected from cold by a thick, double coat, hunted bear, lynx, elk, and straying Lapp caribou. He traveled with the Vikings on their raids and explorations and yet remains a gentle, intelligent, and courageous hunting and house dog in modern times.

The Lapps too wandered, as did most of the mankind in early times. They in time would encounter, somewhere in Asia, the Mongolians out of Africa, who in the days when they resembled Bushmen began their walks from Africa into Asia. Those Mongolians were of the same Bushmen stock — "olive skins, straight black hair and more or less folded eyelids," as Darlington describes them. They arrived in China and ultimately reached the Americas. At some point they may have hybridized with Lapps in central Asia.

Chow Chows, said to have been produced by central Asian nomads, are also from the gene pool of the northern breeds. They became famed for their beauty, endurance, and loyalty to one owner. The blazing red coat of the breed's most popular color phase provides good evidence of its Aureus heritage, says Lorenz.

Their masters were not among the world's warlords, though they eventually would dwell for a time among the Mongols and the Huns.

The Chow Chow was called the "Tartar or barbarian dog" in old Chinese manuscripts. Most likely the breed arrived with Tartars who invaded China during the Tang dynasty, and there remain such dogs on the steppes of Outer Mongolia today. They were depicted, wearing harnesses and guiding humans, on pottery of the Han dynasty of 200 B.C. Such canines served as guard dogs in holy places and were said to guide the dead in the afterlife.

The Lapps and their dogs may have contributed to the domesticated canines of China by a less direct route as they pursued and helped to guide the European reindeer herds north after departing the Baltic area. In northern Sweden, people personally herded, and in a loose manner contained, the reindeer with some help from their dogs, roaming with herds from which they obtained meat, milk, skins for shelter and clothing, and antlers and bones used for tools. They probably brought into the far north a large, Mastiff-type dog that would be an ancestor of the Great Dane (an Aureus dog, according to Lorenz), and they developed a hybrid wolf-dog that would become a progenitor of some of the world's most dependable carriers of people and freight, via the Arctic sled, as well as an efficient, fearless hunter, explorer, and faithful companion. "In Eskimo Society," historian Arnold Toynbee would write, "there are two castes: the human hunters and their canine auxiliaries."

But it remained for the Mongolians and northern Chinese to bring to full scale the domestication of the wolf. They developed unusual canine varieties as well as highly useful working dogs to benefit the general economy, and breeds intended for human food. Wolf-dogs produced by the Chinese became the ancestors of most varieties of *Canis lupus* found in world commerce, and exclusively so in the Americas, where they arrived with their Paleolithic human families during the past 30,000 years.

The authoritative *Man and Animals,* published in 1984 by the University of Pennsylvania Museum Press, concedes that "the origin of the dog is a subject of much controversy," pointing out that "jackals, wolves, and dogs have similar characteristics and chromosome count." But the authors also suggest that it is wolves and dogs that have "a behavior repertoire resembling modern dogs." The similarity of the African wild dog to the wolf in family lifestyle and pack hunting behavior is close, as we have noted, except for the fact that the wolf is more aloof and will hunt with man. The contributors state that since, "like man and dog, the wolf has a highly developed social system based on a hierarchy based on dominance within the group, it was probably this characteristic that allowed man to tame and domesticate young wolves. It thus appears likely that the wolf is the main, if not the sole, ancestor of the dog."

While this may be a fairly accurate deduction regarding northern regions of the earth, it is left for us to assume that the domestication of canines in Africa occurred prior to the arrival of humankind in the Americas—Jeffrey Goodman claims priority only for *Homo sapiens*. By the time Paleolithic man crossed the Berengia bridge, the Asian wolf was indeed one of the ancestors of the modern domesticated dog, as Charles Darwin and Lorenz have suggested. The canine companions of man probably hybridized with the wolf from the time they entered Asia.

Man and Animals reports the arrival of those domesticated dogs in North America at a time much earlier than has been suggested by some scientists. Fossil remains of dogs, coyotes, and a wolf have been found among human hearths in Jaguar Cave, Idaho, carbon-dated at 12,000 years old. "There were two sizes of dogs—one about the size of a modern-day Beagle, the other about the size of a Labrador Retriever. . . . The possibility must be borne in mind that . . . the large wolf specimen may also represent a wolf-dog hybrid," the Pennsylvania researchers write. "Although other finds of remains in North America have been dated even earlier, those from Jaguar Cave constitute, for the moment, the single most securely documented source of evidence that at least two sizes of dogs were present in North America at the beginning of the post-glacial period."

A number of veterinary scholars suggest that the wolf is the main ancestor of the dog but then add that "the way in which the animal first entered the human community is not known." They do not exclude jackal ancestry, saying, "The wolf, coyote, and jackal . . . have dog-like characteristics, and each produces a fertile hybrid when mated with dogs." A great many of the differences now seen between one breed of dog and another can thus be accounted for by the genetic variability present in their wild wolf ancestors.

"There is little doubt that the dog was one of the first domesticated animals," *Man and Animals* continues. "Bone specimens clearly distinguishable from those of wild canids and having features characteristic of present-day dogs have been found in the Middle East, Asia, and North America at human dwelling sites dating to around 10,000 to 8,000 B.C.

"It has been pointed out by S. J. Olsen that the Chinese wolf (*Canis Lupus chanco*) has a jawbone with certain features resembling those of early North American dogs. These features are lacking in the North American wolf (*Canis Lupus lycaon*) as well as other wild canids, suggesting that early dogs in this hemisphere were derived from wolves of Asia and were brought with man in his migration across the Bering Strait."

This American theory appears to be at some variance with that of Lorenz, who flatly declares and reiterates that the earliest domesticated canines were descended from the golden jackal and had little or no wolf kinship at the time these early dogs were brought as far north as the Baltic Sea, as shown by fossil discoveries in that area. Yet it is not difficult for us to reconcile the two viewpoints. Migrating humankind originating from Africa may have been first to domesticate the jackal, creating the Aureus dogs found in Egypt, the Middle East, and on the Baltic Sea shores. Those scavenger animals may have followed scavenging humans and/or human hunters, as Lorenz contends. There would be little reason for man to attempt to hybridize those jackal/dogs with the small desert wolves or foxes of the Middle East or southwest Asia. The hunter needed a fast, strong, large canine with superior scenting powers to find, chase, wear out, and help to bring down the large game that human hunters would not readily capture on their own. But as man moved north, a large, dominant male northern wolf, timber wolf, or tundra wolf would have suited the needs of the big-game hunter. The wolf would have been valued as a hybrid because he had the natural habits and inclinations of that social animal, their own domesticated dog.

"Only wolves had a behavioral repertoire resembling that of modern dogs," the University of Pennsylvania scholars write. "It was probably a characteristic that allowed man to tame and domesticate young wolves." And how did man first come to understand and appreciate this attribute of the wolf? Probably because he'd been able to domesticate the wild dogs of Egypt or central Africa, who look like an American coyote but whose social behavior repertoire almost exactly matches that of the African wild dog and the tundra wolf.

ᏅᎾᏯ

It's time we greet the wolf, a fearless, redoubtable fellow given a bad name in written history and in "fairy stories" composed initially in the Middle East, where early herdsmen settled and prospered. In Anatolia and Persia wolves were blamed for attacks on livestock as well as human beings. Pioneers in all lands learned to fear the wolf. The exploits of "three-toes," a wolf living in the Dakotas, who freed himself from a trap and then took revenge on flocks and herds for sixteen years before he was finally slain, have become legendary. Children were told the sad story of the Scandinavian farmer who returned from a hunt to find his wife and children in hiding, except for an infant son left bleeding and bruised and guarded by their dog, descended from a wolf. The farmer, believing that the dog was responsible, crashed through the door of the house and killed his dog. After the child the dog had been guarding was revived, the father found, under the child's bed, a dead wolf, obviously killed by the protective dog. Obviously, this tragic legend and others like it bode no good for American wolves.

Such stories and fears spread widely, making life precarious for all wolves, animals that were at last exterminated in the British Isles and most of Europe in the nineteenth century. Many immigrants to America remembered the wolf stories, and their superstitious fears crossed the ocean with them. Coyotes, native to North America, who shunned humans but were accused of attacking sheep, have also been relentlessly hunted, except in areas where great increases of harmful rodents occurred shortly after the coyotes had been cleared out. In several such areas the coyotes have been brought back.

⌒⌒⌒⌒

In our mythical walks with Kiwi, pursuing the one goal—to follow the development of dogs and humankind as mutual partners—we also have come upon the wolf as an enemy. But we have learned that some people of the north, our own Scandinavian ancestors in fact, have concluded not to fear the wolf, but rather to befriend him. And we find in the work of Lorenz this evaluation: Those Lapps who had dwelled for a time on the shores and islands of the Baltic Sea provided an early cross of wolves and Aureus dogs, and should be credited for "the Esquimaux dogs of Greenland, and Arctic breeds of the Old World, such as Russian Laikas, Samoyeds, and even Chow-Chows."

So again we visit the Lapps. They may have come into Europe in Magdalenian times, about 15,000 years ago, bringing with them bone tools, their animal-skin fishing boats, and a few of their dogs. Those who departed to follow the reindeer herds went into northern Sweden and may have gone on, with the caribou (attributed to their breeding) to America, while Lapp hunters followed the route of the silk road to roam the tundra all the way to the territories of the Mongols and the Huns in western Asia, where the Chinese also settled. There are now few caribou on the Asian tundra, but a half million can be found in Alaska and Canada.

Those Lapps remaining did much of their own herding, using relatively few dogs. They were no longer great hunters, and they trained reindeer to draw their sledges. The Tungus and Samoyed tribes appear to have been the dog breeders, who may have carried their practices to the Chinese. Those late Stone Age hunters moving steadily farther north and west continued the hybridizing of dogs and wolves, directing and controlling the qualities of their wolf-dogs by careful selection of breeding stock. They were considered to be Mongoloids who produced dogs that seemed to resemble themselves, having the face of a wolf, the slanting eyes and flat snout of a Shar-Pei, and the reddish color of an Egyptian wolfhound. Even the faces of the reindeer seemed to have an Oriental cast.

Wolves provided hybrid canines with great strength, endurance, and size, and, according to Lorenz, inherited the wild traits of wolves, "turning their natural love for the mother into love for humans." Or, for a human: "A *Lupus* dog," he wrote, "who has sworn allegiance to a certain man, is forever a one-man dog, and no stranger can win from him so much as a single wag of his bushy tail. Nobody who has once possessed the one-man love of a *Lupus* dog will ever be content with one of *Aureus* blood."

Today's travelers in the far north have found the sturdy Lupus dog living in closest possible association with humankind. They have continued to be members of the family, though they sleep outside the human habitations much of the time. The Eskimo finds room for his dog in his kayak, and for several to add warmth to an igloo of ice and snow. From the canines brought north from many far-flung places, and the wolves that mated with them en route, have come working dogs recognized today as among the world's finest, the most loyal, and the best adapted to their environment. The sled dogs of the north have been celebrated in world literature. (Jack London devoted his classic *Call of the Wild* to them.) Endurance sled racing is perhaps the most arduous sport known for both man and animal. Men also have been known to risk their lives for these dogs, and few in the north will sell dogs used in their own service. The wolf-dogs will defend their masters and one another to the death, Lorenz tells us, "even when at the point of starvation."

The breeds contributing to the northern hybrids were themselves a hardy lot, able to stand the cold, northern climate as they followed the reindeer herds. When the Lapps departed Denmark they left behind their own sturdy breed, a

European-type working dog whose fossil bones have been found in Danish Mesolithic sites. "This medium size Spitz had a wedge-shape head resembling that of wolf," says Mary Crosby in her *Encyclopedia of Dogs*. The dogs thus left behind may have come from Asia, bred by ancestors of Lapps and Finns as Paleolithic tribes brought them from central Asia into Persia. These tribes are known to have developed large Mastiffs which, reputedly, came from Tibet by way of Persia. The patterns of domestication and migration are indeed complex. But the road to the Americas, Australia, and New Zealand for man and dog is clear, by way of northern China, Mongolia, and Siberia's Lake Baikal.

Why did Stone Age people seek to leave China for North America and Australia when they had no knowledge of lands beyond what they could see from the top of the tallest tree on the highest hill they could climb? Some were pushed along by other migrants who wished to settle, or they did not assimilate with newcomers, or it was simply their nature to wander, always seeking new pastures. There were environmental reasons for their movement. The environmentally inhospitable dryness and intense cold of tundra regions ultimately discouraged these people who merely wished to hunt and settle down with their flocks and dogs. Later we find their traces far to the south in the gravel bed along the Silo River in Java, in the swamps of New Guinea, and along the Malay Peninsula. Ultimately the hunters, except for their dogs, were alone near the end of the trail in Australia. In time, widespread need for canines would arise on that island continent as it had in the rest of the civilized world.

The last of the primitive migrants probably went down the Malay Peninsula to Sumatra, then to Java, where fossils and artifacts have been found, and on to the New Guinea and York Peninsula in Australia. Some of the late arrivals must have come from the "stepping stone" islands via dugout canoes and then sailboats developed in Asia and the South Seas; their tool kits have been found en route. Australian naturalist Mulvaney writes: "First men with stone choppers made by Peking Man and Java Man, then a Mesolithic [middle Stone Age] culture of pebble tools. . . . Artifacts are abundant in caves and rock shelters of the limestone cliffs in the center of the Malay Peninsula. . . . These Mesolithics were probably related to the modern Australian aborigines. They are the primitive men of the Equatorial north who continue to hunt with their Dingo hounds and their spears."

The Stone Age people entering the Americas by way of the Berengia land bridge brought with them only Dingoes, it is believed. They walked in, with relatively few possessions in addition to their canines. Few signs of fossils or artifacts can be found since the crossing point, some 400 miles wide, long ago became sea bottom. This occurred perhaps on three occasions, the most recent at about the same time the British Isles ceased to have a causeway connection with mainland Europe. The first migrants may have crossed the bridge without canines. The new American artifact finds indicate that some crossings occurred between 30,000 and 70,000 years ago. Late Stone Age arrivals brought in Dingoes, as noted by Darlington and others.

The final crossings including Chinese dogs, among them a few large wolf-like dogs such as those found with human fossils in caves of Idaho and along the Newfoundland coast. But most American Paleo-Indians did not require large dogs, or could not transport them from Siberia. Only the Mandans in the Dakotas are known to have had big dogs to pull the travois and snow sleds.

Dingoes, however, had accompanied early migrants across the Bering land bridge and into the south. "The Plains Indians owned many dogs that were cared for by women," *Man and Animals* reports. "Dogs played an important role in the family, assisting with a variety of tasks. Their primary function was transporting supplies, either on their backs or with a travois, a carrier consisting of two trailing poles supporting a basket, to which the dog was harnessed. Dogs carried loads weighing up to fifty pounds, or dragged a travois of about seventy-five pounds and could manage over five miles a day with a heavy load." They accompanied the Indians on hunts, wearing down the prey for the hunter. Later Indians would have horses, taken from invading Spaniards. Indian hunting dogs were trained to ignore raw meat while transferring it to a butchering spot within the village. Some Indians ate dog flesh, but most abhorred such a practice.

The Indian dogs provided an alarm system for the villages but did not fight in wars. The tribes engaged in warfare, but many such conflicts were little more than vigorous games no more fatal than lacrosse. The Indians in some "battles" merely "touched" an opponent, who was then required to quit the contest. Southern Indians in time would meet some of the world's fiercest warriors, who brought to America their horses and war dogs from Spain.

The linkage of Asia and the Americas appears confirmed throughout the southern United States and Mexico by the discovery of fossil bones of canines that obviously came from Asia. Some small animals might have crossed the Bering Strait land bridge on their own, as did large herbivores and predators, but many fossils of smaller canines clearly were those of animals brought in by humankind, some originating in Africa. Lorenz saw evidence of the red dog of Egypt in the Chow Chow, and David Taylor found in the Mexican hairless "much in common with the Chinese Crested, suggesting they may be related." Dog skulls found in Mexico and the southern United States range from those of small, short-nosed animals with rather large brain cases to those similar to the fossil skulls of northern canine types brought into the New World, all thought to be Asian. An unknown, small breed became the ancestor of the Chihuahua, most likely the same as or similar to the small dogs that Mexican Indians used in religious rites and as food. According to Indian legend, "The dead [soul] crosses a broad river on the back of a dog." A famous Mexican work of art, *Kneeling Woman Kissing a Dog,* found in an ancient tomb in Tlacopan, now shown in the National Museum of Anthropology in Mexico City, records the relation of the primitive people to their canines. It is subtitled, *Affection between a kneeling woman and a leaping dog in a happy, sunlit world.*

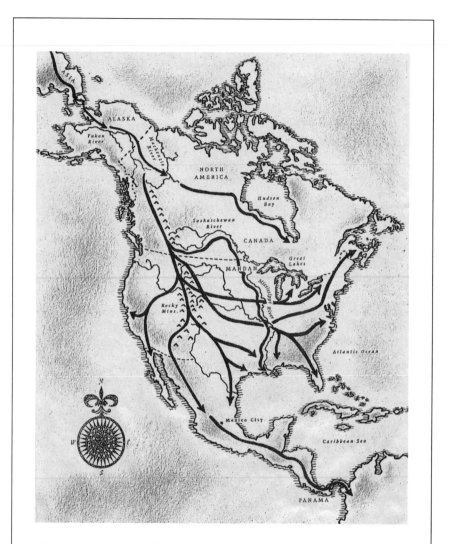

Herbert Boyer's basic map of North America shows the routes of Asian migrants and their dogs as suggested by ethnologists. The Bering Strait land bridge between Siberia and Alaska became submerged about 12,000 B.C., effectively altering all future migration patterns into North America.

9

To the New World

⌒m⌒

We are now relatively sure that the first Stone Age people in the Americas arrived with their Asian dogs in glacial withholding periods, between 10,000 and 70,000 years ago, the peaks of migration probably occurring about 30,000 B.C. They were hunters who made and used crude tools and weapons, knew the uses of fire, and built the kind of shelters developed by nomads of Europe and Asia. They crossed the land bridge created between Siberia and Alaska when the ice caps in the north had locked up seawater to expose a 400-mile corridor of tundra and rock. They are known today as Neolithic people, called Indians or Amerinds since the time of Columbus.

There is no record that the migrants brought with them any domestic animals other than dogs, which in most instances had hybridized with Asian wolves. The people were nomads who persisted in their hunting ways until they reached areas of benign climate in Mexico and Central America where large game was no longer plentiful. There, as in early Egypt, they became collectors and planters of seeds and roots. They had improved their weapons, adding blow guns and the bow and arrow, and made serviceable canoes, but they did not capture and herd animals as beasts of burden except in limited areas of South America.

The hunter preferred to be a wanderer. He studied flora, however, since this helped him to determine which animals might be present. Thus he learned something of edible plants and how to tip his flint weapons and blow gun darts with poison. When the hunting was bad, the hunter and his mate and children would scrounge for food in the form of edible plants. These were more plentiful in the south than in the north, and they readily lent themselves to cultivation.

Darlington's botany chart for the Americas, labeled "Paleolithic—arrived 15,000 B.C. (with dogs)" lists thirty-two plant varieties in wide use and shows that nearly all cultivated plants in the Americas originated south of the Isthmus of Panama, the others—maize, beans, cotton and squash—being first domesticated in Mexico and Texas. Maize, in its varieties, would prove to be one of the world's most popular and essential crops.

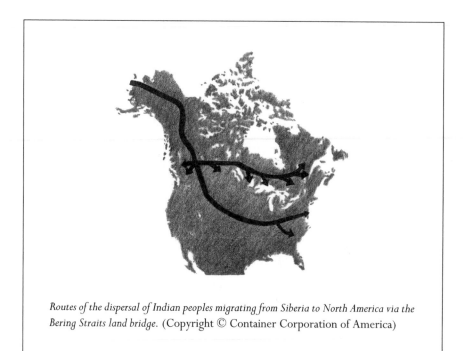

Routes of the dispersal of Indian peoples migrating from Siberia to North America via the Bering Straits land bridge. (Copyright © Container Corporation of America)

Many of the migrants from Asia settled permanently in areas where food crops grew readily. Fossil bone fragments and artifacts of Mongoloid people dated to 17,000 B.C. have been found in the southwestern United States. Some of the settlers returned north, among them hunters who followed the streams and herds in all directions. A dramatic fossil find demonstrating that some migrants returned north or engaged in trade over a wide area was made by A. E. Jenks in glacial Lake Pelican in Minnesota in 1931. Under strata estimated to be 13,000 to 17,000 years old, fossil remains of a young woman were discovered and designated as "definitely Mongoloid," according to Samuel Eliot Morison, in his *Oxford History of the American People*.[1] She without question was one of those people who crossed the Bering Strait land bridge after the glacial ice lowered the seas some 300 feet. She wore a small conch shell ornament; thus, either she had gone south all the way to the Gulf of Mexico or to Central America and returned or someone brought the conch shell decoration to her. Beside her body lay a dagger made from a deer's antler. She may have been the continent's earliest murder victim.

Many Asian migrants crossing the Bering Strait would remain in the north, amid an environment much the same as that of tundra areas left behind. Some would find such an environment in Patagonia, 11,000 miles to the south. Most departed from the line of march as earlier man had done in Africa. The settlers remaining in what would become the Yukon and southern Canada and the Dakotas in the United States soon developed special ways to use their dogs in addition to hunting. They trained them as beasts of burden, to pull sleds, toboggans, and poles of the travois and the light tepees used on the trail. Such dogs were used by the Mandan tribe of the Dakotas in American colonial days, as shown by early artists, and by Indians in the southwestern United States. Early explorers reported that the dimensions of the wigwam were determined by what the dogs could pull on the cedar travois poles.

The migrants who left the main southerly trails to enter the southwestern area of the United States were evidently Mongoloid. The dating of fossils in Mesa Verde digs fix their time at about 20,000 B.C.—6,000 years earlier than the first carbon-dating of domesticated dogs in China. They were Stone Age men who had no bows and arrows, writes Oliver La Farge in his *American Indian*.[2] Yet those "Folsom Men" killed bison and other great animals, including sloths "big as bears," according to La Farge. Some writers deny that any significant human fossils were found at Folsom, New Mexico—only fragments of tool kits and animal bones. The hunters may have driven bison into water or a trap, killed them with their spears, then departed. Possibly they ate their dogs en route south.

The last of the Mongoloid peoples to cross the Berengia bridge with large Asian dogs were Eskimos, whose lives continue to be the most closely related to their canines, historian Arnold Toynbee writes. They began arriving in America with their Siberian Huskies, inured to the worst of Arctic weather, possibly walking or in their kayaks as recently as 5,000 years ago, just before the tundra causeway was again covered by the Bering Sea. The Eskimo lives on in the Arctic, fishing and hunting seals, and some have accepted Alaskan and Canadian lifestyles. The modern Eskimo slightly outnumbers the Lapp of Scandinavia, each having a population of about 50,000.

Some primitive peoples arriving in North America found congenial lands in Alaska and Canada. The migrations continued over thousands of years, as the land bridge was raised and lowered by changing conditions of the earth. Naturalist C. D. Darlington estimates that the most favorable time was a 500-year span enabling the "Paleolithics and Dogs" to continue south to Patagonia in about 8,000 B.C. That does not preclude the possibility that some Asians and dogs arrived much earlier. By 10,000 B.C. many tribes occupied the Canadian wilderness and moved into what is now the United States, passed into Mexico, and were training the llama as a beast of burden in Chile. The spread of these primitive peoples occurred more rapidly in the Americas than in Europe. The hunters had a bit of a start from their China experience, and most were not pausing in the North American continent to capture and herd animals.

The migrants remaining in Canada and the northern United States found an environment much to their liking, as hunters of big game, not as collectors and planters. They used dogs, spears, and, in some cases, bows and arrows. In the extreme north they hunted caribou, moose, and bear, probably with large dogs like those of the later Mandans, as well as hybrids from dogs and northern wolves. Peter Farb in his book *The Land and Wildlife of North America* credits the Canadian tribes with developing the birchbark canoe, the snowshoe, and the toboggan. The tribes reaching the southern Great Plains hunted buffalo as well as smaller game. Naturalists living with the Indians in colonial days later agreed that those Paleolithic people lacking bows and arrows, or even those who used them, could not bring down big game alone. The dogs would track and wear down the prey, finishing the kill of animals wounded by the hunter, as Marco Polo found them doing in Asia. However, Farb maintains, as does La Farge, that many of the migrants did not rely on the dog but instead developed more efficient weapons to take down their own big game.[3]

Darlington describes the earliest Americans as having the olive skin, straight black hair, and partly folded eyelids of the Mongolians. They were probably descended from settlers like those of Choukoutien, China, where the domesticated dogs with their cave-dwelling partners have been carbon-dated recently at 20,000 to 14,000 B.C. The first such primitives may have passed into North America many thousands of years earlier and may have taken with them dogs to be used as food, according to indications in fossil finds in the southwestern United States. Some later migrants were Cro-Magnons who advanced across Asia to Kamchatka. The Cro-Magnons used fire, bows and arrows, spears with fluted flint points, and other evidence of an advanced culture. The legends of North American tribes, among them the Delawares and the Cherokees, indicate they used boats in crossing "the waters"; thus they crossed at a late date when the oceans again had risen to higher levels. The last of dry land migrations, according to Darlington, began when the Asian Australoids took their Dingoes with them about 8,000 to 10,000 years ago, continuing to about 2,000 B.C., when the Eskimos arrived in Alaska. Throughout the period of the Bering Strait crossings, wild animals could have moved both south and north. Asian animal fossils found in America have included mastodons and mammoths, a six-foot-long wolf called *Canis dirus,* and *Amphyicyon,* a huge canid. These creatures disappeared, as did many humans, leaving only fossil remains.

The migrants from Asia, described by Darlington, are credited by Ruth Moore in her book *Evolution* with advanced skills characteristic of many Cro-Magnon tribes that made their way across North America to become the woodland Indians, and who reached Mexico and Central America, where high cultures developed. "Even at the earliest appearance these men were biologically as any men since," she writes. "In brain size, in posture, and in physical organization, the three-and-a-half billion beings who are their descendants today have not basically changed the patterns that evolution had already built in their bodies."[4] Not all qualified, however. Darwin found aborigines at the tip of South America, a few hundred miles from Antarctica, who were dusky olive in appearance and who also hunted with their bows and arrows, spears, and dogs, but Darwin called them the least advanced of any primitive peoples he had seen. They evidently descended from those among the first to cross the Bering Strait on dry land.

There were no native dogs or peoples in the Americas when the Asians arrived. "There is not a shred of evidence that *Homo sapiens* originated in the Americas or that he was preceded here by more primitive kinds of man," Farb insists. "No fossils of primitive man—or of any primates more advanced than pre-monkey— have ever been found in North America. Nor have any fossils of dogs been found, except for canines known to have disappeared prior to the arrival of man." There is fossil evidence of a long-tailed dog, *Daphoenodon,* that may have hunted the *Syndyoceras,* a double-antlered deer, in the Miocene age, about 20 million years ago. Some thousands of years later, canine creatures *Osteoborus* and *Hemicyon* existed. All of these early cynoid species died in catastrophes that destroyed most of the mammals then on earth.

During the decreasing glaciation of the globe and the ensuing melting period that extended many thousand of years, wild dogs and wolves may have crossed into the Americas on their own. Hybridization of peoples occurred in the long years of migration, and undoubtedly occurred also among dogs and wolves. The first arrivals into the Americas are said to have brought no more than crude tools and weapons, as well as their domestic dogs, with them. They found congenial lands in Alaska and Canada. The migrations continued over thousands of years, as the land bridge was raised and lowered by changing conditions on earth.

⚬⚬⚬

The early Stone Age people from Asia created small settlements throughout North America in the days when a high civilization was developing in Anatolia, Mesopotamia, and Egypt. Later, waves of migrants represented higher cultures that had been created in Africa and Asia. The fortunate migrants who paused in the salubrious climate of Mexico and Central America found an environment similar to that of the Nile Valley, the Egyptian deserts, and the Fertile Crescent of Asia. There were few large predators, much small game available, and fertile soil in which wild plants grew, many of them edible. Those settlers, perhaps possessing a cosmic memory in their genes, were farming and building great cities and high civilizations within a mere few thousand years. The Aztecs and Incas created governments, writing, and mathematical systems that provided a calendar required for proper planting of crops. In time large temples were erected, and pyramids were built, either of stone or platform tombs made of logs surmounted by pyramids. In some cases, these pyramids had round roofs resembling those of the roofed huts the nomads learned to build on their way south. Generally, except for the round roofs, the structures were similar to those of Egypt. By the time the Europeans arrived in America, the Asian descendants in Mexico had built the largest urban area in the New World, covering seven square miles. They domesticated only dogs, "which they bred for food," according to Hammond Innes in his study *The Conquistadors*. When the Spanish arrived with their war dogs, the peaceful natives, who used the wheel only for children's toys, and dogs for food, were quickly conquered.

Dogs and their owners in other parts of the New World fared better, though they did not play an important role in hunting or war except among the most primitive of the migrants. The scholars and researchers do not always agree on precisely why or how humankind adopted new ways and new directions. The

Theodore de Brye engraved this scene showing Spanish war dogs attacking prisoners in Mexico, evidently drawing on descriptions from sixteenth-century writings by Bishop Bartolomeo de las Casas. As a young friar, the bishop had come to Mexico with Spanish troops and witnessed the carnage of the perros de sangre *(dogs of blood) against the Indians.*

pressures, constraints, stimulations, and opportunities differed according to the paths taken. Generally the migrations that followed the wild herds were helped by the dogs' hunting skills. The canine sense of smell—thousands of times more sensitive and acute than that of man, as demonstrated by modern testing methods—was a constant in the changing human experience. Man could drive animals into traps by the use of fire, often disastrous to his own environment; he could kill large game that was aged and feeble, wounded, or caught in bogs or brambles. The regular, consistent supply of flesh among people who had not domesticated animals for food and who lacked weapons more effective than the spear or bow and arrow was dependent upon hunting dogs. Most of the Asians, Mongolians, Australoids, and Amerinds, however called, were able, with the aid of their dogs, to follow trails of their choosing as the Ice Age was ending. The routes were varied, yet sometimes were strangely the same.

The Cherokee, called the "Dog Tribe" by the French and American historian Francis Parkman in his histories of England and France in early America, were among the most advanced of the Asian migrants to North America ,and they became the largest tribe in the South. While they lacked the fighting power of the Iroquois Six Nations, they shrewdly managed to maintain a balance of power between England and Spain, and England and France. When they felt betrayed by England, they joined France for a time, ultimately supporting the colonists in the American Revolution. But all their efforts failed. The Cherokee, who got that tribal name from English traders (their own name for themselves was Ani Yumeyd, meaning Principal People), ultimately lost their power and land and walked the long "Trail of Tears" to exile in Oklahoma. A few Cherokee evaded the eviction notices and continue to have their own small but self-governed colony in North Carolina.

These are drawings of fragments of the Walam Olum, *a map found in 1820 and attributed to the Delaware Indians. Like many of the artifacts from the caves of Choukoutien in China, the* Walum Olum *as a whole has disappeared. The map was said to represent the tribe dividing, or migrating, part of them "crossing the frozen waters," probably in longboats.*

A Cherokee legend says that they crossed icy waters on their way to settlement sites in America. They were traveling with a people ultimately called Delaware, who have a similar legend. In 1820 a manuscript was found showing such boats and crossings in crude pictographs. The Cherokee evidently went south and east to a land that Queen Elizabeth I would allocate to her courtiers. They were an industrious people, collectors as well as hunters. They possibly had gone farther south, then turned northeast in their wanderings, since they cultivated agricultural products first domesticated in Mexico: maize, beans, squash, and tobacco. They cleared the forest for farms and mined flint, quartzite, and gemstones to create tools, weapons, and ornaments. Their arrowheads found today are exceptionally sharp and deadly. They made necklaces of shells, bones, and teeth, including those of humans and dogs. They pounded copper nuggets into ornaments but declined to use the gold found within the territory where they established towns. Lewis and Mary Lou Dendy, students of the Cherokee culture at Highlands, North Carolina, where the Cherokees had summer camps, think that the tribe engaged in widespread trade, since their flints and plants are not all indigenous. In their studies of Indians of the Alabama and Tennessee region, anthropologists Thomas M. N. Lewis and Madeline Kneberg reached a similar conclusion. They also provide detailed accounts on the well-developed culture of Asian migrants called "Archaic Indians" (8,000 B.C.) who inhabited dry caves in the Ozarks, tanned skins, and wove fabrics, skills they carried east.

The Cherokee, Creek, and Yuchi were creating a Bronze Age civilization when they were interrupted by foreign invaders in the sixteenth century. Their lives as they were emerging from a late Stone Age culture were reminiscent of ancient Egypt and Mesopotamia, especially their treatment of dogs. "Dogs were the first animals domesticated by man . . . and were immigrants from the Old World just as the Archaic Indians, their masters, were," Lewis and Kneberg write in *Tribes That Slumber*. "The high regard in which dogs were held by these people may be inferred from the careful burial that they received, either with their owners or in separate graves. This regard may have arisen from services rendered by the dogs in hunting and as beasts of burden, or it may simply reveal the human response to the dogs' faithful and affectionate companionship."[5]

Although the Cherokee were one of the largest tribes north of Mexico, their population was relatively small (estimated at 22,000 in 1650), but their influence was great. Their language was close to that of the Iroquois, with whom they had little contact since the days when the Asian migrants followed differing trails 6,000 or more years earlier. Their settlements were in the Carolinas, parts of Tennessee, and north Georgia. The Cherokee, like neighboring tribes, including their enemies the Creek, had rituals and religious beliefs reminiscent of Egypt, Babylon, and Hebraic tribes. But their story of The Flood, as translated by Douglas LeTell Rights in *The American Indian,* credits the dog rather than a deity with preserving mankind when the rains came.

"Man had a dog which began to go down daily to the river to look at the water and howl," begins the story. "At last, man, angry, scolded the dog, which then spoke to him and said, 'Very soon there is going to be a great freshet and the water will come so high that all will be drowned. But if you make a raft to get upon when the rains come, you will be saved, but you must first throw me into the water.' The man at first would not believe the dog, but he became convinced. He built the raft, provisioned it, and placed upon it his family. It rained, the water rose until the mountains were covered. Only the man and his family remained alive."[6]

In another version of the legend, man, dog, and other living things boarded the raft. Either way, the world was repopulated by creatures generally, including dogs. Another Cherokee legend deals with a dog who behaved badly and not unselfishly. "The dog from the North came upon people who had a corn mill, in which they pounded corn into meal, and for several mornings they noticed that some of the meal had been stolen during the night and they found the tracks of a dog. So they watched, and when the dog came they sprang out and whipped him. He ran off howling to his home in the North with meal dropping from his mouth as he ran, leaving behind the white trail we now see as the Milky Way, which the Cherokee call to this day *Giliutsunstanunyi,* meaning 'where the dog ran.'"

The Cherokee, known to historian Parkman as the "Dog Tribe," had many dogs, no doubt, but did not use them in war: They were not compatible with the Indian style of fighting, which required silent approach and surprise, but they guarded the farms, camps, and fields and were always to be found in the homes, and even in men's lodges and tribal longhouses. Emissaries to the Indians, according to Rights, frequently found dogs in the official quarters where various gatherings were held. "When the eatables were assembled, the hungry dogs were kicked out," he says. "After the dog-kicking ceremony, a drum was beaten to summon attendance." Thus Cherokee dogs evidently were treated much like Cherokee children.

In colonial times many Americans believed that the Indians of America were descended from a Lost Tribe of Israel. Prophet Joseph Smith directed his *Book of Mormon* to such Indians prior to his formation of the Mormon Church. The Cherokee not only worshiped the sun, as did the ancient Egyptians, but they had a higher deity, a supreme god, Yowa. "Yowa was a name so sacred that it could not be spoken aloud, except by certain priests," Lewis and Kneberg tell us. The pronouncement of "Yowa" by those privileged priests may have come close to that of "Yaweh" (or "Yahveh"), the Hebraic god whose true name is too sacred for human utterance except by certain priests.

Did the Egyptian and Anatolian masons and tomb builders, the Anatolian and Celtic iron workers who carried their secret skills to much of the Western world, and perhaps some priests of an Israeli-Judean Lost Tribe participate in some of the Bering Strait crossings? Moore writes that the early migrants from Asia made their way south along the west coast of North America to the Isthumus of Panama land bridge and on to "the very tip of the southern continent." Darlington describes a possible route for those taking their dogs—they crossed the Bering Strait during a 500-year warm spell, then moved south, "slipping between the Rocky Mountain and Laurentian ice gap and ranging all the way to Tierra del Fuego," where they arrived as "Paleolithic hunters with dogs" in 8,000 B.C.

Farb suggests other possible courses, noting that "about 750 prehistoric stone tools have been discovered at several sites at a pass in Alaska's Brooks Range and along the Arctic coast of Canada's Yukon Territory. Their design and distribution reveal the possibility of spurts of human migration across Eurasia and deep into the interior of North America." Farb points out that similar tools have been found around Lake Baikal in western Siberia; he also describes the remarkable *Walam Olum* document, found by scholars among the Delaware, which depicted the crossing by boat of the Bering Strait. Thus the crossing occurred late in the meltdown of the ice, possibly after 6,000 B.C. At that time migrants from Mesopotamia and Egypt passing through China and Siberia might have reached the Bering Strait and continued south, until they found lands like those they left in Mexico and Guatemala. Others, after living in the dry caves of Arkansas, may have gone east to the highlands of the Carolinas. Stories, legends, and ideas—Egyptian, Babylonian, and Hebraic in nature—might have been communicated through such lines, or the Archaic Amerinds may have found inspiration from their new environment. Only their dogs may have known.

☙

Recent archaeological digs in the southern United States indicate that many Asian migrants did not linger in the far north, but spread widely from the Pacific to the Atlantic in the lower half of what is now the United States, throughout Mexico and down past the Isthmus of Panama into Central and South America. These wanderings indicate that pressures from the youngest ice sheets continued to determine the migration patterns of the earliest hunters over many thousands of years. The historian Samuel Eliot Morison, like Darlington, characterizes them as Mongoloid hunters with dogs, arriving prior to 10,000 B.C. "The first comers subsisted by hunting big game," he writes, "which they killed by means of spears tipped with flaked flint . . . . Pelts of bison and other animals were dressed with stone scrapers . . . . These people supplemented their diets with nuts and wild seeds, and presumably with fish, but they did not plant corn nor other seeds or keep domestic animals other than the dog . . . they corresponded, roughly, with the early Stone Age man in Europe." Why the dog? Obviously for protection, companionship, finding game, and to hunt large animals.

Some later Mongolians to enter the Americas not only brought their dogs but some evidence of a Megalithic (middle Stone Age) culture. They made and used the bow and arrow, collected plants and seeds, and trapped large animals with fire and deadfalls, and, upon their arrival in congenial climates, many became planters. They retained their dogs, possibly at times using them for food.

Some migrants changed their mode of life as they moved south, developing the use of canoes in Canada, creating skin-covered tepees when they reached the plains, and adopting the travois that the northern Indians employed to make their dogs more efficient draft animals. Not until they reached southern reaches of the United States and Mexico and the Spaniards arrived with livestock did the Amerinds domesticate animals other than their dogs. Only the Incas tamed the llama. The southern Indians later captured and used the Spanish horse, though in the beginning they believed a horse and its rider to be a single monstrous creature that they dared not oppose, as did the enemies of the ancient Scythians centuries earlier.

The American Indians the fifteenth century were no match for the Spanish invaders. Only the Pueblos in the Southwest successfully united to hold off their European enemies through many generations. Some differences among the tribes occurred because the later migrants brought new weapons, tools, and ideas they could adopt. Some developed their own improvements. In Mexico and Central and South America the Paleo-Indians were amazingly successfully in their irrigation and urban building projects. Did Egyptian and Middle Eastern builders themselves migrate to China and ultimately reach what is now Yucatán? Did they also bring the hairless canine of Mexico that historian David Taylor finds similar to Chinese Cresteds?

Most Paleo-Indian migrants to North America continued to live as hunters, declining to attempt agriculture except in the southern areas of the United States and in Mexico. Nor would they unite. "By the time of the European discovery of America," Farb writes, the migrants remaining within North America "existing in 276 tribes had worked out bewildering patterns of life and spoke more languages than are spoken in all of Europe."

The first Europeans to arrive in North America met a Stone Age people who added fishing to enrich their food supply, but planted little in a climate not congenial to domestic crops. Earliest among such visitors to leave a record were the Norse seamen who visited the shores of the New World at the beginning of the eleventh century. One group was led by Leif the Lucky, who by mistake sailed into a North American bay he would call "Vinland the Good," for the vines of a sweet grape he found there, on land where he thought he could successfully sow grain.

Leif's Norse crew remained grounded in Vinland for several months before he could return to take them to Greenland, his original goal. He planned to resupply a colony and thus may have had a few seagoing hounds with him, since canine bones have been found in that northern sea. Or the dogs may have been taken to the island even before the time of Leif by the Thornfinn Karlsefine, who is acclaimed in Scandinavian sagas for having introduced domestic cattle into America in about A.D. 1000. Dogs may also have come with Asians across the Bering Strait bridge and wandered east. The settlements of Leif and Karlsefine, like that of Columbus on Dominica and of the English on Roanoke Island, Virginia, disappeared, leaving little trace.

There is no actual record of Scandinavians bringing canines into America. The British may have left some of their seagoing hounds, but that too is doubtful. In 1577 Sir Martin Frobisher departed England to seek a northwest passage to China. Months later he reached land surrounding what has since been called Frobisher Bay. He had himself rowed ashore at the site of an Eskimo village. The Eskimos fled, but his men were discouraged from seizing booty by some forty Eskimo dogs, described as "Huskies." Frobisher's men managed to capture two puppies. A few years later, Captain John Davis, serving under Frobisher, took three ships into Baffin Bay and attempted to land some coursing hounds in an effort to get venison for his crews. The hounds, soft and fat from sea life, encountered native Eskimo dogs they refused to pursue. ("They waddled a few feet before lying down," their handlers reported.) The Eskimo Huskies, we may assume, came to America by way of the Berengia bridge and hybridized with wolves on their way east.

Large, seaworthy hounds could have been in the background of both the Newfoundland and, later, the Labrador Retriever. These large water dogs carried in their teeth the nets of cod fisherman, and probably reached Canada with Portuguese fishing fleets. In time, both Newfoundlands and Labradors became universally esteemed at all levels of society. Many were shipped out of Newfoundland to England, the world's leading market for dogs.

The Norse sailors themselves did not get far from the sea and thus saw few Indians. The Indians who traveled south, to where the latest of the glaciers advanced and then retreated, along the Ohio River in the United States, never numbered more than an estimated million or so, as compared with the 20 to 30 million said to have populated South and Central America and southern North America. Many southern tribes became advanced in agriculture, some bringing north several Mexican and Central American plants by the time European explorers and adventurers came to the New World. The Indians who welcomed the French to the site of Montreal and those who greeted the British at Plymouth, Roanoke, and coastal Virginia could teach the newcomers not only hunting lore and the uses of dogs in pioneer life, but also how to cultivate food crops. In the beginning the northern natives and the settlers became friends, and one of the early items of American barter was dogs, the Indians especially admiring the hunting dogs that arrived with the settlers.

⚭

In Central and South America, the beginning was not the same. The natives who met the Spaniards on the islands of the Caribbean and coastal America were primitive and curious if not friendly, but the Spaniards sought gold and they brought along their war dogs. These natives could supply quinine, cocoa, cotton, and sisal, and the Indians of Yucatán would provide maize, beans, potatoes, and turkeys. The Central Americans would add plants from which beverages and poisons could be made. But these Spaniards were not interested in agriculture. In time the inland people would be invaded and their high civilization, equal in visual grandeur to that of ancient Egypt, would be ravaged. The people had artifacts of fine gold, but they were reluctant to barter or to change their ways. The invading forces did it for them.

The rediscovery of America by Europeans occurred when native Genoan Christopher Columbus sailed with Spanish support in 1492 from the Canary Islands off the North African coast to San Salvador in the Caribbean, 2,700 miles

Kneeling Woman Kissing a Dog *(circa 1100–550 B.C.) is a fine example of the terra-cotta art of ancient Mexico. The piece, a happy evocation of affection, was discovered in a tomb at Tlacopan and may now be seen at the National Museum of Anthropology in Mexico City.* (Sketch by Mark Sandlin)

This sculpture of an Aztec Indian dog is in the collection of the Museum of Man, Paris. Mexican dogs, especially the hairless types, are believed to have ties to the Chinese Crested. (Sketch by Mark Sandlin)

away. Columbus was sure he had found a new route to the Indies. (He knew the world was round, having read literature on the subject, but perhaps, as J. Bronowski quipped, he just didn't know how big it was.) Columbus claimed San Salvador Island for Spain, returning to receive honors from Ferdinand and Isabella, his sponsors, who conferred rights and titles upon him. Later Columbus returned to the Caribbean with a fleet of seventeen ships, to establish colonies and to find gold. His men expected to see the precious metal lying about on the island beaches, where peaceful Arawak lived—people Columbus called Indians. He intended to establish a colony on Hispaniola (Dominica), but his men did not want to do that kind of work, nor did the natives. So force was used. Within fifty years the population of Hispaniola, estimated at 300,000, became nearly extinct. The colonizers had killed off the population or taken the young men and girls as slaves, shipping them to Europe since they didn't work well at home. More Spanish gold seekers arrived, with troops bringing their ubiquitous war dogs.

Vasco Nunuez de Balboa, commander of the Spanish force in Central America, crossed the Isthmus of Panama and viewed the Pacific, which he thought was the Indian Ocean; he reported to Spain the legends of vast stores of Inca gold and the success of his dogs in destroying Indians. Francisco Pizarro was given command of the Inca venture, and with ships built in Panama he invaded Peru in 1531. He captured and murdered the emperor who had welcomed him, and he then turned his troops and dogs on the people. Earlier, in 1519, the governor of Cuba commissioned Hernando Cortez to lead an expedition of eleven ships, five hundred fighting men, and their complement of dogs to take land in Mexico "to establish a trading post," as the mission was described. "His conquest of Mexico was one of the most amazing military and diplomatic feats in the world's history," writes historian Morison. Cortez and his Conquistadors destroyed the Aztec armies, captured the capital of Montezuma, and made Spain sovereign in Mexico and all land in the western half of what is now the United States.

The Spaniards employed their war dogs in subjugating the Indian people, attacking them in battle and destroying them when their forces took more prisoners than they could control. They also guarded the slaves put into the service of the Spanish military and gold seekers. Friar Bartolome de las Casas was one of the Spanish missionaries who had accompanied Columbus on his first voyage. He returned to lead his priests in their efforts to convert the Indians. In 1552 he wrote of his experiences in *A Relation of the First Voyages and Discoveries Made by the Spaniards in America with an Account of their unparallel 'd Cruelties on the Indians.* Las Casas was an eyewitness to the horrors the forces of Cortez inflicted on victims he described as "a weak and effeminate people not capable of great fatigues . . . their constitution is so nice as small sickness carries them off . . . they have a weakness and softness of Humor like that of Lambs."

His descriptions of the monstrous treatment of fellow humans are provided at length by C. W. Cerman in his book *The First American*. Las Casas, a Catholic bishop when he spoke publicly on the subject and his book was published, was widely denounced by his critics and called insane. He undoubtedly exaggerated the number of Indians killed by the Spanish forces, but perhaps meant to include those stricken by illnesses and lost in famine as a result of the depredations of the Conquistadors. But the death toll in South, Central, and southern North America reached into the millions, later scholars have written. Cerman himself writes, "Recent non-Spanish research has established that in the period of the conquest, between 15 million and 19 million Indians were exterminated. Though none of the figures may be exact, the fact remains, there were millions." [7]

The war dogs, obeying commands and kept from food to make them even more fierce than they had become in their military training, were of a breed that had been brought into Spain originally by the Roman army, so they probably descended from Persian Mastiffs and Greek Molossians. In the days of Spanish rule, smaller dogs, including various types of Basque Shepherds, were brought to America to tend livestock. They accompanied the Spaniards on their marches through Mexico to California and north along the Mississippi to the southern fringes of Illinois and Indiana. Horses and dogs were sometimes lost on the march or abandoned when invaders departed after failing to find gold. The Indians on the western plains thus acquired some of the animals they would use to hunt the buffalo and to protect their villages.

The Spaniards who came to settle the lands and to convert the Indians also left their beneficial heritage. Cities in Mexico and Central and South America became centers of culture and religion. The missionaries left monasteries and peaceful villages in the wake of the marauding Conquistadors and their dogs. The Spanish civilization would leave its imprint throughout the United States from Florida to California, Mexico, and throughout Central and South America, but the brutality of the Conquistadors and their dogs would never be forgotten.

∽⬿∾

The experience of dogs imported into Canada was of a happier kind. Again the canines arrived with the explorers and settlers. Attack dogs were needed but evidently were used by the French as the Indians used them—defensively. Many Indians fought long and well. The Iroquois in the North, the Sioux in the West, and the Tuscarora, Creek, and Cherokee in the South for a time more than matched the invaders, as did the Apache and Pueblo in the Southwest. The American plains Indians, once they acquired Spanish horses, could outride almost any horsemen except those found on the steppes of Asia.

The Indians forced the invaders to adopt their woodland warfare and even showed some knowledge of European military methods. Lieutenant Jefferson Davis, later president of the Confederacy, would credit the Sac-Fox chief Black Hawk with the most skillful maneuver of retreating forces he had ever witnessed. The hostile tribes of the Iroquois confederation constantly menaced the French, bringing even Montreal under attack. Historian Parkman, discussing general conditions in French Canada in his book *France and England in North America,* writes of the grave danger of Indian attacks on French settlements, including Montreal. "This danger was much diminished," he records, "when the colonists received from France a number of dogs, which proved most efficient sentinels and scouts."

The Indians also protected their camps and villages with dogs, sure to give the alarm in the endless warfare among the tribes, long before Europeans arrived. Parkman cites the story of a guard dog at Villemarie, as told by a Jesuit priest assigned there. "The writers of the time speak with astonishment of these animals," he wrote. An example of responsibility, diligence, and good sense was the instance of "a bitch named Pilot, who every morning made the rounds of the forest and fields about the fort, followed by a troop of her offspring. If one of them lagged behind, she bit him to remind him of his duty.

"When she discovered the Iroquois, she barked furiously and ran straight to the fort, followed by the rest." The Jesuit chronicler adds naively that while she was doing her duty, "her natural inclination was for hunting squirrels." Pilot aroused the fort that snowy March day while the Iroquois warriors slinking toward the fort from the east were a considerable distance away. "She was barking with unusual fury," Parkman wrote. "Chomeday de Maisonneuve, the French commander, sallied forth with thirty men—there were not enough snowshoes for more. He was as brave a Knight of the Cross as ever fought in Palestine. He got his men behind trees before the attack by eighty Iroquois with guns and bows and arrows." The French were driven back, but the Indians failed to pursue them under the guns of the fort. Villemarie was saved, and the road to Montreal kept open.

Parkman reports that the French planned to employ "a united force to drive the English from the Ohio, next attack the Dog tribe of Cherokees, who lived near the borders of Virginia." The French struggle with the English in the Seven Years War ended, however, with an English victory in Europe and with General James Wolfe's capture of Quebec, with the Cherokee joining French forces because they felt betrayed by their former English and American friends.

Montreal, nevertheless, would become the capital of a profitable Canadian-American fur trade, rivaling Buffalo, New York. From the city were sent fleets of freight canoes, built in the Chippewa style, manned by farm boys called voyageurs, led by experienced French and Scottish traders. Their pay was low. They powered their craft like ancient galley slaves, but they also sang their boat songs, and talked of "women, dogs, and boats," Parkman says, conceding that the lure of Indian women may have taken them into the fur trade from the start.

In the far north, around Hudson Bay, the voyageurs became the conductors of the dogsled teams that carried supplies to isolated trading posts, gathered firewood, and hauled furs south to stations where canoes could carry them back to La Chine and Montreal. The Indians themselves refused to work for the white station chiefs. They trapped and brought in skins themselves or awaited the arrival of the sled teams to their villages. These came in grand style, as described by Peter C. Newman in his history of the Canadian fur trade: "The voyageurs with their dogsleds decked out their animals in gaudy harnesses and embroidered fur coats, fitting them with tiny deerskin booties to protect their soft paws from cracked ice."

When the voyageurs got back to Montreal, after long stretches of duty in outposts among the Indian tribes, "Their arrival at La Chine (near Montreal) caused great excitement," Newman writes. "The wild appearance of the men and the distance they had come awakened sympathy for them, and hundreds went out (from Montreal) to see them." Newman interviewed an aging, retired voyageur who came to town after years in the Hudson Bay country. He had forgotten the rations of peas and salt pork, the hard times, and evidently had traded in furs a bit on his own, as a few succeeded in doing, far away from their managers. "No one had better wives, nor better harnessed nor swifter dogs that I did," boasted the old voyageur. "I had twelve wives, horses, and running dogs, trimmed in their finest style." He still lived in that grand manner, traveling from one Indian village to another. "He was probably the only voyageur who ever agreed to be interviewed," Newman tells us.[8]

In the War of Independence, little or nothing at all was said of war dogs. They were outmoded by modern arms and perhaps by the Indian style of fighting on the frontier, using silent ambush and stealth often copied by the colonists. Only two dogs appear to have made their way into the history books, one the unnamed canine that may have been the first casualty of actual, organized warfare following early skirmishes, the other a gentlemanly exchange between two generals, George Washington in command of the American forces and British commander William Howe.

Massachusetts Bay Province formed its independent government that met as a provincial congress at Concord in 1774. The formal fighting began in April 1775, when British general Thomas Gage dispatched Major John Pitcairn, commanding a strong detail, to destroy the rebel munitions dump at Concord on the night of April 17. Paul Revere of Boston and other riders alarmed the countryside. "Beginning in the late evening hours of April 17th, a British grenadier quietly hurrying to his assembly place in Boston, bayoneted a barking dog; the next morning at about 6 o'clock, Major Pitcairn at Concord found his horse was slightly wounded after a brief exchange of musketry at Lexington green . . . ." Thus goes the somewhat legendary story of the war's first fatal casualty.[9]

On July 2, 1776, General William Howe moved his British forces from Boston to New York City. General Washington, now commander-in-chief of the American forces, had 18,000 men in place around the city. On August 27, 1776, the Americans were defeated at the Battle of Long Island. During the battle, the small Terrier owned by Howe became lost between the lines. Washington's men found the little animal and identified it. Washington sent the dog back to Howe by an aide under a flag of truce.

The economic outlook was bleak for the thirteen American colonies at the end of their war for freedom. Thomas Jefferson, returning home to Monticello after serving as minister to France, found his own property in difficulties and turned to the task of getting it back in order before he would go to New York as President Washington's secretary of state. Jefferson wished to experiment on his farm to improve the American economy by growing products that the original settlers of Virginia had contemplated; actual trials had to be delayed until he could return from serving his country. Meantime he devoted much land to sheep, importing Bengal, Big-tail, Merino, and other breeds to improve his flocks. His letters concerning the outcome did not indicate much success.

Writing to his son-in-law Thomas Mann Randolph from Philadelphia on May 1, 1791, Jefferson complained: "I long to be free for pursuits of this kind AGRICULTURE instead of the detestable ones in which I am now laboring without pleasure to myself, or profit to others." He thanked Randolph for a promised gift of dogs. "I shall be glad to have a pair of puppies of the Shepherd's dog selected for the President," he wrote. But in later letters he continued unhappy with his flocks, his dogs in Virginia, and his management there generally. The wool was of poor quality, he said, and evidently the dogs were poorly trained. By now he had been chosen president of the United States, thus farming assumed an even lower priority.

In a letter from Washington, D.C., Jefferson instructed his overseer, Edmund Bacon, to add to the cotton acreage, and he also pre-emptorily ordered all but two of his sheepdogs destroyed, as they evidently attacked the sheep. "To secure wool enough, the negroes' dogs must all be killed," he wrote. "Do not spare a single one. If you keep a couple yourself it will be enough for the whole land. Let this be carried into execution immediately." Later, in 1813, however, Jefferson still had some of his dogs and problems with them at Monticello, but few sheep, and those widely scattered. "I have three distinct races which I keep at different places," he wrote to a friend named William Caruthers on March 12. "Merinos, of these I have but two. I have the Big-tail, or Barbarry sheep, I raise chiefly for the table. The large tail encumbers them in getting out of the way of dogs. I have a Spanish race, the ram I received from Spain in 1794. I sent my flock to a place I have in Bedford. If you should wish to get into this breed, and will accept a pair of lambs. . .you will be welcome to them." He kept his interest in dogs, writing his friend William Thornton, "I am much obliged for your kindness in reserving one of the sheepdogs for me."

The southern aristocracy generally had recovered from the war and was able to resume its favored recreations—hunting, riding to hounds, and coursing. Here there was ample work for their canines.

Swiftly, in comparison with developments taking five to ten thousand years in the Old World, the civilization of the Americas moved ahead. The revolt of the colonists demonstrated what many had long believed—that England was more interested in trade with the islands of the Caribbean than with the mainland colonies. Following the Revolutionary War, westward migration accelerated. Thomas Jefferson encouraged an agricultural America, and his policies were generally followed in that respect. Dogs were in demand on farms and ranches for stock and guard work and for sporting pursuits. Machinery took the place of many working dogs in the towns of the East, and they were no longer required in the cotton and cane fields of the South, other than to protect property and slaves. The principal demand for dogs came from the pioneer West.

The rapid rise of civilization in the new American nation was spurred by strife among the major governments of Europe. Western agricultural lands were opened, ores were discovered, and new agricultural products were entered into world trade, some originating in Mexico and the Caribbean. The American colonial exports had been limited largely to tobacco, rice, and grain as well as timber and staves, plus furs and some ores, including gold (prior to the Revolution). A century later, Americans were building ships, producing iron and steel in great volume, exporting barrels of flour and kegs of rum. Yet despite the complaints from New England about failure of the government to protect shipping, they were successfully running the European blockade with their swift American Clipper ships. Skilled migrants were now pouring into America. Carpenters, masons, shipwrights, smiths, and iron workers were needed in former colonial areas to build ships, rope walks, factories, and homes and to supply machinery for farms, cities, and villages.

꧁ꙮ꧂

As water power, wind power, steam, and expanding gases provided for the needs of growing populations in both the Old and New Worlds, the bulk of dogs' work again moved outdoors. The Industrial Revolution in Europe increased requirements for raw materials. The British went to France and Spain for wool for their textile mills and to America for cotton; in the Napoleonic era these countries turned to the United States even for wool.

Recreation and sports continued to stimulate the demand for dogs. Dogs also had entirely new jobs, among them searching for truffles in Italy and France (replacing the pigs that ate too much of their finds) and keeping down rats in palaces and warehouses. (Louis XVI was said to love to hunt rats with his dogs in his apartments.) Small Terriers, Schnauzers, and similar types also found employment as mousers in produce and general food markets until cats and the use of poisons later supplanted them. In America, the southern aristocracy again prospered, especially in Virginia and the Carolinas. Thousands of dogs were imported during periods of peace in Europe. Even the American Indians not dispossessed and moved out purchased imported hunting dogs.

ᏃᎳᎤᎤᎤ

Among the dispossessed were the earliest and most advanced of North American Archaic Indians, the Cherokee, whose territory extended over northwest Georgia and into Tennessee, Alabama, Virginia, and the Carolinas. They had been accomplished diplomats in their alliances and were more "civilized" than many of the immigrants who sought their land. Their independence as a nation had been "guaranteed" by the United States in a formal treaty in 1791. Most, however, were driven from their land onto barren places in Oklahoma in 1838. Some escaped into the hills and returned to create their own enclave in North Carolina, where they have reproduced Oconaluftee, a Cherokee town as it existed in the early eighteenth century.

The Cherokee of the Smoky Mountains area of North Carolina have a long, fascinating history. They may have created their flood legend in somewhat modern times after learning that James Adair, in his *History of the American Indians,* published in London in 1775, had written that Noah's Ark had come to rest in America. Adair also declared that American Indians represented the Lost Tribes of Israel, a view expressed by several early eighteenth century writers and theologians, including Ethan Smith, whose books were popular in America. Joseph Smith, writing his *Book of Mormon* as dictated by the angel Moroni, addressed Indians who had come to America from Jerusalem, though he did not say they were of the so-called Lost Tribes. But the lost-tribe legend has persisted, like that of the dog and the flood in the Middle East.

In archaeological digs in Tennessee and other areas once controlled by the Cherokee Nation, graves have been found indicating that some branches of the Archaic Cherokee frequently buried their notable dead. The bodies were carefully wrapped, if not embalmed in the Egyptian manner, with their dogs, as highly placed Egyptians did, according to anthropologists Thomas Lewis and Madeline Kneberg. The Cherokee worshiped a Trinity, the sun, the moon, and the high god Yowa. Like the Egyptians and Persians, they also revered a sacred number, seven. Their annual harvest ceremony was replete with "seven": Seven men hunted for the feast, seven women prepared it, seven kinds of wood were used for the sacred fire. The priest, dressed in white, led the people in singing the seven stanzas of a hymn dedicated to Yowa. The people sang and the village dogs, like dogs everywhere, howled.

How does it happen that ancient Sumerians and ancient Central Americans thousands of miles apart built similar tombs, temples, and ziggurats? Why do dark-skinned Fuegians, who live like Hottentots in the cold climate of Tierra del Fuego, look and dress like African Bushmen and Australian Bindibus? How does it happen that some branches of the Cherokee bury their dead somewhat in the manner of ancient Egyptians and chant the name of a high god similar in name to that of Hebrew tribes once enslaved in Egypt?

ᏋᎳᎣ

Kiwi is not permitted to visit the Oconaluftee Cherokee village in North Carolina, which simulates early eighteenth century days in the Piedmont of the Smokies and where the excellent Cherokee museum may be found, but my wife Martha and I and our friend geologist George De Vore were warmly welcomed. The Archaic Cherokee were a most civilized people 8,000 years ago and remain so. We spoke with a Wise Woman in the council house. (The Wise Woman, historically high in the councils of the Cherokee, helped diplomatically in times of crisis.) Did her people believe they had crossed the Bering Strait land bridge with their dogs, as suggested by parchments of the Iroquois found in the north? Might they represent a lost tribe of Israel? We were able to ask her a few questions, and here follow her replies.

"We respect the historians and the compliment to our people by those who believe we are related to biblical people," she said softly. "Many of our people became Christians in colonial times and are Christians today. We also believe that we were here in the beginning. Cherokee translates as 'Principal people' in the Archaic tongue. But all peoples may believe as they wish."

"Did your Archaic people seek burial with a favorite dog?"

"We have reason to believe that our people sometimes were buried with a dog or dogs. Since you speak of Archaic people, meaning 8,000 years ago, we may assume there was a religious connotation. Many of our people are Christians today. Some may still wish to be buried with their dogs."

"Do you recall the worship of Yowa, whose name is too sacred for utterance except by an authorized shaman?"

She nodded, pronouncing the sacred name softly, "Yoway. We remember the past. We were here originally."

Back home that evening, Kiwi welcomed us but she was concerned with her own miracle, the resurrection of a possum who, in apparent death, kept her attention for an hour, we were told, until our return distracted her. Then the possum, after the custom of his species, came suddenly and silently to life and fled.

"Okay, Kiwi, it's a small world," I comforted her. "Come on, I just saw a rabbit."

Some Native American tribes learned from the Spaniards the uses of dogs in warfare, as this woodcut clearly illustrates.

10

DOGS COME TO AMERICA

❦

A call to working dogs was heard in the Americas, the Caribbean Sea, and islands of the Pacific and Indian Oceans as new lands were opened in the worlds. The maritime nations with a desire for trade and exploration, gold and spices, sugar and rum, were scrambling for mercantile and colonial outposts as if land were in short supply. Most developing people didn't know that Paleolithic humankind had long since reached still other vast surfaces of the earth yet to be colonized and exploited. The Greco-Egyptian astronomer and geographer Ptolemy had long ago forecast the possibility that lands, perhaps an entire continent, might be found in the lower antipodes, *terra Australis Incognito*. In the late seventeenth century, Dutch and Portuguese mariners would find such lands confirmed, except for the biggest of all, the island continent Australis itself—narrowly missed though the Dutch came close. Captain Abel Tasman, sighting the New Zealand islands and touching Tasmania, proceeded to report and name them in 1642. A century and a quarter later British captain James Cook left Plymouth in the British Isles with copies of the navigational charts of Tasman to find new lands and possibly establish a landfall on an unknown southern land mass to be called Australia.

England had provided the skilled navigator Cook with a ship, charts, navigational instruments, scientists, and various missions and would send him three times into the South Pacific to map and claim lands and establish routes for possible commerce. But England seemed preoccupied elsewhere when Cook accomplished all that was required of him and more. England was having international difficulties much of the time. France, Holland, and Spain were fierce competitors in trade and the search for colonial sites, the competition culminating in costly wars. Ultimately French expansion in India and the Americas would be checked, Holland and Portugal would be limited to scattered colonies in Africa and the Pacific, and the Dutch would be blocked along the Hudson River in North America. But Spain stubbornly persisted in challenging England's power in the Caribbean and along the American coasts even after the defeat of the Spanish Armada by the British in 1588. Toward the end of the eighteenth century, when Cook was returning home to describe great opportunities to be seized in the South Pacific, England focused its attention on its rebelling colonies in America and the victories of Napoleon in Europe, and the nation prepared to fight again.

Mainland America had not been England's favored trading partner at any time except for naval stores—lumber for masts, cotton and hemp for ship rigging, and turpentine for paint were vital and were free of duty, but the sugar, rum, spices, and tobacco of the West Indies were the preferred products in England, or so the American colonists asserted. The British political quarrels with America were annoying, but the troubles at home with the Scots and Irish and local malcontents seemed beyond endurance. Times were not good in England, and the political troublemakers were portrayed in the newspapers and chap books as fighting dogs.

The dogs had a role in all the global competition of the time. Mercantile companies carried them about the world as they did African slaves and European indentured servants in the navies of competing powers. Dogs were needed wherever agriculture was practiced by incoming colonists and for hunting and protection. They were on guard duty in African slaving stations and to restrain and recover runaway slaves on American plantations in the South. They helped to keep order in convict towns and growing cities. The Spanish military brought into the Americas their horses and huge war dogs, called *perros de sangre* (dogs of blood), that were used in the subjection, and in some cases the extermination, of Indians in Mexico and Central and South America. Portuguese fishermen brought their water dogs into American waters, and many remained to hybridize with such canines as seen by navigator Martin Frobisher and his men, creating the famous Newfoundland breed.

The British would import dogs to herd sheep in the American colonies, as well as for use as retrievers and hunters. Holland and Germany shipped dogs along with immigrants into North America—mostly hunters that could take down large game along the Appalachian mountain frontiers. The French sent in military dogs that helped guard frontiers in Canada and Louisiana against hostile Indians, as historian Francis Parkman has noted. Arabs traded their hounds for spices, silk, maize, fine paper, and gunpowder in the Far East, where heads of state admired fine canines. There were wars worldwide, and dogs were kept busy as the century closed.

England appeared always to favor trade with its Caribbean colonies over that of its American plantations and settlements, thus causing the ultimate revolutionary rift. However, trade was resumed with the new United States following the War for Independence, especially in the South. There continued to be a demand for English as well as German, especially the German Shepherd and the Great Dane. The Great Dane is credited by some to Denmark and probably was descended from wolves and early domesticated Aureus dogs brought to the north or taken into Denmark and Germany by Lapps from Central Asia, who first entered Anatolia and then northern Europe. Such were the peregrinations of some canines in early days. Even the Indians of Virginia and the Carolinas in America wanted such dogs and came up with gold, tobacco, and furs to pay for them.

⌒⟋⟋⟍⟍⟋

Great Britain, a leader in the Industrial Revolution, continued in fierce competition with continental rivals for the world's export trade, including dogs, especially those of Germany. The Germans themselves initially obtained much of their canine breeding stock in foreign breeds from England. A notable exception was the Rottweiler, whose ancestors accompanied the Roman legions marching into lands of the Germanic tribes, as herd dogs caring for the army's sheep and cattle and to contain and control captured prisoners of war. Such dogs were so fierce and respected that cattlemen who later used the Rottweiler to take their herds to market tied their moneybags to the dogs' collars on the return trip. No thief would dare approach a Rottweiler, it was believed. The dogs were brought to America by German and other immigrants and were used in large cities as guards for riverboats and warehouses, and as draft dogs, guardians, and companions.

By July 1832, in the administration of President Andrew Jackson, immigration in America had increased considerably. Many dogs entered the country with their owners or were sold from ships without appearing on the manifests. The legal commercial trade in canines, mostly out of England, also expanded, supplying urban dwellers and farmers along the eastern coast who could afford blooded British imports.

The canines were particularly welcomed in what was then called the "Wild West," an area along the Mississippi River from Louisiana to western Wisconsin, where immigrants and war veterans were flooding into the government lands, obtained from the Indians and by Thomas Jefferson's Louisiana Purchase in 1803. Many immigrants were accustomed to having dogs with them at home, and thus required them on the frontier. Herdsmen and their dogs followed time-honored practices of their ancestors: Flocks and herds were created in the piedmont approaching the coastal mountains and endlessly pressed on west. As lands became overgrazed, farmers moved in to bid up prices, and townsmen followed.

Dog breeding increased as breeds with special talents were wanted in pioneer country. Stock dogs, of course, were essential, and any kind of Mastiff was suitable for guard work. Tracking Bloodhounds reared and trained in the South traveled through most states and territories, but especially to the Far West, where they aided federal marshals and county sheriffs in maintaining law and order. As more Central European immigrants arrived, German breeds in America gained in popularity. Many were strong, excellent hunters, could serve as stock dogs for small flocks or herds, and also could manage to draw sleds and carts over mountain roads in cold climates.

Artists' sketches preserved in collections and magazines and later by working photographers have provided a visual history of canines in the West. Some immigrants could afford to bring in their own dogs, as shown by *Scribner's Monthly* and *Harper's:* sketches of people from central Europe and the British Isles boarding ships with their dogs at Liverpool, Hamburg, or Le Havre for New York, or they were pictured on arrival at Ellis Island, having trouble with immigration officials as they attempted to sneak their pets into the country. Some evidently succeeded; many did not. A series of three sketches in *Scribner's Monthly* magazine tells the dog story of a trip made in 1877 that ended happily at a dollar-a-night hotel near the New York Battery: A weeping immigrant child was reunited with his pet.

Legally or illegally, thousands of immigrants and their canines entered America. Few family portraits were taken, whether in Eastern towns or in the Wild West, without dogs included. But photographers seeking general reportorial photographs avoided dogs whenever possible: The animals moved about, blurring the picture. They disturbed people, who were required not to move. Only a few canines sitting in carts, watching the photographer suspiciously, appear in E. H. Henry's great contribution to photo history—his coverage of boomtown Leavenworth, Kansas. His sharp, clear lens provides some of the best photography of the Old West. He caught dogs, clutched proudly by their owners, in many of his general Western scenes. Thereafter, when a dog appeared in any early Western photo, a child usually was holding it—an irresistible combination, as advertisers of goods for sale would discover. In photos taken of homeless children in New York City, a dog shares a windbreak with them, or a child shares a crust of bread with a scruffy canine friend.[1] *The London Illustrated News,* reporting on life of the newly rich in America, depicts a New York family and servants enjoying a Christmas vacation in St. Augustine, Florida. The two Rottweilers with the family loll on the carpeted floor of their splendidly furnished verandah.

Dogs played a significant role in the westward movement in the United States during the ninteenth century. They accompanied the covered wagons of waves of determined settlers, furnishing companionship, recreation, and protection of life and property. It was, however, a dangerous undertaking, and by 1830 trains powered by steam began replacing the "prairie schooner" for cross-country travel. (From *Harper's New Monthly,* June 1867; Courtesy The Westerners, Chicago)

During the War between the States, Matthew Brady, with his improved camera, demonstrated what could be done for history by good photography. A few stray dogs appear in Brady's pictures. His work was followed by wandering photographers who recorded history in the developing West, and canines again came into the historic record. Artists and practioners of the new art of photography showed dogs in their portrayal of American life, from Back Bay mansions in Boston to a blacksmith shop in Washington-on-the-Brazos, where a sentry is shown on guard with his dog "while a convention of Texans" gathered inside to mark readmission to the Union. Photographers continued to have troubles with dogs in motion. An entire naval training company has been known to have stood at near attention for a half hour as recently as 1942 until the cameraman could be assured that the company pet would stay motionless long enough for him to press his camera shutter. (The men refused to be photographed unless their adopted dog mascot would be included. I know—I was among them.)

Dogs traveled with Conestoga wagons en route to Missouri, Oregon, and, finally, California. They guarded the cattle and campsites and ran with scouts who were to make sure of the trail and that it was free of enemies. The dogs guarded tortilla makers and their children working beside their adobe homes while the Americans were storming San Antonio, according to scenes painted by artist Theodore Gentil. Dogs walked with the defeated Mexicans when General Winfield Scott led his mounted troops into Mexico City. There were no war dogs shown; they were outmoded, except as messengers. Hunting dogs traveled with the wagons and the cattle and aboard small boats of all kinds.

Fernand Mery, historian and celebrated French veterinarian, in *La Chien,* his excellent treatise on the dog and its history, credits the Americans with excellent care of their canines in return for their long and faithful service. "It is in America," he writes, "always at the forefront of progress, that concern for dogs, indicated by the affectionate interest shown in them by man, has provoked the setting up of an important and perfected network to insure their better care." He commends the veterinarians, clinics, hospitals, and laboratories of the United States and Canada—high praise since France led the way in the establishment of the first modern veterinary school at Lyon in 1762 and for a time would lead the world in veterinary science.

The practice of veterinary medicine, initially directed to cattle and other large farm animals, began in India, according to historian W. W. Armistead. "Of all ancient civilizations, India had the most distinct veterinary profession," he writes.

Some westbound migrants believed dogs could "smell" water, as Charles Darwin would later suggest. In this vignette titled A Desparate Situation *from* Century *magazine, a group of unfortunate travelers and their lead dog take stock of their plight. The artist's composition implies that the group is saved, however. In parts of the Southwest, it is still believed that a good dog can smell water.* (Courtesy The Westerners, Chicago)

Emigrants Crossing the Plains, *from* Picturesque America, *Vol. II, 1874, shows the ever-trustworthy lead dog in the vanguard of the group. When cameras were used to record historical milestones, dogs were often excluded, as they rarely would hold a pose for the photographer's count of ten.*

"The first veterinarian whose name was recorded was Salihotra, who lived about 1800 B.C. and achieved very high standards of practice for his time. During the reign of King Asoka, many well-equipped veterinary hospitals were built, the first in 238 B.C. But schools which taught veterinary medicine as a separate branch of learning . . . did not appear until the fifteenth century."[2]

⁂

The concept for animal hospitals may have followed the first known hospital, the Temple of Saite in Egypt, attended by dogs as well as priests. Armistead reports provisions for medical care for animals in the Code of Hammurabi, consisting of 282 articles for the governance of the Babylonian Empire, in 2200 B.C. They basically protected people and animals from unjust treatment. "The Veterinary Papyrus of Kahun, written in Egypt about 1900 B.C., contains the oldest known veterinary prescriptions," he writes. "But neither Babylonia nor ancient Egypt made any lasting contribution to veterinary medicine."

The Royal Veterinary College of London is said to have trained nearly all early veterinarians in America, with a few also training in France. Historian D. M. Drenan, also a former official of the American Animal Hospital Association, states that there were only fifteen graduate veterinarians in the United States in 1847. He reports that dogs accompanied the earliest European immigrants to America, "arriving on the Mayflower in 1620."

Known for his own work in controlling overpopulation of pets, a problem continuing to beset human populations that are fond of dogs, Drenan observes that American laws to control free-running canines were first enacted in Salem, Massachusetts, in 1644 and notes that the state of Pennsylvania was next to pass such laws, in the early 1800s.

"Obviously, some of these dogs were companions and were given the same medical care that was available for people," he continues. He adds a list of remedies used, though comments that many were of value "open to question." But pet owners, early on evidently recognized their responsibilities not only to their canines but also to their human neighbors. "Distemper and rabies were major worries for pet owners," Drenan writes. "Diseases were often caused by swine running wild in the streets of Boston." He notes that George Washington, in his diary in 1786, describes one of his hounds as "going mad and biting his servant's arm, although the dog's teeth did not penetrate the skin." The victim stayed at work and survived. Drenan credits Benjamin Bush, colonial physician and a signer of the Declaration of Independence, with writing an analysis of rabies causes for the first veterinary medical manual published in America.

"Two significant events occurred in the mid nineteenth century that had an effect on small animal medicine," he writes. "One was the organization of the United States Veterinary Medical Association in 1863 [becoming the AVMA in 1898] . . . that had direct influence on education standards that influence the care of pet animals. The second was the founding of the American Society for the Prevention of Cruelty to Animals by Henry Bergh in 1866." A union of local anti-cruelty and humane groups took place in Cleveland, Ohio, in 1877 with the organization of the American Humane Association as a clearinghouse for such organizations. In the next twenty-five years, says Drenan, small animal medicine made great strides as did the whole veterinary profession.[3]

Early in the twentieth century, interest in veterinary schools dropped as farmers and herdsmen could afford fencing and new machinery to help with their work. Railroads carried sheep and cattle to market, and gasoline-powered trucks replaced horse-drawn wagons. But, as Armistead points out, dogs were still required, as agriculture, including raising livestock, was extended into newly arable parts of the earth and the need for small animal maintenance vastly increased. "Medicine's future lay not so much with the horse as with food-producing animals and pets as populations increased," he writes. In midcentury, following the World Wars, it was realized that veterinarians in military service had done more than care for horses and dogs; they had been assigned a wide range of "health-related responsibilities," he reminds us. "After World War II, veterinarians were being graduated with a minimum of six years of college education. Subjects added to the schedules of veterinary schools included public health, epidemiology, laboratory research in animal diseases, toxicology, and animal hospital management."

Mery's estimation of American consideration for animals would be fully met in succeeding years. By 1993 there were more than 50,000 certified veterinarians in the United States and 13,175 animal hospitals.

ᏮᏯᏯᏉ

Increasingly canines were required in fields closely related to the care of the sick, infirm, and elderly. Johann Klein, author of a book on training dogs for guidance of the blind, opened the Institute for the Blind in Vienna in the nineteenth century. The first center for the training of dogs for the blind was established in

Potsdam, Germany, in 1916, primarily for the benefit of soldiers who lost their sight in World War I. German Shepherd dogs—renamed Alsatians by the Allied forces—won fame aiding the wounded in all the armies involved as that war ended, and were later called into peacetime training. A school for the training of dogs for the blind was opened in Nashville, Tennessee, in 1929 and later was moved to Morristown, New Jersey, where it became internationally known as the "Seeing Eye" school.

Future Seeing Eye dogs and the sightless humans they would serve were first trained separately for their planned partnership. The dogs, carefully selected for good health and temperament, first received a general education in deportment among humankind.

Communication among blind persons, attendants, and dogs is not a major difficulty as far as guide-dog training is concerned. but hearing dog trainers must have extensive training and experience in communication with the deaf. The applicant for a hearing dog must also qualify. "A person must be emotionally, physically and financially able to undertake this relationship," *The Hearing Journal* warns. "It might mean a commitment for the next ten years." Training such dogs can be expensive, though the dogs themselves are frequently contributed free to the training center. Some sponsors of training programs, such as the Florida Dog Guides for the Blind in Bradenton, make dogs available without charge, says Arlene Dickinson, manager. Contributions of dogs and cash cover the costs. The Directory of The American Humane Association, listing training centers, can be found in public libraries.

CXXXXO

Many thousands of dogs continue their service in the military forces and investigative agencies of most nations, and more are used by police departments, sheriffs, and various agencies employing the powerful canine sense of smell to find and aid those in need, sniff drugs and explosives, and trace and capture law breakers. During World War II, animals suitable to such duty were contributed to the armed forces of France, Great Britain, Canada, Australia, and New Zealand. Germany employed 60,000 dogs in military and police work and to guard concentration and prisoner-of-war camps. Following the war, great attention has been given to training dogs for all manner of rescue work in natural and manmade disasters. Wherever and whenever humans need help, these trained dogs and their handlers stand ready.

ᏩᏫᏃ

The future of the canine, working dog and pet alike, appears to be bright. Dogs will continue in their hereditary work, in agriculture for the most part, and they will be required in greater number as protectors, guides, guards, and caretakers of the young, elderly, and disadvantaged humans of every age. They undoubtedly will increasingly add to their roles in search and rescue, entertainment, communication (including advertising), and their paramount role of protector, friend, and playmate within the human family.

A new field of activity is developing on a wide scale—called "new" though it was in process in Egypt and Greece thousands of years ago. Those ancient canines served in temple hospitals, especially in Greece, not only as guardians of the institution but as healers to calm the patients. They soothed the sick, licked patients' wounds (with their supposedly hygenic tongues), and gave them hope of recovery. In recent years, properly trained and attended therapy dogs have been made welcome in hundreds of hospitals, nursing homes, shelters for abused persons, retreats for the elderly, and, recently, public schools. They have provided attention, affection, and other psychological benefits by their presence and behavior.

The work of the animals and their handlers has been the subject of numerous case studies demonstrating the effectiveness of canine influence. A University of Iowa study, designed to evaluate a dog's contribution to victims of one of the world's most difficult ailments, Alzheimer's disease, indicates the benefits of a canine presence for patients in an Iowa veterans' home. Researchers Kongable, Buckwalter, and Stolley observed the patients and measured eight categories of behavior under controlled conditions. The therapy dog first merely visited the patients once a week; later the animal lived with them. In both instances there were beneficial geropsychiatric results. Surprising was the conclusion that the patients benefited about equally during the course of periodic visits and during the course of the extended "live-in" visits. The benefits were measurable in all categories, and only two of twelve patients exhibited occasional negative reaction to the therapy dog. Other institutions have covered various aspects of canine help in health improvement and control of various psychiatric disturbances, generally and in specific cases. J. M. Siegel's study of the benefits of canine visits to 938 Medicare enrollees showed benefits of stress reduction for the patients visited and also for the visiting dog's owners. Other animals also were used, but "the dogs, more than any other pets, provided their owners and patients with companionship and as an object of attachment," Siegel writes.[4]

Kathy Diamond Davis, who does therapy-dog work, advises those who wish to engage in the contribution of "four-footed therapy" to seek advice as to the training and handling of the animal.

The benefits dogs can provide for the ill, elderly, and disadvantaged are many, some psychological. University of California writers report in *Child Development,* December 1989, a survey of benefits for children and add, "While service dogs are known to perform important tasks, such as retrieving dropped items or pulling a wheelchair, they may also serve [the elderly] as an antidote for social ostracism. Adults in wheelchairs are known to receive many more social acknowledgments when a service dog is present than when no dog is present. *The Journal of Behavioral Medicine,* October 1988, reports: "Recent research on human-dog interactions showed that talking to and petting a dog are accompanied by lower blood pressure in the person than in human conversation. Blood pressure levels are lower and heart rates are lower when petting or talking to the dog." The tests were conducted by J. R. Vormbrock and J. M. Grossberg at the University of North Carolina.

⚬〜〜〜⚬

In 1910, Thomas Hunt Morgan of Columbia University in New York would change the world's conception of human and animal behavior when he discovered a means for reading the secrets of chromosomes in the blood of mammals. He found that ordinary fruit flies could produce new generations so rapidly that a thousand-year evolutinary span and possible change could be studied in a few weeks using the flies. He learned he could map the four pairs of chromosomes carried by the fruit fly that determined its characteristics. He and a few assistants bred millions of the fruit flies in their research, and H. J. Muller, in his "fly squad," using ultramicroscopic X-rays, bombarded the flies, causing mutations and revealing the secrets of their genes. The genes, in a complex process, produced a chemical composition called deoxyribononucleic acid, or DNA, that assembled amino acids which control the structure of the genes.

Marshall Nirenberg of the National Institute of Health solved the code of one amino acid, producing ribonucleic acid, or RNA. Ruth Moore, in her book *Evolution*, likens and differentiates the two: DNA "is an architect's master plan, preserved and guarded, and RNA, like a blueprint, is used for everyday work."

The various studies indicate that dogs may be relied upon for a certain level of predictable response in the performance of their duties based on a genetic behavior pattern. This pattern is traceable to the beginning of dogs' association with humankind, with allowance for mutations and environmental change. Study of genetic behavior resulting from the discoveries of the influence of chromosomes and the control of genetic pattern by DNA and RNA can forecast the likely behavior of all living organisms. For the future of dog breeding, the applications of DNA and RNA could impact the well-being and utility of our canine partners in ways and to extents hitherto unimagined.

A research project now under way in California, called Dog Genome Initiative, is expected to develop information on the varying DNA and RNA of the dog breeds that determine genetic behavior. Results are expected as this book goes to print. Jasper Rine of the University of California, who heads the research project, disclosed the details in a lecture at the National Institute of Health in early 1993. The project is being conducted in the U.S. Department of Energy's Lawrence Livermore Laboratory in Berkeley, California. The dogs, Border Collies and Newfoundlands, will provide "about seventy third-generation descendants" for the tests. Border Collies are widely known for their endurance and intelligence in working with livestock. The Newfoundland, famed for its rescue work at sea and for retrieving fishing nets along the Newfoundland coast by swimming out to seize the lines, is known for its courage and gentleness. "I think we will even be able to gain access to genes that control behavior and personality," Rine reported.

Various dog breeds have been deliberately emphasized by human control over breeding for many years. Traits such as loyalty, reliability, responsibility, affection, and aggression have been sought in these breeding programs. Genetically controlled traits such as dogs' incredibly superior sense of smell, protective instincts, and adaptability to close relationships with mankind have been safeguarded in breeding to the extent of existing knowledge. The Genome project is expected to extend that knowledge.

Rine summarizes the Dog Genome Initiative as an attempt to match breed differences with variations in dog DNA. The DNA and RNA acids can be "seen" only under an electronic microscope. The wire model constructed by scientists looks like a spiral staircase, Moore suggests. The effect is to dictate the order of amino acids that "determine the 'shape' and specific gravity of proteins . . . that dictate the forms of living things . . . [and] control life's infinite variety," she explains. Hereditary diseases, caused by aberrant behavior of DNA, may come under control of man: "Even the physical course of evolution might be influenced . . . ." The role of the Genome dogs is an immense one.

However, man cannot be sure of an ability to change dogs' behavior by genetic control though much can be done by selective breeding, Rine has conceded. Inherent instincts as well as mutations do occur: "The Beagle's free-spirited love of wandering away is the result of a gene or a group of genes. You can take a Beagle at birth and give him to a female sheepdog to raise, and when he is grown he will not behave like a sheepdog. He will have a Beagle's wanderlust, and he will always be gone off to God knows where."

But control has worked with hunting dogs. "Dogs bred for use by hunting clubs have to be willing to hunt with any member," he said. "Those that were attached to an individual were not suitable. Some of the wonderful hunting dogs in the club you visit are in fact probably loyal-minus mutants."

What may the Dog Genome Initiative accomplish?

"Complicated behaviors such as herding may break down into individual components, different genes or groups of genes for such activities as showing eye, crouching or opening the mouth," he suggests. As an example, breeding patterns may change when large predators are no longer a significant threat to livestock. Smaller, faster, more adaptable canines, such as Border Collies, fit the need where traffic is heavier, and "heading" (one or two dogs taking responsibility for a large flock) principles of herding can be used.

Karl von Frisch, a famed biologist who has studied dogs, tells us that the sense of smell is greater in dogs than any other animal ever scientifically tested. "The dog," he writes, "can perceive certain scents in dilutions a million times below our own threshold." We continue to use the dog's acute sense of smell as an aid in hunting and protection, and in such military applications as sniffing explosives and dangerous gasses. This primary skill is also employed in discouraging and preventing illegal commerce, such as drug trafficking. Thus patrol dogs, first used in modern times by European police, continue to be widely employed in civilized nations to find, track, and capture law breakers.

Such trained dogs protect humankind in millions of private and public places. At the Tribune Tower in Chicago, dogs have been employed as buiding guards. Paul Stellato, director of corporate security for the widely spread Tribune Properties, says his canines are preferred over armed guards "because they are a non-lethal weapon." Larry Reynolds, trainer of the dogs, had experience with canine patrols in Vietnam. "It was truly arduous duty for the canines," he recalls. "We had about a thirty-five percent casualty rate among dogs searching for booby-traps and buried bombs. The war dogs saved the lives of many of our troops." Guard dogs today continue to save civilian lives, while keeping order, deterring possible criminal trespass, and protecting property.

～

While war dogs no longer do much fighting in the world's armies, they continue to be needed by the military. Mery estimates that 15,000 canines were called into service by Allied forces during World War I, and almost one-third were killed in action. In World War II, Germany alone used 60,000 dogs trained by the military, to guard munitions plants, war factories, prisons, and concentration camps, as well as finding use on patrol among the public and on the front lines. The French employed their dogs to carry messages, munitions, and medical supplies to the front lines, "and also to catch rats," recalls Mery, himself an organizer of the French canine corps.

"During the Second World War," he writes, "the Russian army employed dogs in true kamikaze fashion. The dogs were deliberately kept starved, then trained to enter armored vehicles to obtain food. Borrowing from the technique of their countryman, Ivan Pavlov, the Russians used the conditioned reflex to get the same dogs to enter enemy vehicles, again in search of food. This time, however, electro-magnetic mines were strapped to the dogs' backs."

Pavlov's experiments on dogs to obtain data on "conditioned reflexes" won the scientist world fame but were said to be almost as cruel for the canines as the armored car killings. Pavlov surgically introduced tubes into the gullets and stomachs of laboratory dogs. When the animals healed and were fed, the food did not reach the stomach, but pure gastric juices flowed and were drained for testing. Various stimuli caused the "conditioned reflex," including the sounding of a piano note. A familiar note, signifying feeding time, caused the gastric juices to flow. The "conditioned reflex" was demonstrated. Years later Karl von Frisch describes other experiments less harmful to the dogs providing similar data. The Russian military conditioned their dogs to expect to find food in every armored car, a kamikaze kind of sacrifice matching those of the Hittites and Persians, who sent dogs with baskets of "Greek fire" strapped to their backs into the enemy cavalry lines.

The war dogs died for their respective countries by many thousands in World War II, but one is known to have achieved honor and appreciation while living to enjoy it. The German military had specially trained a few dogs, described as "giant wolfhounds," for duty under a plan to kidnap Marshal Tito (General Joseph Broz of Yugoslavia), whose forces were holding back the Germans in an area of choice industrial plants they wished to take unharmed, in order to use them in supplying their own armed forces.

One such dog went into action where Tito was reconnoitering. The dog penetrated beyond enemy lines, and Tito's men captured it. The dog was taken to the commander-in-chief, in this case, Tito. The commander and the dog he would call Tiger became instant friends. Thereafter, writes Fitzroy McClean (the British agent who parachuted in from a bomber to bring a message of support from British prime minister Winston Churchill), Tiger devotedly served Tito, whom the Germans had hoped to capture. McClean recalls, in his book *Eastern Approaches,* "Tito had two other bodyguards, but Tiger was his closest companion." The marshal's staff arrived for a conference with the British agent, but all of them kept their distance from Tiger. "He was in a bad temper," McClean remembers. [5]

Mery praises the work of American K-9 Corps dogs used in Vietnam, especially in finding enemy ammunition caches, which they discovered by sense of smell. On my own journalistic visits to areas under enemy attack, I saw no war dogs in captured areas, nor among the South Vietnamese population generally, though canines are known to have lived among the boat people in early times.

Americans brought their dogs along from the start of action in the recent Desert Storm conflict, some seen by the world's television viewers when they dropped with parachute troops into the American embassy grounds in Kuwait City to sniff out hidden explosives. Fewer than 200 American canines were in action in the Middle East, none of them lost. The French fielded "a division of 1,177 highly trained canines," most of them German Shepherds serving as "mobile radars," patrolling grounds where the French Jaguar planes were parked. "They know the scent of their comrades," said Alain Colorado, commander of the division. "They can detect an intruder." The Israelis use dogs as well. While Saddam Hussein of Iraq was sending Scud missiles into Israel, the Israelis protected their "civilian" dogs as well as their children from chemical warfare by placing them in special portable aluminum compartments until the "all-clear" was sounded. Meantime, the Israeli military dogs were on alert.

In all nations, dogs' military work goes on. In the early dawn on October 3, 1993, a line of lean canines and their Black Beret handlers could be seen moving swiftly and silently toward an entrance to the Russian parliament building in Moscow, where rebel legislators had held out since September 24. On the Kalininsky Bridge a quarter of a mile distant, a T-22 tank opened fire. The headquarters room of hard-line rebels on the thirteenth floor took a direct hit. The dogs and President Boris Yeltsin's loyal assault troops began the ten-hour battle that would end the threat of revolution and civil war. Vice President Alexander Rutskoi and Speaker Ruslan Khasbulatov, leaders of the rebels, were taken prisoner. Again the Russian war dogs had done their duty, as had seven canines sent into orbit in Russian rockets in the mid twentieth century. (Only two survived, parachuting safely to earth; poison pills mercifully dispatched the others before re-entry.)

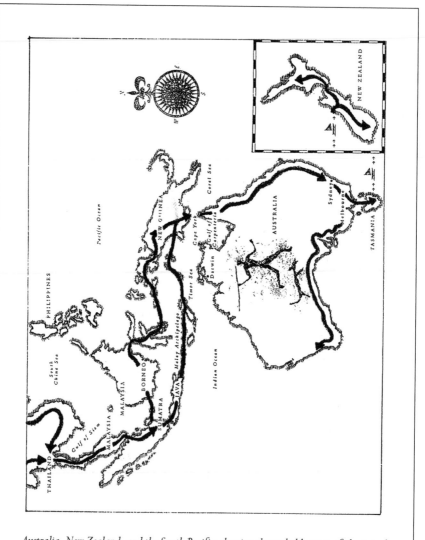

Australia, New Zealand, and the South Pacific: showing the probable route of aboriginal peoples that settled in these areas.

11

END OF THE ODYSSEY—TO AUSTRALIA
AND NEW ZEALAND

ⱺℳℒ℗

Early southeast Asians traveling ever farther south about 30,000 years ago by way of South Pacific island "stepping stones" to New Guinea and Australia found something less than paradise when they reached what would be called Arnhemland on the Gulf of Carpentaria. They were in the tropical north of Australia, having walked to the Cape of York by a land bridge from New Guinea. It may have seemed like home in the genetic memory of many, home in the highlands of Kenya and Ethiopia back in equatorial Africa. They came with Stone Age tool kits, and some would continue south across the island continent to another island (then land-connected), Tasmania. They arrived early, probably more than 30,000 years ago. "The Tasmanian tool kit packed such typical Australian items as the spear-thrower, boomerang, shield, axe, and adze," historian D. J. Mulvaney writes in his *Prehistory of Australia*. "Stone tools apparently consisted of hand-grasped flakes, cores, or pebbles, and though these reflect skillful shaping, techniques of grinding and delicate blade production was unknown . . . . They used wooden spears and clubs. Tasmanians lacked the company of Dingoes. It is evident that many colonized Australia during an epoch of the larger fauna and that they possibly co-existed."[1]

Mulvaney tells us much in that brief summary. The earliest known people to arrive in the farthest extension of land south of Asia did not equal in their culture those tribal members whose artifacts were found by the Leakeys and others in East Kenya. Thus the earliest Australians evidently began their trek out of Africa

---

in a migration that passed through Kenya about 100,000 years ago, and continued on without acquiring hunting dogs, the people surviving as scavengers following a variety of predators. Such scavengers are known to still exist today in the Middle East, India, and Australia. Without dogs to help bring down big game, the early Stone Age people spent their time foraging and collecting food, with no time to develop tools and weapons beyond the kind found in Tasmania about 70,000 years later. Why did they walk halfway around the world? They probably were pushed by environmental changes and the pressure of other tribes' having dogs and improved weapons. At long last those defenseless people reached a land where there would be no human enemies and the only predators were crocodiles. Small marsupials, small flightless birds, abundant fish, insects, and slugs provided their food needs.

"Tasmanians lacked the company of Dingoes . . . but evidently not by choice," Mulvaney writes. Later arrivals did bring such dogs into Tasmania, their fossil bones dating 8,000 years ago. Their coats were tan or a patchwork of colors, black, white, yellow, and tan, as seen in Australia today, the latter colors matching those of African wild dogs, though Bindibu dogs appear to be descendants of the African Greyhound types. The earliest of the settlers may not have brought in canines, or they may have used them as food in the final days of passage across the island stepping stones into New Guinea. Later migrants, a Mesolithic people with dogs, reached Australia near Cape York. They settled in the mountains above the Afura Sea, and the rock shelter art and tool kits they left behind have been dated back 20,000 years. Some probably walked from New Guinea even earlier, and more came later by raft and canoe when the glaciers melted and raised the oceans.

Later Neolithic peoples brought their Asian dogs and more efficient weapons: the bow and arrow and their own invention, the boomerang. They lived in the warm, northern climate with their hunting hounds as they continue to do today, recording on the escarpments of their rugged land their "dream time" experiences of a timeless past. They have been "discovered" in modern times by Dutch, British, and American explorers but managed for centuries to generally evade close contact with intruders, until World War II brought in the scouting forces of Australia and its allies to block the threatened advance of Japanese forces. The Japanese losses in the Battle of the Coral Sea in May 1942 reduced that threat. In the twentieth century, scientists from the Museum of Natural History in Chicago reported on natives called the Bindibu, described as "the world's most primitive people," who survived there in the wet lowlands and western desert beyond the mountains.

The Bindibu, hunting naked with their Dingoes, had arrived in a perverse land where climate changes were severe and unpredictable. The native animals were totally unfamiliar; the north was warm and humid, and the south was cool and dry. But these hunters with their dogs and improved weapons could kill kangaroos and flightless birds. Unlike earlier wanderers, these travelers chose to stay in Arnhemland and the desert beyond.

⌒⚭⌒

The island continent where the Asian migrants settled, like other islands of the South Pacific, had drifted away from a super-continent called Gondwana, a continental mass that about 65,000 years earlier included Africa, Eurasia, and the Americas. In the second century B.C., the Egyptian geographer and astronomer Ptolemy assumed that the earth was global and that vast lands existed in a distant south. Dutch and Portuguese navigators confirmed this in modern times. The Asian aborigines who preceded them did not keep astronomical track of time, but carbon-dating fixes the time of their ancient work in the Arnhemland caves. Hunters and explorers who visit these aborigines today marvel at their endurance and contentment in a difficult, forbidding wilderness. Their carved sculpture and handsome bark paintings are being created in an increasingly civilized state, now a part of the organized commonwealth, and are shown in museums worldwide.[2]

Stone Age fossils found in the Mount Burr area in South Australia, dating between 7,000 and 8,000 years old, indicate that aborigines with Dingoes had crossed to the island continent in the north, many settling in the tropics, while others later moved south to cooler regions. The dogs evidently found little to hunt on the trip south, as the inland plains were dry and windy. The Asians and, later, Europeans made conditions worse by using fire in their attempts to hunt the kangaroo and caused further destruction of flora by introducing sheep, cattle, and rabbits, the latter the worst scourge of all.

Many Dingoes returned to the wild and subsequently were blamed for the destruction of other wildlife. "Possibly the most serious blow to the conservation of native fauna in the prehistoric Australia was the introduction of the Aboriginal dog, the Dingo," Mulvaney writes. He adds, however, "There is no evidence of its presence during the Pleistocene [the Ice Age] that also destroyed both flora and fauna probably prior to the detachment of Australia from Gondwana. Their later role in eliminating the smaller species . . . cannot be underestimated. It is unlikely that hunters could eliminate game totally over the continent, and the Dingo was a later-comer [15,000 years ago]. It seems probable that the solution lies in a vegetational change induced by human activities which affected herbivores and flightless birds."

Thus, the Australian Dingo, like the American coyote, stands accused and partly absolved. They did well the work allotted to them by nature. Mulvaney's "indictment" is somewhat equivocal, nor does he mention another destructive possibility, sheep and cattle herding, in which domestic dogs with some Dingo blood served. The rabbits introduced for "sport" and "a change of diet" also devastated the ecology. When the verdict on the dogs was turned in by New Zealand years ago, it was "not guilty." And Mulvaney, in final evaluation of the domestic dogs on the island continent, concludes approvingly that "in Australia, of the one thousand generations of men that have elapsed, at least the last three hundred of them have had the companionship of the dog." He then adds, somewhat begrudgingly, "The Dingoes [that] they introduced but apparently never fully domesticated ate more of the master's food than he retrieved for them." It is true that in Australia there were not many game animals, but the Bindibu and other aboriginal tribes still needed dogs in the hunt.

Fernand Mery gives somewhat higher marks to the Dingo. "Certainly this very beautiful, intelligent and brave . . . dog is only to be found in Australia . . . surprisingly, as it is the only higher animal on a continent inhabited exclusively by placental mammals," he said. "It is tempting to believe that the Dingo is descended from the Phu Quoc dogs of eastern Asia and was brought to Australia by seafaring men. Ill-adapted, decimated by disease and the habits of nomadic hunters, these men disappeared, but the dog remained behind and, in order to survive, reverted to the wild.

"Explorers studying the habits of native tribes around the River Herbert," he continues, "noticed the primitive people liked very young Dingoes. They reared them patiently, caring for them as for their children, and kept the pups with them when they pitched camp. When the young Dingoes are fully grown, the natives use them, without schooling, to hunt. The Dingo cooperates with man, but it never becomes fully attached."

Generally the Dingo has been helpful to primitive hunters in Australia. Interestingly, today's residents of the Australian north country, as far south as

Brisbane, report occasional sightings of Dingoes that are not the usual tan in color, but a patchwork of yellow, orange, white, and black—the coloring of many African wild dogs. Such dogs continue to hunt with the Bindibu and may be of Indian, Chinese, or African origin. "The Dingo has been a valuable animal, keen-scented, reliable on the hunt," reports an explorer among the Bindibu. "Temperamental, too, sometimes refusing to go on, so the native hunter carries it on his shoulders. The hunter never complains."

In Queensland it is common to find aboriginal children receiving and keeping as pets the pups of wild Dingoes found in burrows or hollow trees. "In southern [colder] areas, the family slept with its dogs. Few of the aborigines wore any kind of clothing. On a chilly night, three to six dogs might sleep with their nearly naked human family."

The aboriginal loved his dog. Journalist Freeman Lloyd, reporting in *National Geographic* magazine, cites an aboriginal hunter in Queensland with his wives and hunting dogs, asleep together after feasting on proceeds of a successful hunt, "their stomachs distended . . . embers of three fires still warm, found spears leaning against a tree. . . . Here was a living picture of primitive savages with their canine allies."

How did the partnership begin? Lloyd provides a Bindibu legend from the seared central-western desert of Australia: The earth split in two shortly after creation. Man was left on one side, animals on the other. No four-footed animal minded except the dog. He ran up and down, whimpering, seeking a way across. At last the dog leaped and caught the edge of man's side, but began slipping down. Man then pulled the dog to safety beside him. "You shall be my companion forever," man said.

The first of the domestic dogs to accompany the hunter into Australia must have found life perplexing. Most of the marsupials inhabiting the place were too peaceful to be worth chasing, and one variety, the kangaroo, was too evasive and sometimes downright dangerous, while possums, koalas, and marsupial rodents could be had for the taking. Discontented Dingoes went back to their wild state in vast numbers and would cause endless trouble when Europeans finally discovered Australia and brought in domestic livestock. Wild dogs earned the hatred of the new immigrants, though many of the canines continued to join the naked Bindibu in the hunt and to play as puppies with Bindibu children and to help warm aborigine families who wandered into the cold temperatures of the south.

Early Caucasian settlers in Australia and New Zealand experienced difficulties with the native fauna and bred Kangaroo Hounds to keep wildlife under control. (Alexander Turnbull Library, Wellington, New Zealand)

In time, the Dingoes would help control the rabbit scourge brought on by the European immigrants themselves. Settlers imported rabbits for their favorite sports, pack hunting and coursing, and as a change from a dull diet of fish. The rabbits, finding themselves in a new environment, nibbled the ground bare and had to be destroyed. Dingoes, imported Greyhounds, and other European dog breeds spent several satisfying years checking the rabbit population. Eventually cattlemen in Australia introduced a line of Dingo blood into Basque and Scottish shepherd dogs to create a tough, small Australian cattle dog that would develop the fierce tenacity and intelligence characteristic of that modern breed, possessing ability to nip the meanest bull in the herd and to control the sheep with the skill of a Lapp hound among Arctic reindeer. Herding history would be revised upward by such Dingo hybrids, especially those with a bit of Kelpie added in Australia and New Zealand. In time Australia created the Kangaroo dog, a manufactured sighthound— big, bony, and "as fierce as a tiger"— that could bring down both kangaroos and wild dogs. They ultimately were introduced into New Zealand to destroy rabbits and remaining Maori "wild dogs."

ᏅᎿᎻᏅ

The circumnavigation of the globe by humans traveling with dogs was completed in 1769 when a pair of English hounds traveled to New Zealand and Australia with Joseph Banks, a young British botanist. They sailed aboard the *Endeavour* with Captain James Cook, commissioned to make navigational and botanical studies in the South Pacific. The group of botanists were passengers put aboard by the Royal Society, and Banks, a wealthy adventurer and avid hunter, brought along his household servants and his dogs.

Captain James Cook, whose navigational fame ranks with Abel Tasman, Vasco de Gama, Ferdinand Magellan, and Christopher Columbus, set sail from Plymouth, England, on August 27, 1768. After calling at the Canary Islands off North Africa and a brief stop in Rio de Janiero in Brazil, Cook rounded Cape Horn at the tip of South America, skirted the rim of Antarctica, and headed for Tahiti. There he set up transit equipment to correct his set of Tasman's charts.

Cook, on his own course to New Zealand, reached a cape at forty degrees south latitude, where hostile natives in double-hulled war canoes came out to meet him. Their chieftain's aides carried staffs bearing white tails of animals that botanist Solander, reporting the incident, had learned were from sacred Maori white dogs, called Kuri. The chief wore a splendid cape made of the skins of such dogs, and his warriors brandished spears and clubs decorated with white dog hair. Cook held off after one native had been shot. The huge Maori war canoes carried 200 men; Cook could muster only 88. His mission was not combative but to map the coastlines of the islands that Tasman had merely touched yet had named for his homeland and himself.

In a warm December, Cook rounded the northern tip of North Island, and in January 1770, he took advantage of summer temperatures to replenish water and food supplies and clean ship. Banks probably got his dogs ashore at that time if not earlier. Cook named his stopping place Queen Charlotte Sound, for England's royal lady. In early April 1770, Cook set out on a northwesterly course to Tasman's island. After three weeks of sailing, the lookouts saw the lurid lights of campfires ashore, and the following day *Endeavour* dropped anchor in a fine harbor. Banks and his botanists found so many plants that Cook would name the location Botany Bay after the abundance. The dark-skinned aborigines were not hostile in the beginning; they simply ignored the ship and its crew as though they didn't exist. Banks evidently took his dogs ashore with the botany team since they brought back kangaroos, "enough for the ship's company," Solander reported. "The meat tasted like venison." It would become the staple food for explorers of Australia and the settlers who followed. The hunter and his domestic dogs had encircled the earth.

Eighteen years later the first free settlers from Europe arrived in Australia, the island continent that Cook had claimed for the British Crown and carefully mapped along its eastern coast. England was having troubles with its fractious colonies in America and showed little interest in exploiting the half of Australia it claimed. In time it resumed a policy once tried in America—sending its debtors and convicted law breakers to the most distant land it owned, New South Wales in Australia. The site of Botany Bay was chosen for a first settlement. It would become part of the beautiful city of Sydney in the century following, and was pleasant enough at the start, situated on the sea coast in a temperate latitude. Soon farmers and adventurers, dissatisfied with religious strife, wars, and life in general in the Old World, arrived from England and other European lands. Some had become enchanted with Cook's descriptions of the woods and meadows along the Australian coast, where farming and sheep and cattle runs beckoned and hunting was good, but most found only sandy beaches, interior deserts, limited trees suitable for masts, and little to hunt but the elusive kangaroo. Yet Sydney became a growing town as whalers and traders found subsistence there.

Fifty years after Cook's arrival at Botany Bay, the free settlers in Australia numbered only 1,307 persons, but explorers had ventured inland, some had circumnavigated the coast, showing Australia to be an island, and John MacArthur, a naval lieutenant attached to the New South Wales Corps, had introduced domestic sheep in 1797. Sheep, cattle, dogs, whaling, lumber, and mining in time would change Australia into a land of fabulous entrepreneurs and a tough, redoubtable people who would show the world the way to political independence and reform. Yet there were many problems. The land was relatively benign and beautiful along the coast, but only the whaling industry could make a quick start as the sole producer of import revenue until MacArthur brought Merino sheep into the country and until gold was found inland a half-century later. Early shepherds saw little land immediately adaptable to their flocks. Water was limited, and wild dogs roamed and attacked the sheep. The distance to world markets was great. The importation of convicts increased. Some escaped to become outlaws and squatters who conducted guerrilla war against the "aboriginals." European settlers brought with them the scourge of rabbits, along with rats like those carried everywhere around the globe in unclean ships.

Farm work in Australia from the beginning was hard. The English and Scottish immigrants who in early years began to find ways to get water in the desert "outback" had first to drive out nomadic aboriginals, then dig wells to find artesian supplies, and finally protect their sheep or cattle from the threat of wild dogs. The livestock imported from Europe was subject to disease in the new environment, and few trained shepherds and no veterinarians were available. The incoming shepherd was among the first of the settlers to meet the native tribes who were being deprived of their hunting grounds in the limited arable land, and the tribesmen themselves raided all settlers. The land that was not actual desert was covered with a vegetation that absorbed the limited water supply and had to be cleared. The shepherd in the beginning worked with few or no domestic dogs. There was little wood for fencing; flocks had to be kept apart to retain identity of ownership and to avoid the spread of disease. The shepherd usually was required to take his flock miles into the bush and often for weeks could not return to his station.

The importing of dogs improved the lives and income of the sheepmen. Cattle were also introduced when lands in the north having more moisture were taken from the aboriginal tribes. Scottish stock dogs, as well as breeds from England and Wales, were brought in. Cattlemen adapted these breeds by introducing Dingo blood, giving their animals added toughness and stronger jaws that enabled them to nip and control cattle and horses as well as stubborn sheep. They became known as Australian Heelers or Cattle Dogs—small, tough, and intelligent.

⟲⟳

Life in Australia was difficult. The beginning population came from the impoverished classes of England. When the first census was taken in 1828, the population numbered 36,590, with possibly a few thousand unaccounted for in the desert outback and 300,000 estimated aborigines in the tropical north.

From the beginning, the new distant colony of Australia, like some of England's American possessions, had been populated largely by men, with few women and fewer children (mostly those who had "failed" at home, victims of incredibly harsh British "peer laws"). Many were accused simply of failing to pay their debts, of vagrancy, or of minor misbehavior such as petty theft or loitering at work; others stood convicted of actual offenses against the state or individuals, usually employers of labor. Many were habitual criminals, said to exist at the time in a ratio of one to eight in the city of London. Historian Robert Hughes, in his stark but compelling history of early civilization in Australia, details the dark days when the island continent and adjacent Tasmania were deluged with "convict" populations. Entire districts, including most of Tasmania, were inhabited by outcasts from the English working classes; it was said that living was so crowded that there was scarcely room to bury the dead.[3] Even the dogs lived better—those in the British Isles hunted in the farm country on great land reserves owned by royalty and the nobility. The canines brought into Australia hunted in the Outback with the aborigines or ran wild in the rest of the country. There was some doubt, however, as to which suffered most—unfortunate humans in a promising but difficult land, or the dogs, many deserters from their aboriginal masters. Crime increased as prisoners vanished from their camps and collected wild dogs to assist them in their depredations in the settled towns or the seizure of lands from the aboriginal tribes.

Fierce Mastiffs were imported to guard the prison camps, government property, and roadways. In Mitchell Library in Sydney, a contemporary drawing shows such animals chained to posts beside their barrel-shaped kennels, baring their fangs and lunging on their chains at Sir John Franklin and Lady Franklin, who were inspecting them. These canines lined Eagle Neck, the land bridge to Van Dieman's land (as Tasmania was then called), where Sir John was lieutenant governor and ruled the colony's vilest prison, Norfolk Island off the southeastern coast of Tasmania, commonly known as "Convicts' Hell." Some said that dogs were treated better than the convicts. But dogs may not have been that lucky, since often the cry of the men themselves, when they escaped, was, "They treat us like dogs."

In the regime of Captain William Bligh (of *Bounty* fame) as governor of New South Wales, England at last took note of some of the horror stories from the Australian prisons, about the time that Lieutenant John MacArthur, jailed by Bligh for indiscretions as an officer of the New South Wales Corps, was arousing the free settlers to near revolt. In fact MacArthur, while in his cell, planned the coup that caused the deposition of Bligh. MacArthur, serving as a military paymaster ashore, had been accused of using military funds to help finance the activities of a gang of former prison officials in bringing untaxed rum and other contraband into the country. The group was wielding power and growing rich.

By 1799 officers of the New South Wales Corps were found to own 77 percent of the sheep, 32 percent of the cattle, and 59 percent of the horses in Australia, according to Hughes. No governor out of England could control them, however, though Bligh had made a start by jailing MacArthur. Bligh was deposed by the powerful conspirators who called themselves the New South Wales Corps and succeeded by a British naval hero, Lachlan Macquarrie. MacArthur himself was ordered to return to England to face a court-martial. He bequeathed his land and flock of 1,200 sheep to his wife, Elizabeth, collected some wool samples, and took them with him to London, where he faced charges and was acquitted of any illegal association with the New South Wales Corps.

MacArthur meantime kept busy in London. He persuaded the British Treasury to allow him to purchase Spanish Merino sheep from those that had been brought to England as a gift to King George III. He convinced Lord Camden, of the wool council, that he could produce Merinos in Australia and was granted 20,000 acres of land. The British wool barons, including spinning-mill owners, were convinced that Merino wool made the best cloth, and Napoleon was cutting off supplies of Merino wool to England. MacArthur got sheep, dogs, land, and permission to return to Australia aboard his own ship, the *Golden Fleece*.

MacArthur's banishment from Australia ended in 1805. The time was right for the advancement of the sheep industry in Australia. His wife, Elizabeth, had been an excellent manager of the family sheep runs in his absence. Shortly after the return of her husband with his Merinos, the MacArthurs created a splendid sheep station on 60,000 acres along the Napean River. They named their estate Camden, grand in true British style, for their good friend in London.

By the mid ninteenth century, Australia had advanced generally in world commerce, exporting wool and minerals and even building ships for world trade. The production of wool, led by the MacArthurs, expanded from 40,000 kilograms shipped out in 1821 to 4.5 million kilograms in 1840. Many graziers were able to follow the MacArthur's style of Georgian elegance. In 1850, gold was found at Bathurst in New South Wales and later in Kalgoorie in Western Australia, and the Hamersley Range of mountains provided a rich iron ore. Australia was prospering, providing great wealth to the settlers who managed to hold their lands in days when drought and inexperience would bring down many. Others survived by bringing in experienced Scot and Basque shepherds and their dogs.

The lifestyle of some of the 34,000 major sheep station proprietors was modeled on that of the English gentry. Agriculture, with its requirement of trained dogs to handle sheep and cattle, and for household pets and protection, to keep public order and serve the military, care for the elderly, the disadvantaged, the hard of hearing, and the blind, as well as to hunt and run in racing and coursing events, continues to be the largest and most profitable industry on the island continent. The well-bred canines of Australia are doing well.

☙

Little is known of the earliest settlers in the two islands now called New Zealand. They arrived by boat, which indicates they came from the canoe making castes of Asia, who created the outrigger canoe with sails. They hunted the now-extinct moa bird and probably helped bring about its fate. A few primitive tool kits have also been found. The Maori arrived in about A.D. 600 in splendid, double-hulled sailing canoes that could carry up to 250 men, women, children, and dogs to the beautiful mountainous islands 1,000 miles southeast of Australia, islands they called "land of the long white cloud." The Maori culture was far above that of their predecessors. They sailed thousands of miles in their sophisticated canoes that may have been designed in the Mekong River delta, where outrigger canoes with sails are still used and where dogs similar to those of the Maori may still be seen. Some may have found their way through the Aleutians and on to Hawaii.

The Maori venerated their dogs but also devoured them when the supply of moas and other flightless birds ran out. The Maori's route may have been from Tasmania, as has been suggested, but also may have been via Hawaii, as can be deduced from Captain Cook's journal, which describes his fatal meeting with vengeful, dog-worshiping Maoris there.

The Maori tribesmen who fastened tails of sacred Kuri dogs to their spears and wore the hair in their headdresses caused problems for Cook when they met his forces in battle in New Zealand and again in Hawaii. Cook was killed in Hawaii by tribesmen similarly garbed, except for their capes—also white, but made of bird feathers. Evidently the islanders, thousands of miles apart, were members of a similar dog-worshiping cult.

Cook's journal records fighting in the course of his early New Zealand landings in which several Maori were killed and also describes, in the captain's own hand, the strange beginning of the scene proceeding his death in Karakakooa Bay, Hawaii, on January 17, 1779, ending his third voyage into the South Pacific. Cook's final journal entry relates his initial welcome as a god, Orono, by native chieftains wearing the same kind of regalia as did the New Zealand Maoris, headgear ornamented with tufts of fur from the Kuri and dog teeth used in armbands and necklaces worn by the priests. The dignitaries of the dog cult may have intended to honor Cook as the foreign god of their legend, Orono, but members of the entourage also included troublemakers who precipitated a fight in which Cook was killed. Since he recorded the details of the above visit, describing a welcome by large Maori chieftain, as well as of the honors that evidently mystified him, just prior to his death, the true cause of the tragedy remains unknown.

Cook, in his final journal entry, had taken notice of his hosts as "men bearing wands tipped with dog's hair." Had he recalled his often unpleasant encounters with the Maori in New Zealand? Were the wand bearers and priests chanting "Orono" under an impression that a Maori dog-cult chieftain was returning home? Or did they consider him an enemy, to be lured by guile to his death? Were the Hawaiian islanders closely related to the Maori of New Zealand? The tragic encounter remains a mystery and may have been an unfortunate accident, rather than a vindictive plot.

Thus the Maori may have come to New Zealand by way of Hawaii, a considerable distance beyond the 1,200 miles out of Tasmania estimated by some historians. Whatever their course, they brought with them the advanced culture of the boat builders of Asia and added their own religious practices. The Maori considered dog flesh a sacred dish, obligatory for the *tohunga taa moke*, their priesthood. The priests and tribal males also prepared the skins of their Kuri dogs for the ceremonial cloaks worn by the chiefs and their shamans, and attached the white tails to the headdresses worn by leaders and to the "wands" or spears carried into battle. The teeth of the dog were used as ornaments for the privileged wearers of dogskin capes. Maori legends explain that the pelts and tails of their dogs were worn by leaders because they represented the care and concern as exemplified by their canines for the good of all the people.

"The first dogs to arrive in New Zealand leaped from the canoes of the early Maori voyagers," says author Miriam MacGregor in her fascinating history of the island canines. "It is said that Ilhenga, of the Arawa canoe, discovered Lake Rotoiti in the Rotorua district with the aid of his dog."[4] The Kuri has been described by Julien Crozet, an officer in a French expedition reaching the islands in 1772, as a "sort of domesticated fox, quite black or white, low in the legs, thick tail, long body, full jaw—they do not bark like our dogs."

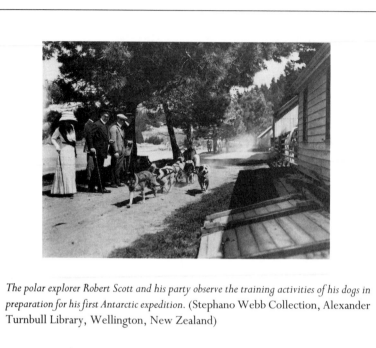

The polar explorer Robert Scott and his party observe the training activities of his dogs in preparation for his first Antarctic expedition. (Stephano Webb Collection, Alexander Turnbull Library, Wellington, New Zealand)

Bound for the Antarctic. (R. Wall Collection, Alexander Turnbull Library, Wellington, New Zealand)

Crozet continues: "Dogs with white hair of the tail was also highly esteemed. The hair was used for ornaments, decorations for weapons, the teeth served as ear pendants and necklaces . . . . It was believed that these favored animals were endowed with spirits that traveled to the World of Shadows, but by a different route from that taken by humans." Only men were permitted to make and wear dogskin cloaks, but women were allowed to weave the flaxen linings and to wear dog-teeth ornaments. In modern times the sacred Kuris are shown less respect.

"The Kuri was not very intelligent," says the authoritative report of the Maori Ethnological Research team, "nor did it have a well developed sense of smell." It served well, however, as an object of religious veneration, as a pet for the women and children, and, at times, as food.[5]

Maori legend credits Ngatero-Rangi, "high priest of the Arawa canoe," with bringing two types of dogs to New Zealand, the small foxlike Kuri, which resembled the tame dogs of Burma in Asia, ate fish, and did not bark; and a larger canine, Putiki Pa, also a dog that did not bark but was an excellent hunter and guardian. Thus the Kuri and Putiki Pa representing domestic dogs near the rim of Antarctica, where, early in the twentieth century, the sled dogs of northern Asia, many with wolf ancestry, would take part in the progression of mankind to the South Pole.

One such breed, the Siberian Husky, is credited to the Inuit people of Siberia who inhabited the Chukchi region en route to the Bering Strait. They probably were related to the dogs of the Samoyed and Lapp tribes. These dogs pull sleds, assist in the hunting and fishing expeditions, and make excellent house dogs, although they are usually made to sleep outdoors, even in the most extreme cold. Robert Peary led twenty-four men and 133 sled dogs to the North Pole, using the best of the dogs and four men for the final miles to the spot where he planted the American flag on April 6, 1909. Robert Scott approached the South Pole without using dogs; he was reported to have said "they ate too much," but his close friends revealed that Scott feared he and his men might be reduced to eating dogs, as the members of an expedition that earlier failed to reach the South Pole were forced to do. Scott substituted Siberian ponies—and failed regardless. Roald Amundsen, experienced in arctic and antarctic exploration and an expert dog handler, took ninety-two Greenland Huskies pulling four sledges into Antarctica. He and his men had killed all but eighteen dogs before their final dash to the pole was made. On December 14, 1911, Peary had won the race with Scott.

Mankind learned that dogs provided the solution for travel in polar areas. Ibn Butata, an early Arab trader, had stated the reasons: "In Mongolia people travel only with small sleds or carts drawn by great dogs," he wrote. "The steppes are covered with ice, and feet of horses and man slip, whereas dogs, having paws, don't slip on the ice. The guide [lead dog] is yoked to the vehicle by his neck, three others being harnessed with him. He is chief, and all other dogs with the carts follow his guidance and stop when he stops. The master of this animal never abuses or scolds him. At feeding time the dogs are always fed before the men."

⁂

As a result of human encroachment, considerable fauna of the New Zealand islands were diminished, though fish remained plentiful. Many Maori dogs running wild were killed for food. There was much tribal warfare, evidently for the possession of remaining canines, especially those with white coats. "The theft or killing of dogs often led to bloodshed," MacGregor writes. "Dogs with white hair were prized . . . they were provided with clean mats to sleep on lest the tail should lose its whiteness and luster." The white Kuri was a pet of the women and children and watchdog of the village; the Putiki Pa hunted with the men and served as war dogs. The dogs enjoyed traveling by canoe and usually stood erect in the bow as they watched the river bank for hidden warriors, she continues. Evidently all canines were at risk, and many were killed in the endless tribal fighting. "They were the only dogs in New Zealand until the 1830s when the sealers, whalers and traders came to these shores," she says. The traders kept watchdogs on their ships to warn their crews of trespassers when in port, though "at times the dogs found their way ashore and they visited the furry females there."

On May 20, 1773, Cook returned to New Zealand, bringing a ram and ewe as symbolic gifts to the Maori along Queen Charlotte Sound. They did not survive long. Not until John Bell, a Sydney merchant, successfully established a station for running sheep under Maori herdsmen on Mana Island was a sheep venture on a large scale successful. In the following decade missionaries and European settlers, mostly Scots and a few Basques bringing in their Merinos, tried running sheep in various New Zealand districts. The flocks anywhere near the Maori tribal enclaves were sure to be attacked by wild dogs. The depredations of the "escaped" Maori animals reached near disaster proportions in the mid nineteenth century. Entire flocks of sheep were lost. "Then came a period when many New Zealand settlers imported Kangaroo Hounds from Australia," MacGregor writes.

"[A cross of English Greyhounds and Irish Wolfhounds] were as game as Blood-hounds, as fierce as tiger cats, and a match for any kangaroo that ever leaped from the plains." Kangaroo Hounds finally solved the problems, killing off the wild dogs and helping to control kangaroos and the rabbits.

The grazier industry continued to grow in New Zealand and mainland Australia. Problems of sheep management kept the flocks down until the arrival of Scot shepherds and their Border Collies. These men were very experienced and qualified to manage thousands of sheep. One or two men and a few muster-ing dogs were sufficient to handle huge flocks. Until the dogs arrived, the shep-herds lived alone in the open or, on cool North Island, in small, poorly heated cabins. "[The Border Collies] were never bred as house pets," says MacGregor, "but as assistants and companions for the shepherds in their lonely lives . . . although they were found to be highly strung and of reserved nature, they have always been known for unsurpassed intelligence." While not herding, however, some Border Collies demonstrated their aptitude for a variety of tasks in the houses of the growing number of sheep and cattle stations. Eventually something of a caste system developed, the house dog making sure no herding dog could be allowed to linger inside once feeding time was passed, and the herd dog rarely permitting a house pet to get near the sheep.

"The typical New Zealand shepherd," as described by author MacGregor and illustrated in the paintings in the Alexander Turnbull Library in Wellington, took over much of the management of the New Zealand grazier industry. "For centu-ries the shepherds led their flocks, [which] were small, and the dogs were kept to guard against wild animals rather than to work the sheep," she writes. The dogs brought out by early shepherds could not be compared with the highly trained animals working the flocks today. "A tame sheep wearing a collar with bell [the bellwether] led the flock, following the shepherd. There were no fences . . . and stopping dogs worked in a wide and silent manner to get to the head of a straying mob to stop or hold them from going further afield."

Border Collies were at once popular in New Zealand since they could gather the sheep, bring them to the shepherd, guide them on the move, and find and return straying animals. They were selected for their capacity to learn commands and obey them from a distance.

Dogs imported since the 1790s showed surpassing ability to control sheep, MacGregor notes: "Some believe it was bred into them from matings with the Gordon Setter of Scotland." The "strong-eye" sheepdogs actually mesmerize sheep,

Shepherds on horseback or motorcycle are a familiar sight driving the vast flocks. Responding to whistles, the dogs "bark up" to acknowledge that they got the message. (Alexander Turnbull Library, Wellington, New Zealand)

Today, many a working sheepdog gets to the job in the relative luxury of a well-used pickup truck. (John Pascoe Collection, Alexander Turnbull Library, Wellington, New Zealand)

A group of sheep, under the control of the shepherd and his vigilant dog, await dipping. (John Pascoe Collection, Alexander Turnbull Library, Wellington, New Zealand)

The Border Collie is a natural stock dog and is widely used in the sheep raising industry in New Zealand. (Thelma Kent Collection, Alexander Turnbull Library, Wellington, New Zealand)

The Gordon Setter was blended into the genetic mix that produced the Border Collie and could account for the collie's celebrated "strong eye."

staring them down in any kind of confrontation. The Marquis of Huntley, who later became the Duke of Gordon in Scotland, sought to improve his hunting dogs and discovered a neighboring squire who owned a "highly gifted Border Collie"; the Duke "put her to one of his most successful Setter sires." In time the "strong-eye" breed was taken to New Zealand and later to Australia, which already had the Kelpie. The typical New Zealand sheepdog thereafter set high standards in New Zealand.

(The paintings at New Zealand's Alexander Turnbull Library and MacGregor's words rang a bell for us. Kiwi! The "typical New Zealand sheep-dog" pictured in the Turnbull Library has the look of the dog my wife, Martha, and I know so well, touched with the tan of the Gordon Setter, possessing the "strong eye" that seemed to have hypnotized me from the beginning.)

A characteristic picture of early New Zealand pastoral life shows the lone shepherd leading his flock. Two dogs watch over the scene as the bellwether follows the shepherd, ahead of the flock. Thus is a flock of several hundred sheep run, with two gathering dogs keeping order at the rear. Not all dogs can lead the "mob" or flock. They must be mature, judging the speed their individual sheep can maintain and walking them at a proper pace. The dog must always be ready to pull the sheep to the shepherd and to hold them. The heading (or lead) dog is the drover, able to work alone all day and meet emergencies. The strong-eyed dog is not the best to put into the lead because it is not usually a natural barker. The duty of the lead dog is to discipline and communicate. He is an assistant to the shepherd, who knows not only how to manage the sheep and bring them up, but how to report by barking what is going on in the distance. The work is hard: Sheepdogs are known to live for up to twenty years, but "mustering dogs" live an average of ten to twelve years.

MacGregor has written superbly of the life of the New Zealand dogs. She describes the specialized work of modern shepherds who prepare their canines so well for their work that human direction in the field seems almost superfluous. "When riding [in New Zealand]," she notes, "it is a common thing to meet a large flock of sheep guarded by one or two dogs, at a distance of some miles from any house or man."

In the beginning both the sheep and the dog are removed from the mother at an early age, she tells us. When a visitor approaches a flock, the dog barks his authority and the sheep draw together behind him. The dogs know when to bring in the flock to the shepherd. They will not allow the house dogs at home to come near. Only the shepherd can approach. Shepherd puppies sometimes begin their training by herding ducks at home. Boys of the shepherd's family early on learn the whistles, calls, and hand signals that will control the dogs. The dog learns to know sheep, understanding that if a sheep looks in a certain direction, it is likely to go that way, and that the sheep are very stubborn animals. The heading or mustering dog also watches the shepherd, or boss, when he is present. If the boss levels his binoculars in a certain direction, the dog looks for action in that direction and is ready to go. The dogs learn to act on their own.

A typical Border Collie in New Zealand, circa 1899. (Blackburn Collection, Alexander Turnbull Library, Wellington, New Zealand)

The Border Collie's "strong eye" in action. (Courtesy Ben Roy Ousley, D.V.M.)

In training, the New Zealand shepherd dog learns to use his judgment as well as the techniques of his job. The dog learns to conquer a series of obstacles and then takes his trainer through or over them. If training for work with the blind or hearing impaired, he learns to stop for traffic by recognizing the sounds of its advance. Sometimes the dog will disobey a command in heavy traffic if he decides from the noise of its approach he can't get the flock, or human, through in time. Consequently, shepherd dogs make excellent guides for the blind and deaf persons. They willingly accept responsibility for the welfare of dependent humans or livestock. Sheepdogs have been known to be away for several days hunting lost lambs and they do not return to their station without the missing animals if they can be found at all.

Then there's the routine of getting the animals home for shearing or to the cattle market, with special problems. The shepherd, when present, controls it all because he is expert at communicating with his dogs, with whistles, voice, and hand signals. "Sometimes it takes a couple of hours of walking before the sheep are even seen [in the high country of the south]," herders say. Growth, such as bracken or matagouri, can trouble the dogs. The Wild Irishman bush is covered with thorns and grows above three yards high. Needlelike grasses spear the paws— "sometimes the bloody paw tracks seem to be everywhere." A dog will pull a claw off during the run at times, but keep going to finish the run, though it's painful. "A dog can stand a lot more than a human being, but with the continuous crossing of the creeks their feet are constantly wet and dry, wet and dry. They become sore, the sun comes out and the shinge (dry turf) scorches or burns the dogs' pads. No pad, no dog, but the biggest thing is its heart—the will to go on and on." For the best of reasons, the shepherd is intensely proud of his dogs.

"Good dogs under good command can hold their own in any country. Command does not mean making a dog sit down or go, it is controlling it and directing it from extreme distance." Out of whistle range the dog will keep an eye on the shepherd and pull the sheep in the direction the horse is moving (modern shepherds are usually mounted, some on motorcycles)—the movement of the horse indicates to the dog the way to draw the sheep. The "mustering dog" that can perform these tasks is highly valued. The "heading dogs" will never leave the sheep in storm or snow, leading the sheep toward the shepherd. They are capable of working alone all day, bringing up sheep spread out along a trail.

The "strong-eyed" dog will confront the sheep, forcing any stubborn, wayward animal to obey. There is a truism the New Zealand shepherds know: "Any puppy descended from a line of head and lead dogs is a natural worker, half educated before it is born." Also: "Don't use a strong-eye or other dog that is not a natural barker as a lead dog. Your assistant, the shepherd dog, must understand why it has been sent 'up front' to work and do what is expected by speaking up and giving loud tongue—it must be a natural barker. Watch the puppy when playing about the yard; it should herd any fowl without prompting. This is something it has not been taught to do—it is an inborn talent." We know this now, but I had thought we needed to teach Kiwi what to do! No wonder she separated and drove away the Muscovy ducks from the mallards after just one lesson. She was born to it.

The list of requirements for New Zealand and Australian Sheepdogs is long and demanding. The dog meeting them is, accordingly, quite valuable, bringing a high price when it is for sale at all. The shepherd, alone for perhaps months at a time with his dogs and flocks, must be part veterinarian and part pioneer. He must have the ability to communicate competently with his "assistants" and make responsible judgments, as must his leading dogs. There must be no driving stock over a cliff, no worrying of sheep and no over-working good dogs. The last, however, would be difficult to do, as these dogs are tough and enduring, and some can run fifty miles a day, the New Zealand shepherds say. Paper and pedigrees mean little when dogs are traded Down Under, as the prospective buyers keenly watch them work. They'll buy the progeny if they have observed and approve the performance of the parents.

The dogs are worked hard but cared for well. Many of the big stations have an airstrip and a small plane for the owners and family and help and also to take the dogs to a veterinary clinic if needed. The dogs must not only herd and care for the sheep, find lost animals, and make sure no lamb is harmed; some are ordered to go rabbit hunting to prevent the rabbit scourge of past years from recurring.

Most shepherds live along with their dogs most of the time. They get to talking to an understanding animal as if it might be an understanding human. And many seem to be. ("I guess some people will think I'm getting goofy, talking to our dog," I mentioned to Martha a few years ago. "No they won't," she replied firmly. "Not when they see Kiwi answering you." True, in New Zealand at least.)

We cannot turn from the dogs of New Zealand without mentioning one of the country's most famous canines, Freefall, a black Labrador/German Shepherd mix owned by Major Albert Kiwi of the New Zealand Army. Freefall was the first dog to run from one end of New Zealand to the other, 1,250 miles as the roads go. Freefall, who earned his name by parachute jumping with his master, wore a World War II victory medal and wore out twenty sets of special boots created to protect his paws. Major Kiwi and Freefall ran over hot pavement and through brush and brambles, taking thirty days traveling ten hours a day to cover the distance, averaging sixty-nine kilometers a day and ultimately winning $28,000 for charity. At the end Freefall was given the privilege of "anointing" the finish post at Reinga—and did.

Some things never change, and the life of the modern shepherd can be as lonely as that of his ancient predecessors. The scene is in North Auckland. (Northwood Collection, Alexander Turnbull Library, Wellington, New Zealand)

When the mountain shepherds and their dogs do get together, everyone is glad for the company. (John Pascoe Collection, Alexander Turnbull Library, Wellington, New Zealand)

New Zealand, having some of the world's most industrious and talented canines, whose day-to-day working feats seem beyond belief, can also make a claim to metaphysical accomplishment. Ancient Egyptians, Greeks, Nabeteans, and other primitive people thought their dogs had an ability to conduct human souls to a peaceful haven. The Aztecs of Mexico believed their canines guided human spirits across wide waters to eternal bliss. The Maori of New Zealand, a more pragmatic people, allowed their dogs to determine proper conditions for the hunt and warn them of enemies and dangers ahead. They also believed the dogs could be helpful in appeasing evil spirits.

Maori mysticism involving their sacred dogs may have led to the final obscure paragraphs of warning and doubt in the journal of Captain James Cook, who knew them well. The Maori shared with their dogs a fear of ghostly apparitions. No Maori would remain in a house where a suicide had occurred. However, immigrant shepherds from Scotland were not superstitious. Historian MacGregor relates the story, in *A Dog's Life,* of Vern, a South Island shepherd, who rented a small cabin at a low price without knowing that Maori had deserted it following a suicide there. He moved in with his dogs, but they were uneasy, whined to be freed, and gave him no sleep. The day following, Vern learned something of the history of the cabin. He had no choice but to return to get his needed sleep, but his dogs rebelled. One by one, ignoring his commands, the dogs leaped through a window, and at last Vern followed them. Thereafter no one would live in the cabin, said to be haunted.

Vern's own feelings may have alarmed his dogs, but another account of death and a canine, vouched for by MacGregor, is even more mystifying. Cuddles, a coursing Greyhound owned by the Masterson family, was beloved by their four-year-old son Raymond, whom the dog adored and considered his master. Raymond suffered an accident away from home and was taken to a hospital, where he died. He was not returned to his home, but received final rites in the family church and burial in a cemetery several kilometers away. Following the burial service, his parents realized that their dog was mysteriously missing. They returned to the cemetery to attend the flowers there and were surprised by Cuddles, who stubbornly resisted their attempts to take her home. Thereafter Cuddles mourned and howled when she was tied at home and rushed to the cemetery when she was freed. "Raymond had not returned home from the hospital, so how did Cuddles know where he had gone?" MacGregor asks. "And how did she know which was Raymond's grave?" It is as Canon Bib Lowe said: "Dogs do have something that gives them an uncanny ability to sense the unknown, and this should always be regarded with the respect it deserves."

The hunting dogs of the American South were strongly influenced by Old World scent-hound breeds. Shown here are the Black-and-Tan Coonhound (top), *an obvious relation of the Bloodhound; a Blue Tick Coonhound* (center), *which traces to the elegant hounds of France; and the Plott Hound* (bottom), *with German roots that probably go back to the various Brache varieties and hounds of Bavaria.* (Photos by Doyle Calloway)

12

VIRGEORGOLINA—THE LAND THAT LOVES DOGS

ᏀᎳᎳᎤ

In Virginia, Georgia, and the Carolinas dogs are not worshiped as they were in ancient Egypt, but you'd better not belittle anyone's coon dogs, nor any other canine found wandering through a downtown store or elegant antique auction room along the Blue Ridge Trail. A dog's life is mostly a good life in the Great Smoky Mountains, the Blue Ridge country, the Piedmont, and the Barrier Islands. Dogs are beyond criticism here, even from their owners, who are allowed, however, to cuss them out privately now and then. People love their hounds. Natives even smile benignly on visiting flatlanders who walk their dogs on mountain roads and along Main Street. The fundamentalists, comprising about 79 percent of all Virgeorgolinians, worship God and adore their pets.

The first hunting hounds were brought to the Blue Valley about 5,000 years ago by the Dog Tribe, as the Cherokee have been called by Francis Parkman and other historians. There were Indians along the southeastern seaboard 10,000 years ago, but settlement of the area by Europeans did not begin seriously until the close of the sixteenth century. A great mercantile war was under way between England and Spain. The English had missed a chance to control the Caribbean and had fallen behind France in the development of Canada. It was time for a mercantile flanking movement. In 1496, John Cabot, the Italian-born navigator, sailed west with the backing of Henry VII of England to discover a northern passage to India, China, and the Spice Islands and to establish trading posts. Instead he found a short way to North America, as Jacques Cartier had done earlier for France, landing on what was probably Newfoundland, the island previously visited by the Vikings in about A.D. 1000. Cabot brought back reports of a fine warm climate and excellent cod fishing. Cabot was a summer visitor. He and his men saw no natives, but they found fishing nets. Those nets had been set by the descendants of migrants from Asia who had crossed the Bering Strait before the land bridge closed. Possibly those Amerinds had hybridized with the sailors who accompanied Leif the Lucky but then disappeared from his colony there. These people may have helped develop beautiful, sturdy, seagoing dogs that helped the fishermen by bringing in nets, carrying the lines in their teeth. The ancestors of these dogs later earned universal recognition as the Labrador Retriever.

Cabot's discovery of rich fishing banks off an "Asian" island was not exploited until sometime later, however. Henry VII claimed the island, gave Cabot a pension, and sent him on a second journey from which the intrepid navigator and his men did not return. In 1584, almost a century later, Sir Walter Raleigh, a young favorite of the Virgin Queen, Elizabeth, sent a small probing force to mainland America that entered into Pamlico Sound. Raleigh's captains brought back a fine report—good climate, good soil, and friendly Indians. They also were summer visitors. But Roanoke Island appeared to offer an excellent strategic base flanking the Spanish to the south. Elizabeth gave Raleigh permission to establish a colony there, calling it Virginia, and to establish proprietorships that would include as much of North America as he could take. He in turn sent out a colonizing expedition that landed 100 men who settled on Roanoke in 1585. His rival for Elizabeth's favor, Sir Francis Drake, scourge of the Spanish in the Caribbean, dropped off to visit Raleigh's little settlement, found the men there dispirited, and took them with him back to England. In 1588 the dreaded Spanish Armada would sail against England to meet destruction by a British naval force that took advantage of a vicious storm at sea. Meantime, Raleigh in 1585 had sent out three ships carrying 117 men, women, and children. They settled on Croaton, a low-lying island about 100 miles south of Cape Hatteras, later to become known as the Cape of Storms. When Sir Walter was able to send a supply ship two years after the defeat of the Armada, the sailors found no colony, only destruction and ruin. The mystery of the "Lost Colony" has never been solved, though Indians and fearful storms off Cape Hatteras may have settled the fate of the colonists.

In 1604 James I, the new king of England, made peace with Spain. Two years later he granted a Royal Charter for the Virginia Corporation, a stock company that landed 120 male settlers on low, swampy land to establish a settlement called

Jamestown. Within two weeks it was attacked by Indians. Six months later nearly half the population was dead. The romantic rescue and saving of Jamestown colony is known to almost every American schoolchild able to read. Captain John Smith found a way to become a friend of the militant chief Powhatan. John Rolfe, who introduced tobacco seeds from the Caribbean into Virginia and then hybridized them with the coarser Indian variety, married Chief Powhatan's daughter Pocahontas. A supply ship arrived with needed food, tools, and dogs as well as 100 fresh settlers, including women and five Polish men skilled in the production of pitch, tar, and turpentine. The tobacco and the Poles' creation of naval stores soon gave the colony a profitable trade with England, governed by the British mercantile policy of "you trade with us, we'll protect you."

The colonists also found they had a product that could be sold for gold to the Indians—English hunting dogs. Just when the dogs arrived, or the exact breed, is not recorded. However, by 1670, the dogs were a major consideration in a peace settlement between Powhatan's people and the colonists. The Indians desired fine hunting dogs. The English wanted gold, discovered in the Carolinas and Georgia, as well as Indian maize and furs. The conclusion of a peace treaty in which dogs were specifically mentioned is still celebrated by the annual October dog trade fair in Fredericksburg, Virginia, the first of its kind in America.

ᏬᎥᎥᎥᏉ

Following the defeat of the Spanish Armada, England could attend to the development of her generally faltering colonies in America and those prospering in the Caribbean. Britain's basic commercial interest continued to be spices, sugar, lumber, and indigo. In the reign of Charles II, England made plans for settlements, not mere trading posts, in America. Several good friends of King Charles, including Lord Ashley, Earl of Shaftsbury, interested him in the possibility of establishing proprietorships where subtropical products, such as "sugar canes, orenges, limons, and almonds," as well as wine grapes and olives, could be grown—in southern Virginia. The British were consistently wrong about climatic conditions in North America, based on misleading reports from John Cabot and other explorers.

Lord Ashley with the aid of his secretary, the brilliant young writer and philosopher John Locke, after obtaining a Carolina Charter in 1863, drafted a constitution for the new colony in southern Virginia that would create not only a government for the land but also a system of nobility based on land ownership

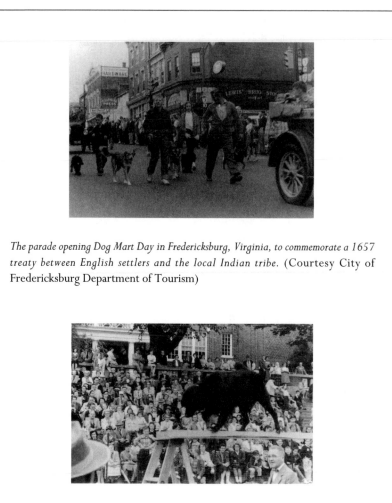

The parade opening Dog Mart Day in Fredericksburg, Virginia, to commemorate a 1657 treaty between English settlers and the local Indian tribe. (Courtesy City of Fredericksburg Department of Tourism)

The Dog Mart Day crowd loves to watch the various events available. An exhibition of canine agility is always a popular favorite. (Courtesy City of Fredericksburg Department of Tourism)

that had long been under attack in Europe. Samuel Eliot Morison describes it as "the longest, most fantastic and most reactionary of all colonial forms of government." Wealthy men who could purchase 3,000 acres of Carolina lands would become barons. The owner of 12,000 acres could become a *cassique* (chieftain). A purchaser of 20,000 acres could have the German title of *Landgrave* (count).

Later, John Locke became the respected, though radical, English philosopher who enunciated principles that would in America be implemented by the leaders of the Revolution. Only forty wealthy men made actual use of the titles, and few of them ever set foot in America. Some of their agents, however, who retained for themselves much of the revenue intended for the owners, were able to create the noble lifestyle for themselves that had been achieved by successful planters in Virginia. This Carolina and Virginia aristocracy used dogs for hunting and protection of their urban homes and country estates, to keep away Indians and predators, and to control their slaves.

◔▥◑

The Carolina colony came into being, with Captain Joseph West as governor, in the spring of 1670, the year that Virginia settlers concluded a tenuous peace with the local Indians. While the British government desired to block Spanish expansion in North America, West declined to base his capital at Port Royal, as owners recommended, calling it "too near St. Augustine," the Spanish base. Instead he located near what is modern Charleston, South Carolina, naming his trading post for his king. Eventually the Carolina project got under way as an establishment of common people who could fish, raise livestock, cut timber for the king's navy and barrel staves for the northern flour grinders and the Caribbean rum trade, and trade for furs with the Indians. The Virginians had ignored Indian skills in agriculture, though some tribes, especially the Cherokee, brought from the South such produce as maize, cotton, and squash. Carolina and Maryland did not make the same mistake. The Carolinians were well situated to grow on their coastal islands a superior cotton. They also planted Indian maize, rice, indigo, hemp, and tobacco.

The need for dogs was not great until the seaboard populations began to seek land to the west, in the Piedmont and highlands. In the beginning English, Scot, and Irish settlers moved up the rivers to harvest lumber and farm and herd cattle. The Huguenots, driven from France by religious persecution, and some Scandinavians arrived in the Carolina coastal towns to find work, and many continued west, where such craftsmen might be needed. The migrants also included Germans and others from central Europe who arrived in the North, found that booming immigration following the Revolution had taken up most job and land opportunities and moved on to enter what was then the Wild West—the highlands of the Carolinas—going south down the Blue Ridge valleys as fast as trails and roads could be opened, and into a new territory to be called Georgia.

Some such migrants had gained a stake in the coastal towns or as tenant farmers in the Northeast. They brought livestock—their capital—to the Shenandoah Valley. The Carolinas grants extended west to the Mississippi, as the Indians had been for the most part conquered and driven from their lands. Some settlers moved in too fast and too far, and their villages met the kind of fate meted out to the Indians. But the migrants from Pennsylvania kept on coming. The Germans brought their sheep-herding, bear, and boar dogs; the Scots and English their stock dogs, foxhounds, Spaniels, and Setters.

Baron Graffenreid of Bern, Switzerland, who bought Carolina land and was made a *Landgrave,* opened thousands of acres along the Neuse River, and welcomed Swiss and German pioneers who began a town they called New Bern. The new settlers brought in dogs to control the flocks and herds that were not confined in pastures and to drive them to holding pens established along rivers and new roads to handle trade with the North. The Carolinas began to have a diverse population that in time would match that of Virginia and Maryland in the production of exportable goods. Charleston became a city of fine homes, built by wealthy rice and cotton growers. There were gold seekers among the new immigrants, and some discovered what they sought, though in limited amounts, in the Carolinas and Georgia.

By 1776 all of the original proprietors of Carolina but Lord Granville had sold out, and North and South Carolina were reconstituted as Crown colonies. As the highlands opened to settlement, Granville sold 100,000 acres of his land in North Carolina to the Moravian United Brethren, who settled in what became known as the Wachovia Tract. Despite devastating Indian attacks, settlers stayed on to produce lumber, cattle, and hunting dogs, but most remained farmer-hunters. They planted in acreage left by the Cherokee or turned to farming after clearing the land of timber, which itself was floated eastward down the rivers where the production of wooden products would soon rival that of the New England colonies.

Tobacco and rice growers and agents of the large landholders in the Carolinas enjoyed the lifestyle of the wealthy Virginians. However, the craftsmen, shopkeepers, and farmers generally had to be content with limited incomes. A few could afford slaves and horses as well as hunting dogs. Nearly all the small farmers found a way to keep a dog or two for protection and companionship.

Pioneer women complained about the loneliness of life in the country. Western North Carolina was isolated from the rest of the country and the world, except where the rivers ran to the sea, taking lumber, cattle, and some farm produce to market. The coastal Carolinas had their own aristocracy, imitating that of Virginia, who brought in the many English dog breeds for their hunting pleasure. Since Spanish horses and pigs ran wild in southwestern parts of the Carolinas, some Spanish dogs may have survived there as well, hybridizing with Indian dogs. However, the Indians' eagerness to acquire English hunting dogs may indicate that their own dogs were not much used for hunting before the Europeans arrived, instead used primarily to protect Indian camps and hovels. It remained for the upland Germans to produce the right dogs to help in the hunt and as protectors.

☙

Michael Frome, author of *Stranger in High Places,* describes his own experience with modern-day bear dogs, which appear to have changed little from colonial days. "They were not the kind of dogs that one would ever find in a show," Frome writes. "The members of this pack were lean, on the scrawny side. One was minus an eye (lost in a fight with a bear). They were whipped, kicked, treated fiercely. In the relationship between hunter and dog, however, the harsh disciplines do not reflect the full feeling of the man. He also protects his dog from abuse by another person. He placed a high price upon his bear dog . . . but wouldn't sell him at any price . . . he'd sooner have parted with his wife."[1]

Bear hunting in the Smoky Mountains is not a sport for the timid, man or dog. Early breeders and trainers of bear dogs were descendants of Johannes Plott, who immigrated to the United States from Heidelberg, Germany, to Philadelphia, then later followed the wagon road to Goldsboro, North Carolina, there settling on Jonathan Creek. Sheep and cattle raising was slow, and gold mining was running out, so the Plotts brought in Bloodhounds and German hunting dogs to supply game hunters and also to track runaway slaves. Frome learned from the Plott descendants the methods of bear dog training, conceding that the family "was very guarded about their ways of training the hounds." Basically, the bear dog learned to fight by fighting other dogs. The rule was that a dog must never quit; thus they fought to exhaustion or death. Older dogs, nearly fought out, would go out with a pack of young animals that never had tracked a bear. Frome quotes a veteran Plott trainer: "Dillard and me took out a New York buyer. I gave the old dogs a chance before turning the young loose. . . . Jack Dillard cut two loose, I cut two more, and then the other two. There was a big fight. They got a bear in a hole. The dogs charged in, one after the other. They got bit up pretty bad, but they stayed at it and charged till they got him. That flatlander bought 'em all."

The training followed the pattern of the fighting pits in Europe. The young dog learned from his mates, then was on his own. He had to learn never to quit. "If the dog wouldn't stay all day, he's no good," the trainer said. "This breed won't quit. He may git chewed and clawed but he'll be back next week. He's got to have a good owner. The man who ain't game ain't fit to have him."

Sam Hunnicut, a grizzled veteran in the Smokies who is credited with killing 33 bears alone and 104 more with help, lists dependability as a top virtue in a bear dog. He wanted a staying hound, one "thirsty for game. . . . If you want a good hunt, get a thoroughbred hound." But then he added, "The best dog I ever owned was a Redbone Beagle, crossed. A Cherry Redbone, which is known as a Florida Tan—a mixed breed." That often included plain mountain cur. Hunnicut was a demanding master. "If anything would cause me to kill a dog," he said, "it would be when I told it to go after game across the ridge outa my sight and hearin' and then I should climb the ridge and, instead of hearin' him after game, meet him comin' toward me. It would cause me to shoot him right on the spot."

Early in the ninteenth century, Horace Kephart, the great chronicler of Smoky Mountain lore, wrote his account of a bear hunt on the Tennessee border. The hunt was to start in Tennessee but a high wind caused the veterans to think of heading for the North Carolina side of the mountain.

"Why hunt on the Carolina side?" Kephart asked.

"Thet's whar we're goin'," he was told, "but hit's no use if the bear don't come over."

"How is that?" Kephart asked. "Do they sleep in one state and eat in the other?"

The answer, according to Kephart in his book *Our Southern Highland,* ran this way: "Yes, you see, the Tennessee side of the mountain is powerful steep and laurely, so t'man nor dog cain't git over it in lots o' places, thats whar th' bears den. But the mast, sich as acorns and beech an' hickory nuts, is mostly on th' Carolina side; that's whar they hafta come fer food. Now, when th' wind blows like this, they may stay at home an' suck their paws 'til th' weather clars. We gotta go wait fer them."[2]

The disgruntled dogs got into a fight. "They flew at each other's throats," Kephart wrote. "They were powerful beasts, as dangerous to man as the brutes they were trained to fight," but their master soon booted them into surly subjection. Kephart asked, "Have these dogs got Plott stock? . . . I've been told the Plott Hounds are the best bear dogs in the country."

"T'aint so," the boss hunter told him. "The Plott curs is the best; that is half hound, half cur—though what we'uns call a cur, in this case really comes from a big furring dog that I don't rightly know the breed of. Fellers, you can talk as you please about a streak of the cur spilin' a dog; but I know hit ain't so—not for bear fightin' in these mountains, where you caint foller up on hossback but hafter do your own runnin'."

"What's the reason?"

"Waal, hit's like this; a plumb cur, of course, cain't foller a cold track—he just runs by sight. And he won't hang, he quits. But, t'other way, no hound'll raelly fight a bear—hit takes a big, severe dog to do that. Hounds has the best noses; they'll run a bear all day an' all night, an' th' next day, too, but they'll never tree—they're afeard to close in. Now, look at my dawgs—foller a trail, same as them hounds; but they'll run right in on the varmint, snappin' and chawin' an' worryin' him till he gits so mad you can hear his tushes pop half a mile. He cain't run away—he haster stop every bit an' fight. Finally he gits so tired an' het up that he trees to rest hisself. Then we'uns catches up an' finishes him."

Bear hunting in North Carolina and Tennessee began in days when bear meat was essential to the mountain family and when the cattlemen killed bears and wolves to protect their stock. They also hunt destroyers of crops, the wild boar and the raccoon and wild turkey, the latter mostly in Georgia. Some believe the Spaniards first brought pigs to America, along with cattle and horses. Late in the nineteenth century, some northern hunters and Carolina associates undertook to create vast hunting preserves stocked with big game, including wild boars. They also brought in proper hunting dogs from Austria and Germany. The projects were failures. The boars killed many dogs and broke free to range the mountains, and poachers invaded the preserves. The boars continue to thrive, having hybridized with escaped domestic pigs.

The hunting is by permit in the Cherokee National Forest and in parts of Nantahala National Forest in modern times. Some hunters assert the boar is the most exciting of all prey, "fleet as a deer, cunning as a bear, elusive as a fox." What concerns the hunter most is that an enraged boar will fiercely charge both man and dog, and it can cut a young, inexperienced dog to pieces. But the dogs can bring down a boar, and in the Nantahala Forest, bobcats and black bears prey upon boars to the extent that the season has been closed from time to time to insure continuity of breeding stock. The great hunting sports in the Smokies remain, in modern times, coon, quail, and turkey. Bear and boar hunting are for the hardy few.

Lewis Dendy, a genial, burly, soft spoken native of Macon County, has the look of a highlander in his eyes. He recalls the stories of life in the Smokies in early days as told by his great-grandparents, the McCalls. His father, Floyd Dendy, was a minister in the mountains. "We are mountain people," says our neighbor Dendy (his grandfather built the sawmill that cut the timber for the house that is now the summer home for Martha, Kiwi, and me). "Every family had a dog or dogs. It was lonely in the woodlands, there were few roads, you needed protection and company. Dogs were needed to run cattle and sheep." The best times came when Lewis was old enough to go grouse hunting with his grandfather—hunting for coons, bears, and boars came later.

Dendy took the morning off from his golf game, his second-favorite recreation these days, to talk about his prime sport, coon hunting. "They hunted them for food and skins in early days but not anymore," he says. "They're just nuisances now, especially down in the low country of Georgia where several of us go to hunt. It's a kind of fellowship and social event, and the fun is working with dogs." There were no hunting camps with bunkers and showers in the early days. "We'd walk," Dendy said. "We took along a rifle, twenty-two-caliber, or a twenty-gauge shotgun, an ax, a four-pound shortening can to make coffee in our campfire. We'd start out evenings about eight o'clock and not get back until early the next morning. Working the dogs is the thing in raccoon hunting. When the dogs are trailing, the hunter knows exactly what's going on by their cries. 'Old Butch is trailing,' he'll say. 'Or so-and-so has got one treed.' When they tree a coon, the hunter will sometimes drop him with a gunshot, or he may climb the tree, high as fifty feet, and shake him out for the dogs. That coon will land on his feet and take off, but this time the dogs will have an even start and there is a fight. It's a fight to the finish.

"I'm not certain about the original stock of a coon dog," Dendy said in reply to a question. "We have fox hunters that are English, shepherds that are German or Scot, Bloodhounds that are English. Some of the animals that are running loose or are seen sleeping by the roads are called coon dogs, but you don't see a real, proud coon dog running around loose. For one thing, they may cost a thousand dollars or more. They're bred by those who regard raccoon hunting as the world's best sport. There are many breeds: Blue Tick is bluish gray, weighs forty to fifty pounds; Black and Yellow Tan, about the same size. Generally they are crossed mountain cur. They can lick their weight in wildcats; they're one-man dogs, and proud. You work as a team—one man, two dogs. They won't tolerate another dog, except when older dogs take out the young for training. You bring in an outside dog without preparation and you don't have a coon hunt; you have a dogfight.

"You have a dog with a cold nose lead the way. He'll get on even a cold track within ten minutes. Mountain dogs run in two styles. The trail dog follows the track runs by scent. You begin in the swamp where the raccoons find their food, crayfish, any freshwater fish, and vegetation. When the dog runs a coon to the ridge, and the coon disappears, he'll raise his head to sniff for the scent. The hunter tries to keep up. He knows his dog can scent a deer at 250 yards, the coon at a bit less. The hunter knows what his dogs are doing by the manner of their yelping and barking.

"The dogs tree the coon. Working with the dogs is the fun of it. In twenty-four hours or so, you're back home, or in camp, tired, happy, and your dogs are content."

Another native-born mountain man, based in the Piedmont of Georgia, agreed that the best of coon hunting is "working the dogs," not destroying the coon. Bruce Nix, a veteran of the Vietnam War, had seen enough of the killing. "I enjoy the sport, I like working with the dogs. I don't like to shoot the coon," he said, "but now and then you have to bring it down or the dogs won't work anymore."

Dendy recalls his Great-grandfather McCall and friends having specialized dogs, "a kind of bulldog-retriever" that would follow grouse in the woods, deer hounds, and a brace of bear or boar hounds, sometimes one caged and taken along, fresh and fit, to fight the bear or boar after the trail dogs were weary. "Black bears and wild boars were taken then for food, or protection of children in the area, as well as sport," he recalls.

Our own dog Kiwi demonstrates her "strong eye" and natural ability as a stock dog as she works a protective cow and her calf on the Zay Ranch in northern Georgia. (Photo by Alice Jean Zay)

Kiwi in a moment of togetherness with Martha. Her observations leave no doubt as to Kiwi's status in the Wendt "pack." Says the lady of the house to the author, "I am her mother; you are her sibling." That says it all.

13

THE SIDE OF DOGS
WE WILL NEVER KNOW

⚬⚬⚬

When you walk your dog in the town of Highlands, North Carolina, you are greeted with a friendly smile of approval, even though you may be a stranger and your dog is not on leash. Highlands, founded July 14, 1875, rescinded its pre–World War I leash law a few years ago because it was never enforced. The grand symbol of this dissidence, in a state known for flouting mandates that are obviously unfair or unreasonable, is Artie, the town mascot, who has rarely known the touch of a leash in his long, happy, and productive life. Artie is the putative town pet of Highlands. He wanders the streets freely (or did until his recent semi-retirement); he visits shops and stores as well as residents who welcome him as a dinner, breakfast, or luncheon guest; and on occasion, it is said, he has dropped into one of the nine churches between Shortoff Mountain on the east of town and Gold Mine Road on the west. Only in the restaurants and shops of France and on the campus of Cornell University at Ithaca, New York, have dogs had equal freedom on such a scale.

Artie is the associate of Highland's native son Leon "Deadeye" Potts, who was said by some to have won the animal, part Husky and part Labrador, in a poker game. Not so, says Potts. He was won in a bingo game, then legal in this town of many churches and one municipally owned liquor store; furthermore, the dog was won at a benefit bingo game for the Highlands Studio for the Arts. "That's why I named him Artie," Potts explains. "I'm not home much and neither is Artie," he adds. "Sure, Artie wanders a lot. He likes people."

239

Artie, whose presence has enriched the life of his North Carolina friends and family, disdained leash laws all his life but consented to wearing a leash and red ribbon for his community's annual Christmas parade until he retired and went to live with an equally retired local chef. (Sketch by Mark Sandlin)

Journalist Carson Lindsay, writing for our local newspaper, *The Highlander,* describes Artie as "regal—a king-sized white dog the size of a grizzly bear who holds court with all of the grace of an emperor, allowing the attention of the masses." Actually, says Potts, Artie rarely weighs more than 100 pounds, stripped. "If he sometimes gets overweight it's not my fault." Artie is gracious and friendly, especially to small children. At one time some newly arrived entrepreneurs in booming Highlands wished to keep Artie from entertaining crowds before shop doors, but none dared to propose it officially. Anyone who has ever seen Artie lead the Highlands Old Mountain Christmas parade with a beautiful Christmas bow around his neck and heard the cheers and applause would never consider trying to limit Artie's freedom. So, not only has Artie not been curbed in any way, but the leash law was abolished. However, Artie has restricted himself somewhat and has consented to a leash for the Christmas parades.

One home, where Artie had been a breakfast guest almost daily during the summer and fall months, is that of Clyde and Hope Frick, in Carolina Court. The dog dropped in on them one evening while they were cooking hamburgers, and Artie, of course, had one or two. In time he changed his schedule and came in almost daily for breakfast. In the summer of 1991, Clyde was delayed returning to Highlands from his home in Florida. Coincidentally, Artie did not call on the

Fricks, that anyone remembers, until Joyce Tolbert and other neighbors saw him sitting in front of the Frick place on a certain August day. Frick had not come back earlier because of his wife's death. He had not advised his Carolina neighbors of his plans but returned with his daughter Becky in August. Artie was there that day to greet them. "It was eerie, seeing Artie there," Mrs. Tolbert said.

⟋⟋⟍⟍⟍

William "Bummy" Bumgardner, a Highlands summer visitor from Wheeling, West Virginia, and Stuart, Florida, is a former business executive who may be either one of the most gifted animal trainers in history or owner of the world's most brilliant dog. Bummy taught his pet Sandy, a "Collie farm dog," to play poker. Sandy has never lost.

Bummy began working with the family's new pup early in 1957. "We worked together one hour every day, learning how a dog should perform and how a master should teach and give commands," he writes in his own memoirs. "I bought a book on how to train dogs but couldn't find one on how to train a master." Within months Sandy could do all the tricks the family had seen Lassie do in the movies. "All seven of them," Bummy says. He took Sandy to a fair and won a performance blue ribbon. (He insists that the judge handing him the award whispered, "Too bad you aren't as smart as your dog.") Sandy continued his training, learning to play properly with Ruth's three daughters, pulling a cart, finding lost objects (including Bummy's keys and wallet), jumping, and climbing ladders. "I could send him after any one of the three girls, asking him to bring back a certain one, and he'd come back with the right girl," he writes. If a refractory child did not wish to return home, Sandy would gently "add just the right amount of pressure on her arm with his teeth."

Sandy was in general demand as a performer. At a party, all guests would be invited to remove a shoe, and the shoes were then piled in the center of the room. Sandy, on command, would select and return each shoe to its proper owner. Sandy also appeared in several of Wheeling's Little Theater presentations. In one play, Sandy won fame by portraying a dead dog through the entire production. That was all that was required; nonetheless, such a role would not be easy for any actor. Sandy performed perfectly in the somewhat heavy melodrama, requiring a reverently emotional climax. Sandy never stirred, hardly breathed. Then, still "dead," Sandy appeared with the cast for curtain calls. The cast was receiving polite applause when Sandy opened one eye and saw his family in the front row. He sprang from the stage into daughter Karen's arms while the theater rocked with applause, cheers, and laughter. Sandy continued throughout the run of the company's most successful play of the season.

"He was on TV's *Romper Room* for several years," Bummy writes. "He was a winner of a cup in a Wheeling pet show, and when the master of ceremonies said, 'Sandy, come up and get your prize,' he went by himself to get the cup."

What about the poker playing? I asked Bummy.

"One time I was at the club where some men were playing poker, and some of them were losing quite heavily," Bumgardner replies. "I undertook to show them how easy it could be to win, with the proper attitude. Even a dog could do it. I got Sandy and spread out a shuffled deck on the floor. Then I asked Sandy to bring me a good poker hand and he brought me back four aces and a joker."

"So Sandy always won?" I asked.

"Every time," Bummy assured me.

I knew that since Bummy had told me the secrets of metallurgy procedures in the ancient world, where the bronze and iron smelters withheld their secrets over thousands of years, there was a chance he might explain Sandy's feat.

I was wrong, momentarily.

"I could control him by voice or signals, and toward the end of training he could read my mind, which was really my facial expression," Bummy began.

"I've read your book," I said. "It was a long time ago. Wouldn't Sandy want you to disclose the secret now?"

Bummy agreed. He'd marked cards with varying scents. Sandy practiced picking up the scented cards with his paw and nose, no easy feat in itself. The rest was easy. Sandy simply laid the cards face down a few feet away.

"He had openers and he could bet his whole stack of chips?" I suggested. "He'd win the pot and then quit?"

"You said it," Bummy replied.

"What special quality about Sandy do you best remember?" I asked.

"He made it on his own," Bummy replied, beaming proudly. "And he was the runt of the litter."

⌒⊶⊷⌒

In my newspaper days I was made aware of the strange and wonderful ways of certain dogs and wrote of one canine incident I never quite understood, the feat of a hunting dog called Dan. I can credit that published story for the unexpected visit of a pleasant, shy, but famous man shortly after my return to Chicago from navy service in World War II. Joseph B. Rhine was the popular parapsychologist of Duke University in North Carolina. I had bought his book that I hoped to read, and I knew of an "extrasensory" card game originating from his laboratory tests. He briskly explained that he was between planes, acting on impulse, and wished to speak briefly with me on "dogs, trailing, and PSI." He understood that I was scheduled out of town that evening. Not much time would be taken.

I was pleased to meet him. "I have your book; your extrasensory cards are the rage here in Chicago," I said. "But I doubt I can help you. I don't think I understand psychokinesis and PSI or even extrasensory."

He smiled. "I'm checking on a dog story you wrote years ago," he said. "As for PSI, it's a general term to identify a person's extrasensory motor communication with the environment. PSI and psychokinesis define extrasensory perception. Your dog story covered almost all of it."

I recalled the story. "You're referring to Judge Sigler and his hunting hound Dan," I said. So I filled in the details. As a beginning reporter I had known well Probate Judge Emmanuel Christopher Sigler, a fine and honest man. He liked to hunt. When he lived in Leola, a small town in northeastern South Dakota, he had a speaking engagement in Aberdeen, a relatively large city twenty-seven miles

This 1914 photo shows Judge E. C. Sigler's dog, Dan, with some members of the Sigler family and their vintage Ford touring car.

away. It was November 1913, and he took along Dan, his faithful hound, and they got a duck or two to be stowed in his open touring car. Dan would guard them.

On Sigler's return following his talk, the ducks were there but Dan was gone. The judge loved his dog, but no amount of searching produced him. Sigler informed his friends and drove home through an early Dakota blizzard that blasted across that part of the plains.

Back home, Sigler told his family about the unfortunate loss of Dan. He was desolate, couldn't sleep, and tried by all possible means in that pioneer area to locate his dog. It was just four days later that he heard a familiar bark outside the darkened house. The judge turned on the porch light and there was Dan, weary and limping from a cut forepaw. Dan was dirty, matted with pine needles and briars and pieces of Dakota tumbleweed, but he quickly recovered. It was a grand reunion.

How could Dan have done it? He'd never before been on the rutted roads to Aberdeen. He'd found his way out of town—a metropolis compared with Leola—and made his way across a prairie swept by savage weather. Possibly Dan got a clue, once he determined the right direction to Leola generally. Then, perhaps, his sense of smell told him he had passed the duck hunting spot. However, he was following a cold trail over an unknown area, and an old-fashioned open touring car wouldn't leave much of a spoor, even with frozen wild ducks aboard.

Dan's feat, however, did not make the reports of Rhine and Sara R. Feather, published in the *Journal of Parapsychology,* titled "The Study of Cases of PSI-Trailing in Animals." "Numerous claims of 'talking,' 'calculating,' and 'thinking' dogs have been explored in the attempt to arrive at adequate methods for ruling out sensory cues," the authors write. "However," they add, "the question of PSI in animals has not been answered in a decisive way by the lines of exploration so far attempted, although generally significant, and in many respects valuable, results have been obtained."

A few of the 500 cases of PSI trailing studied by Rhine and Feather provide examples of inexplicable trailing even more dramatic than Dan's feat. The incidents all had a common weakness: They could not be checked while under way, only as a successful result. Witnesses to PSI trailing stories did not want their names used, fearing ridicule.

Thus the memory of a retired minister, recalling his experience as a young divinity school student years earlier, is credited to "R.O.F.," no full name given.

The young divinity student entered school in Washington, Tennessee, 100 miles from his farm home where the dog, Old Taylor, did an excellent job of herding cattle and generally looking after the security of the farm. He also looked after the boy. Old Taylor was lonely and deeply depressed after his young companion departed. Several weeks later the dog appeared at the house near the campus of the divinity school where the boy was a student, whining and scratching at the door. How the dog got to Washington, Tennessee, no one could guess. Since dogs were not allowed on the campus, and R.O.F. could not keep his friend with him, he fed Old Taylor well and then told him "solemnly and sternly to go home to George," evidently the boy's father. A few days later the dog was back at the farm. "A beautiful tale as it stands on the word of F," the writers tell us. "But," they concede, "the members of the family were gone and with them the means of checking on F's memory."

"One moderately good mark of identification in an animal is its manmade collar if this is still retained on arrival," authors Rhine and Feather state. They tell the story of Tony, in Aurora, Illinois. Tony was left in Aurora when the D. family, parents and children, moved to East Lansing, Michigan. Friends agreed to keep Tony, who could rejoin his mother, since Tony was of her litter. Six weeks later, a member of the family in Lansing noticed a familiar-appearing dog at his heels. The animal looked like Tony, and when his friend turned, Tony came bounding up, most eager to see him. Mr. D. took Tony home and there his sons removed the collar. Tony's collar identified him as a current resident of a neighboring county. Mr. D. and his sons were certain that the dog was their own Tony, who responded to that name. The dog's markings and stub tail were the same. Mr. D. had cut down the collar and thought he recognized the markings of his knife. He then threw away the collar and got a new one. Some friends in East Lansing were critical, asserting that Mr. D couldn't be sure. But Tony, we're told, lived happily ever after in East Lansing.

Long distance trailing by dogs has been the subject of many legendary accounts. A Greyhound named Cesar is said to have followed his master from Switzerland to the court of Henry III in Paris. He arrived months after his owner had traveled there by coach. "Prince" in 1915 found his way across the English Channel to his master in Paris. A *Parade* magazine account, dated April 20, 1991, relates the odyssey of Fido, a Belgian sheepdog that spent two years crossing Europe to find his owners, Jose Redondo and Lise Deremeir, who had moved to Gijon, Spain. Lise almost stumbled over their former pet in the doorway of their new home. Fido was welcomed to stay.

In 1952, the Parapsychology Laboratory at Duke University in North Carolina was called upon by the armed services R&D Laboratories at Fort Belvoir, Virginia, to conduct PSI tests on the ability of dogs and man working as a team to discover the location of landmines placed under six to twelve inches of water covering a similar depth of sand—a problem experienced by forces in military landing operations. The tests took place on a isolated beach north of San Francisco, observed by scientists Rhine, Luman Ney of Stanford University, Wilbert Toole from the Fort Belvidere Laboratories, and others. All were well hidden from the trainer and dogs who were making the searches. The dogs, Binnie and Tessie, both German Shepherds, had been trained to search for such hidden objects. The test location "was selected not only for its isolation and the presence of sand banks and low dunes but also to provide a typical landing beach of the kind American forces found in the Pacific and in Europe in World War II." Strong prevailing winds would also remove the possibility that strong sensory stimuli would remain from the planting. Since the mines would be under water and sand, the chances of sense of smell guiding the dogs were limited, if not obliterated. All other signs of humans on the beach were removed, and the mine laying took place well before the tests to reduce the possibility of spoor of any kind.

There were 108 buried mines. The conductors of the search estimated that skilled mine search teams, without dogs, might find 20 percent of the mines with various types of sweepers used by persons having experience in such work. The addition of dogs raised the score to 38.9 percent in the initial test when wind and water conditions were severe. The dogs had been trained to "sit" on discovery of a mine. That spot was marked and the dog went on. When the target line had been run with one dog, another dog tried; the movement of the water erased the traces of the first dog's stop. After each stop, the handler praised the dog for its work, but the handler did not know whether the dog had been right or wrong.

There were 120 trials, occurring under differing conditions, including some in shallow pools in the sand, as well as those in sand washed with heavy breakers. The tests in sand or shallow water yielded a record high of 51.7 percent. The tests in heavy breakers fell to 37.5 percent success. In complete calm, one dog found two of five hidden mines, and the other located all five, for a mutual score of 70 percent success. "What seems to stand clear," Rhine reported in his paper presented to the Winter Review Meeting of the Institute of Parapsychology, January 3, 1970, "is that the success in the water was most probably an ESP performance." However, Rhine conceded that ESP in the handlers may have played a part. "So it stands," he concluded, "the experiment shows only that man-dog combinations did for a time produce a very significant order of success in locating the boxes (mines) under conditions that rather strongly indicated ESP."

Can dogs find mines? One way or another they do. Television viewers who watched the first American forces entering the United States embassy compound in Kuwait City in the Persian Gulf War—to search for mines and explosives that might have been placed in that compound by Iraq after the besieged embassy officials departed—saw that German Shepherds arrived with them. They could be seen darting about the compound, doing their job.

ᏬᎢᎳᎥᎧ

Earlier it has been mentioned that dogs in the Carolinas and adjacent states enjoy sometimes difficult but general happy lives to compare only with those of ancient Egypt—or perhaps with modern-day Cornell University in Ithaca, New York. Cornell not only has one of the best veterinary facilities, giving extensive attention to research about dogs, but it has been a haven of freedom for the canines since its founding in 1865. Dogs wander about the campus and in the past have attended chapel and many lectures on subjects not likely to have been of intense interest to them. It was said that Ezra Cornell, whose gifts helped Cornell to be established as a college of agriculture, decreed that dogs must at all times have free run of the campus. Later it was said a few of the professors living on or near campus allowed their pets this privilege, creating a precedent. Unquestionably the dogs ran free, and some possibly attended more classes than did some students.

A story told by the students may be apocryphal. A certain professor in the university, whose subject was the English Lake poets, required an exceptionally large classroom because of his dramatic presentations. The students appreciated his frequent theatrics, and the dogs seemed to enjoy them also. Professor R.'s singular exploitation of the aposiopesis left students in breathless suspense. On one such occasion, an otherwise drab presentation that had some listeners in a kind of mindless stupor, a sleeping mongrel awakened in the deathly silence, and lifted his head as if awaiting the next words in extreme anticipation. Hearing none, the dog arose, sniffed his way to the podium, lifted his leg, and anointed it.

There was pandemonium in the classroom, the aroused students shouting, laughing, applauding, and otherwise demonstrating their agreement with the canine visitor. Professor R. surveyed them grimly, then at last spoke. "Keep

Thanks to her service dog, Zambelli, Becki Bushnell can attend college and enjoy skiing and other activities, in spite of her inability to walk due to injuries she sustained in an auto accident at age fifteen. (Photo by Marshall Harrington)

Tony Maranon continues in the war against drugs with the help of his service dog, Quadrille. A member of the Sunnyvale, California, police department, Maranon became confined to a wheelchair after sustaining injuries in a motorcycle accident in the line of duty. Now he and Quadrille appear before groups of youngsters to lecture on the dangers of drug addiction. (Photo by Marshall Harrington)

in mind," he suggested, "that's only one dog's opinion." He then completed his lecture.

Like many legends, that of the Cornell dogs is askew. Cornell definitely is friendly to canines and does great research beneficial to them, but Ezra Cornell left no injunction favoring dogs in his will. "Nobody knows the origin of the myth that money was given to Cornell on condition that dogs be tolerated on campus," says Herbert Finch of the department of manuscripts and archives at Cornell University. "But everybody abides by it. There are no records of any such bequest or endowment. There have been professors—linguistics, medieval studies—who lived on campus and used to bring their dogs to class with them." A countywide leash law, and increased numbers of handicapped students whose guide dogs can be distracted, have caused the number of dogs on campus to be reduced over the years, Finch explains. "The university has a laissez-faire attitude on dogs—takes no action. Cornell does extensive research on dogs and many give money for research in the name of their dogs."

Lulu Chye, deaf since birth, is still able to enjoy life thanks to her hearing dog, Zephyr. Lulu says that Zephyr gives her a sense of safety. He wakes her every morning and provides faithful companionship both indoors and out. (Photo by Marshall Harrington)

This photo, and those on page 248, kindly furnished by Canine Companions for Independence of Santa Rosa, California, are wonderful examples of how specially trained dogs today can make life more meaningful for people with special needs.

Hail Cornell! With such American friends and the praise of Europeans like Fernand Mery, it cannot be doubted that even the ancient Egyptians and Greeks would give high remarks to the developing civilizations, including the British Commonwealth, France, and the United States, for their treatment of canines. In New Zealand especially, oldest of the true democracies after Greece and Switzerland and last of the nations to be discovered by domesticated dogs, the whole of the adult populace, men and women, have fulfilled the conditions of the Platonic dialogues: the entire population of the state possessing equal rights under franchise and embracing the virtues of the well-bred dog.

While in history women have ruled nations and empires, some have risen only recently to the level set by the Greek philosophers. A right to vote was first granted nationally to adult women in 1893 by New Zealand, a land also according high value and responsibilities to its dogs. New Zealand was soon followed by Australia. The women of the United States were granted their franchise to vote by the Ninteenth Amendment to the constitution in August 1920, some 2,000 years after Plato wrote that women were the equal of men when each is measured by the standard of the well-bred dog. Yet it must be granted that the British continue to be considered the most dog-loving nation, according to many writers, including the Russians, who have become dog fanciers once again after the disintegration of communism. "The Russians know the English as keen gardeners, but they are also celebrated dog lovers, and the typical Englishman in Soviet films and popular imagination has one or two dogs in his home," Michael Binyon writes in his *Life in Russia*. "Nowadays, this applies equally to the average Muscovite. A mania for dogs, cats, birds, and pets of all kinds is gripping the country. Almost every household boasts some four-legged creature. Dogs are especially fashionable."[1]

However, journalist V. S. Prichett takes a slightly dimmer view of the British way with dogs. "The British attitude toward foreigners is like their attitude toward dogs," he writes. "Dogs are neither human nor British, but, as long as you give them their exercise, feed them, and pet them, you will find their wild emotions are amusing and their characters are interesting."

As the historians Christopher and Jacquette Hawkes have written, half of England loves its canines, while the other half does not. But in England, royalty has set high standards for pet dogs, Queen Elizabeth II herself possessing and caring for her seven Pembroke Welsh Corgis. The British press reports that she personally bathes and feeds them.

Groups such as Canine Companions for Independence are forming all over the United States to help physically challenged people. This specially trained little dog lets her deaf owner know, by tapping her leg, that a caller is at the door. These dogs also warn their owners about any potential household hazards and even provide wake-up service. (Courtesy Florida Dog Guides for the Deaf, Inc., Bradenton, Florida)

Modern studies in gerontology have shown that dogs have a positive effect on older people, just as they do on autistic children and others in need of special therapy. Charles Nolan lives in a senior citizens' residence with his Golden Retriever, Barney. Nolan and Barney reflect on the quality of life that comes from interaction with pets. The policy of allowing seniors to keep their pets in managed facilities speaks well for the vision of those who operate such residences. (Courtesy Westminister Asbury, Bradenton, Florida)

It was early morning and darkness hovered above Blue Valley. I was back at work early despite the long trip of the day before and the interruptions of the night and early morning. Soon I felt the gentle pressure of a canine nose against my thigh just as the lights again dimmed and went out. Kiwi, sleeping in a dark closet in another room, was up again after the hectic night. Now, as usual, she was telling me something was wrong with our power line, as often happens. Why and how she has first knowledge of a power failure is a mystery. She took refuge under my desk, and I went to trip our power switch after assuring her we'd still go squirrel hunting later.

We had just returned to Kiwi's favorite place, overlooking Sassafrass Gap, where the Cherokee hunted ages ago, the smoke of their campfires lingering. It was her time for hunting, in the glorious colors of mid-October after a somewhat dull season of chasing swamp rabbits in the marshes of Florida. Late that afternoon we found our favorite trail. The maples of Nantahala Forest below us blazed yellow, red, and orange against the dark green of fir and hemlock, the tulip poplar tracing a network of pale gold, the sourwood glowing russet red. The colors were never better.

Only birdcalls, fitful and questioning, punctuated the twilight as we returned. Was Martha checking the feeders at the rim of the forest? Had our friend Steve remembered them? He had, and she was. Kiwi inspected the perimeters as was her custom, and that cool night she slept soundly with us. We were still weary from a long drive and were resettling. Late at night, Kiwi was again suddenly awake, growling angrily, then yelping and finally barking loud and fiercely. Then, there was a gentle tapping on my feet. An intruder! An intruder, as seemed to have been lurking in the woods the night before now indeed, had happened by. I grabbed slippers and opened the door to the screened porch. Kiwi hit her own dog door and was racing toward the woods.

And while we're solving mysteries, there's one from Florida to be added. Bronson and Frisco, a pair of splendid Labrador Retrievers, are Kiwi's special friends there. Owners Duke and Karen Pangborn walk them twice daily, but not at the precise same time each day. Their route from home a quarter of a mile away passes our house. Kiwi inside, even when asleep, rouses and dashes to the door to announce their coming minutes before they can be seen or heard. How does she know the exact time they will come into view? Our friend Duke, a former

U.S. Navy Seal who could find enemy mines under water, has only a partial explanation. "She's got radar," Duke says.

⟨∞∞⟩

All canine mysteries are solved in time; there are natural causes. Kiwi is ready to go squirrel hunting before we go up the mountain for a formal meeting with our neighbor Nora's wandering white cat but shows no mystical anticipation of my need to work. She evidently has what a zoologist might designate as distichal levels of activity, running in the same direction, in her case the natural and the mystical. Dogs understand their owners, simply because they focus on us with unremitting devotion. Proposition 1: Kiwi grows excited and guards the door and begins joyous barking when close friends are arriving because she senses and reads our expectation and discussion—the natural level. Proposition 2: The mystical level, she hasn't yet explained to us. How can she know the exact time they will arrive as it seems she inevitably does?

Truly, even after all these centuries, there is a side of dogs we will never know.

NOTES

ᏬᎢᏬ

CHAPTER 2

1. Bronowski, Jacob, *The Ascent of Man* (Boston: Little Brown & Company, 1973).

2. Stern, Philip Van Doren, *Prehistoric Europe* (New York: W. W. Norton, 1960).

3. Saur, Carl C., *Agricultural Origins and Disposals* (New York: 1952).

4. Zeuner, Frederick, *Dating the Past* (London: Methuen & Co., 1946).

5. Bourliere, Francis, *Land and Wildlife of Eurasia* (New York: Time-Life Books, 1964).

6. Hawkes, Jacquetta, *Atlas of Ancient Archaeology* (New York: McGraw-Hill, 1974).

7. Hawkes, Christopher and Jacquetta, *The World of History* (New York: New American Library, 1954).

8. Keaton, William T., *Biological Science* (New York: Norton, 1967).

9. Hawkes, Christopher and Jacquetta, *The World of History* (New York: New American Library, 1954).

CHAPTER 3

1. Erman, Adolph, *Life in Ancient Egypt* (New York: Dover Publications, 1971).

2. Schwaller de Lubicz, Isha, *Her-Bak: Egyptian Initiate* (Rochester, Vt.: Inner Traditions, Ltd., 1968).

Chapter 4

1. *The Quest for Sumer* (New York: Putnam, 1965).
2. Rine, Josephine Z., *World History of Dogs* (Garden City, N.Y.: Doubleday, 1973).
3. Glueck, Nelson, *Deities and Dolphins* (New York: Farrar, Straus, and Giraux, 1965).
4. Durant, Will., *The Life of Greece* (New York: Simon & Schuster, 1939).
5. Hull, Denison B., "Hunting in Ancient Helas," *Greek Heritage Quarterly*, vol. 1, no. 1.
6. Childe, Gordon, *Pre-History of European Society* (London: Cassall, 1958).
7. Newark, Tim, *Celtic Warriors* (Poole, England: Blandford Press, 1986).

Chapter 5

1. Pugnetti, Gino, *Cani*, translated in *Simon & Schuster's Guide to Dogs*, Elizabeth Merriwether Schuler, ed. (New York: Simon & Schuster, 1980).
2. MacNamara, Ellen, *Everyday Life of the Etruscans* (New York: Dorset Press, 1973).
3. Polo, Marco, *The Travels of Marco Polo the Venetian* (Garden City, N.Y.: Doubleday).
4. Freemantle, Ann, *Age of Faith* (New York: Time, Inc., 1965).
5. Hale, J. R., *Renaissance Europe* (New York: Harper and Row, 1971).

Chapter 6

1. Mery, Fernand, *Le Chien* (London: Cassell, 1970).
2. Robbins, Ann (Wikkiughty, Australia: Rigby, 1982).
3. Crosby, Mary, *World Encyclopedia of Dogs* (Secaucus, N.J.: Cartwell, 1977).
4. Hull, Denison B., "Hunting in Ancient Helas," *Greek Heritage Quarterly*, vol. 1, no. 1.
5. *The New Complete Great Dane* (New York: Howell Book House, 1972).
6. Reader's Digest Association (Great Britain), *Reader's Digest History of Man: The Last Two Million Years* (London: Reader's Digest Association, 1973).

CHAPTER 7

1. Hawkes, Christopher and Jacquetta, *Prehistoric Man in Britain* (New York: Society of American Historians, Inc., 1954).
2. Churchill, Winston, *A History of the English-Speaking People* (New York: Dodd, Mead & Company, 1965).
3. Rine, Josephine Z., *The World of Dogs* (Garden City, N.Y.: Doubleday, 1973).
4. Taylor, David, *Ultimate Dog Book* (New York: Simon & Schuster, 1990).
5. Creighton, Michael, *The Age of Elizabeth* (New York: Charles Scribner's Sons, 1891).
6. Bayne-Powell, Rosamond, *Eighteenth-Century Life* (New York: E. P. Dutton, 1938).

CHAPTER 8

1. *Science* magazine (June 1992).
2. Mulvaney, D. J., *The Prehistory of Australia* (New York: Frederick Praeger, 1969).
3. Goodman, *American Genesis* (New York: Summit, 1981).
4. McNeish, Richard, from *Science* magazine (July 1992).
5. Taylor, David, *Ultimate Dog Book* (New York: Simon & Schuster, 1990).
6. Wallo, Olav, *The New Complete Norwegian Elkhound* (New York: Howell Book House, 1987).

CHAPTER 9

1. Morison, Samuel Eliot, *Oxford History of the American People* (New York: Oxford University Press, 1965).
2. La Farge, Oliver, *American Indian* (New York: Crown, 1957).
3. Farb, Peter, *The Land and Wildlife of North America* (New York: Time-Life Books, 1964).
4. Moore, Ruth, *Evolution* (New York: Time-Life Books, 1962).
5. Lewis, Thomas M. N. and Madeline Kneberg, *Tribes That Slumber* (Knoxville, Tenn.: University of Tennessee Press, 1958).
6. Rights, Douglas Le Tell, *The American Indian* (Durham, N.C.: Duke University Press, 1947).

7. Cerman, C. W., *The First American* (New York: Harcourt, Brace, Jovanovich, 1971).
8. Newman, Peter C., *Caesars of the Wilderness* (Markham, Ontario, Canada: Penguin Books Canada, Ltd., 1987).
9. *Journal of the American Veterinary Association* (July 1976).

Chapter 10

1. Phillips, David R., ed., *The West* (Chicago: Regnery, 1973).
2. Armistead, W. W., from the *Journal of the American Veterinary Medicine Association* (JAVMA), vol. 169, no. 1.
3. Drenan, D. M., from JAVMA (July 1976).
4. Siegel, J. M., from the *Journal of Personality and Social Psychology* (June 1990).
5. McClean, Fitzroy, *Eastern Approaches* (Boston: Little Brown & Company, 1949).

Chapter 11

1. Mulvaney, D. J., *Prehistory of Australia,* (New York: Praeger, 1976).
2. O'Farrall, Michael A., *Keepers of the Secrets* (Perth, Australia: Art Gallery of Western Australia, 1990).
3. Hughes, Robert, *The Fatal Shore* (New York: Alfred A. Knopf, 1987).
4. MacGregor, Miriam, *A Dog's Life* (Wellington, New Zealand: A. H. & A. W. Reed, 1980).
5. Board of Maori Ethnological Research, *Evolution of a Maori* (Plymouth, New Zealand: Board of Maori Ethnological Research, 1926).

Chapter 12

1. Frome, Michael, *Stranger in High Places* (Garden City, N.Y.: Doubleday, 1961).
2. Kephart, Horace, *Our Southern Highland* (New York: Macmillan, 1913).

Chapter 13

1. Binyon, Michael, *Life in Russia* (New York: Pantheon, 1983).